DEVELOPING LEADERSHIP
IN PRIMARY SCHOOLS

Christopher Day is Professor of Education and Co-Director of the Centre for Teacher and School Development in the School of Education, University of Nottingham. Prior to this he worked as a teacher, lecturer and local education authority adviser. His particular concerns centre upon the continuing professional development of teachers, school and teacher development, leadership and school cultures. Recent publications include *Research on Teachers' Thinking: Towards Understanding Professional Development* (co-edited with J. Calderhead and P. Denicolo; Falmer Press, 1993); *Curriculum Leadership in the Primary School* (co-authored with C. Hall, P. Gammage and M. Coles; Paul Chapman, 1995); and general editor of *Developing Teachers and Teaching*, a series for the Open University Press. He is editor of *Teachers and Teaching: Theory and Practice* and co-editor of the *International Journal of Educational Action Research*.

Carol Hall is a lecturer in Interpersonal Skills for Management at the Centre for the Study of Human Relations in the School of Education, the University of Nottingham. She is currently Deputy Head of School with responsibility for development. She has worked as a teacher, lecturer and educational consultant with schools, LEAs and other organisations on aspects of human relations training. She has written and researched in the areas of human relations training and management, including *Human Relations in Education* (1988), *Scripted Fantasy in the Classroom* (1990) and *Leadership and Curriculum in the Primary School* (1993). Her areas of interest are in organisational effectiveness, integrating personal and professional development and interpersonal skills training.

Patrick Whitaker is an educational consultant and writer, formerly a primary school teacher, headteacher, LEA adviser and Director of the Educational Management Development Unit in the University of Nottingham. He currently works with schools, colleges, businesses and LEAs throughout the UK and has written widely on management, leadership and learning in schools, including *The Primary Head* (Heinemann, 1983); *Managing Change in Schools* (Open University Press, 1993); *Practical Communication Skills in Schools* (Longman, 1993); *Managing to Learn* (Cassell, 1995); and *Primary Schools and the Future* (Open University Press, 1997). He is currently directing the Primary Headship Project at the University of Derby.

DEVELOPING LEADERSHIP IN PRIMARY SCHOOLS

Christopher Day, Carol Hall
and
Patrick Whitaker

Paul Chapman
Publishing Ltd

Paul Chapman Publishing Ltd
144 Liverpool Road
London
N1 1LA

British Library Cataloguing in Publication Data
Day, Chris, 1943-
Developing leadership in primary schools
1. Elementary school administration
I. Title II.Whitaker, Patrick III.Hall, Carol, 1951–372.1'207

ISBN 1 85396 3550

Typeset by Anneset Ltd
Printed and bound in Great Britain

ABCDEFGH   321098

Contents

To our families for all
their love and support

Preface

A great deal has happened in primary schools since the first edition of this book was published in 1985. In the early 1980s, books on the management of schools were somewhat rare, but by the time the second edition was published in 1990 the landscape of education was experiencing considerable upheaval and change, and the literature on school management was growing rapidly. It was in part as a reaction to the predominantly rational model that we emphasized the importance of professional development in that edition. In this third edition, we have retitled the book *Developing Leadership in Primary Schools* and have set out to consider the demanding challenges facing schools as we move into a new century and a new millennium. We continue to believe in the importance of continuous professional learning as a key dimension of effective management, but in this edition we also emphasize the central role of leadership. We see leadership as being the clear focus for the whole professional team of a primary school, applying equally to the work of classroom teachers as to that of the headteacher. We believe that the processes of leading and managing primary schools are extremely complex, defying easy analysis and simple solutions. In particular we see the future success of primary schools depending increasingly on leadership as a shared and collaborative process, drawing on the talents, skills and qualities of all those involved in the life of the school.

Underpinning all the chapters in the book is a belief in the life-enhancing possibilities of management and leadership. It is our experience that human beings are at their best when they encounter conditions designed to draw out and express their undoubted capabilities. We believe that people prefer to be led than to be managed, and what we have set out to explore in this book are the intricate and sometimes fragile processes involved in helping people to be at their best. These challenging processes can be both baffling and disturbing. Leadership is not a task for the faint hearted. Rather it implies a commitment to growth and achievement for children and staff. We believe that leaders must be judged not only by outcomes but also by the quality of their relationships, plans and policies.

Our first chapter, 'Building the team: sharing roles and responsibilities', proposes that effective management is about teamwork and shared leadership, the working with and through all members of the staff team. As an alternative to the individualistic approach to management responsibilities currently practised in the majority of primary schools, we offer a model which, we believe, provides the basis for a more cohesive team approach.

In Chapter 2, 'Managing the learning lives of children', we examine the core activity of any primary school – how the processes of learning and teaching are managed. Traditionally there has been a tendency to view the learning and teaching life of the school as separate from those activities designated as management, and management development as something that relates to senior roles and responsibilities. This is a false distinction, for nothing in primary schools is more demanding of management and leadership skills than the processes of bringing about continuous learning within a curriculum framework among thirty or so children at the same time in the collective setting of the classroom. Primary school classes are sizeable organizations in their own right and no less susceptible to complex forces than any other sort of institution, and primary school teachers are their chief executives and managing directors, responsible for virtually every aspect of their endeavour and enterprise. This chapter explores the variables involved in managing the learning lives of children and proposes a comprehensive framework for understanding the demanding management and leadership work of teachers.

Chapter 3, 'Leadership: principles and practices', considers the headteacher first and foremost as a leader of adults, with responsibility for ensuring continuing opportunities for professional development that are related both to individual and to school purposes and needs. It asserts that leadership is about the head and the heart. Staff will, like children, have both intellectual, personal and social development needs. They will be in different phases of development. Schools will have to respond to these needs as well as to externally generated demands. We explore the complexity of leadership roles, offer practical assistance in planning and reflect on the task of leadership in which all staff have an active part to play.

At the heart of the headteacher's role is a responsibility for ensuring that every child and teacher in the school receives the best possible education. In order to achieve this, he or she needs not only to keep up to date with developments in both curriculum and in the understanding of effective teaching and learning but also to have the knowledge and skills to enable staff to do the same. Such information and new understandings will, from time to time, challenge the existing theory and practice of one or more members of staff, and it will be for the headteacher to ensure that his or her particular leadership and strategies provide the best possible spur and support for change. There are no known 'recipes' for successful change, but there are a number of different cultures and practices that seem to have achieved success in a variety of schools and other institutions – and these are all based on principles of leadership, intervention and professional learning proposed in Chapter 3. Chapter 4, 'Change processes', relates these principles to innovation and change. The focus is on change processes first, because change involves people in a re-examination of values, attitudes and feelings that, arguably, are not governed by rationality nor are amenable to prescription; and, secondly, because attempts to promote change are unlikely to meet with success unless there is an active consideration by the headteacher of the psychological and social dynamic in its planning, processes and evaluation.

In Chapter 5, 'The inner experience: developing self-awareness', we continue the theme of change, probing beneath the surface of self-defeating, quick-fix, one-step management recipes and linking managerial effectiveness with the emotional, physical and spiritual health of headteachers and their staff. We focus primarily on the human skills' dimension to leadership, while acknowledging that such approaches are also directly transferable to the relationships between teachers and their pupils in the classroom described in Chapter 2. Many texts on school management offer limited rationalist models of managerial skills which deny the complexities of human behaviour in organizations and perpetuate simplistic myths of how to become a successful manager in schools, without acknowledging the complementary knowledge of self and others required by successful leaders. We argue that when teachers are prepared to take responsibility for their own personal and professional development within emotionally mature school cultures then staff relationships will flourish. In order for such a culture to thrive, understandings of the importance and use of interpersonal and intrapersonal intelligence, too often neglected areas in the theory and practice of management development, are needed by teachers with leadership roles within the school. This focus on 'personal intelligences' can give us an insight into understanding the processes of personal and professional growth in the self and others. Such insights can enable leaders both to chart their own development and be a catalyst or role model for the development of others. We acknowledge that the process of developing the human relations skills necessary to become a person-centred leader is likely to be one which is both stimulating and challenging. One form this challenge will take is to confront teachers with their own resistance to breaking out of habitual patterns of interpersonal behaviour and to experience the discomfort of growth as well as the benefits of improved relationships. The chapter combines practical exercises designed to develop self-awareness with a discussion of theory in order to prompt constructive action-planning. It deals with issues of self-management, self-esteem, interpersonal skills, living with pressure – coping with work-related stress and personal support systems.

Chapters 6 and 7 apply considerations of leadership and change processes to two cycles of development which are fundamental to the ongoing organizational health of schools – appraisal and the staff development cycle. Chapter 6, 'Appraisal for development', recognizes that because appraisal is legislated as a means of 'marking' teachers' developments and contributions to the school at two-yearly intervals, there is a temptation for it to become a bureaucratic exercise linked to contractual accountability. We believe, however, that it is potentially a close ally of professional development, a powerful expression of the school culture and a demonstration of the importance the school places on providing a reflective space for all staff, both individually and collectively, to audit, reassess and plan. The chapter places appraisal within the context of professional development, asserting that it represents more than an individual's and school's contractual accountability procedures. We discuss key design and implementation issues and suggest that school leaders must place teacher autonomy (and thus self-appraisal) at the heart of the system of professional development if its outcomes are to be of long-term benefit to the quality of teaching and learning. Suggestions as to how this may be achieved are provided alongside practical examples to assist teachers and schools in processes of appraisal and career-long professional development planning.

In Chapter 7, 'Renewing the team: managing the staffing cycle', we encourage school leaders to see the recruitment, selection, induction, support, development and loss of staff as part of a dynamic, evolutionary cultural process which is central to the life and continued vitality of the school as an organization. The educational reforms of the 1980s, which devolved much of the personnel function formerly carried out by LEAs to schools and their governing bodies, have given headteachers and their staff the opportunity to grapple imaginatively with the increased responsibility that actively managing the staffing process brings. The ways in which this organic process is planned for, managed and conceptualized will reflect both the existing culture and aspirations of the school. We consider the impact of organizational culture on the recruitment process and suggest practical strategies for managing the staffing cycle, focusing upon the appointment of all staff, irrespective of their role, contract or status within the school. The process of staff selection and induction may seem like an additional chore for overburdened senior staff in a school. However, school leaders with a poorly conceptualized view of staffing as a fundamental aspect of school renewal will invariably manage the process in a way which results in a poor fit between meeting the needs and aspirations of the school within its community and the needs and aspirations of individual candidates.

Our final chapter, 'Connecting with communities', conceptualizes primary schools as one part of an intricate nexus of services, both public and private, which exist to serve the changing needs of families and children within society. While the core tasks of each organization may be different, each in their own way will have a powerful and enduring contribution to make to the development of children's learning in schools. Interagency collaboration, resource and information gathering are important aspects of school leadership but do not reside with the headteacher alone. While a fundamental dimension of the role of headteacher is to develop opportunities for working in partnership, every member of the school community has a part to play in this important process. In any partnership there exists the possibility for both costs and benefits. Ways of acknowledging areas of possible tension and providing the means to resolve them are explored, as well as ideas to develop good practice.

Christopher Day
Carol Hall
Patrick Whitaker

1

Building the team: sharing roles and responsibilities

Inherited traditions • Current realities • Limitations of the current model • The headship collective • Management structure • Role definitions and job descriptions • Professional development

Inherited traditions

In recent years, the structure of roles and responsibilities in primary schools has settled into a remarkably consistent pattern. What we now find in most primary schools is a configuration of roles and responsibilities which gives each member of staff, in addition to their class-teaching responsibilities, an area of the curriculum to manage. This system has grown and developed over the years as successive pay awards have extended and rationalized the allowances available to teachers. Extra allowances are awarded for responsibilities over and above the main professional grade and these sometimes involve some organizational responsibilities in addition to curricular ones.

By the late 1970s a pattern had emerged which reflected three distinct types of extra responsibility:

- curriculum leadership and co-ordination
- organizational work
- welfare work and pastoral care

It was in the report of the Bullock Committee, *A Language for Life* (DES, 1975), that the recommendation that each primary school should have a language co-ordinator was made. This was later reinforced by the HMI survey into primary schools, *Primary Education in England: A Survey by HM Inspectors of Schools* (DES, 1978). This report did much to rationalize a model of allowances based on curriculum responsibility, but it noted only a limited impact of such posts:

> In a quarter of the schools in the survey teachers with positions of curricular organizational responsibility were having a noticeable influence on the quality of the work in the school as a whole. In the remaining schools there was little evidence that the influence of

teachers with curricular responsibilities spread beyond the work of their own classes.

The initial response to this observation was one of concern that as many as 75% of teachers were receiving allowances and not significantly influencing the work of their colleagues. On reflection, this could be regarded as something of an achievement, for with no non-contact time available for the crucial processes of consultation, monitoring and professional development, as many as 25% of teachers with responsibilities for curricular management were having a significant influence on their colleagues. Perhaps the criticism said more about the model of allowances than it did about the holders of them.

Two developments during the 1980s did much to reinforce further the model based on subject co-ordination. The first of these was the School Teachers' Pay and Conditions of Employment Order (1987). This established that all teachers, whatever their pay level, would have in their contracts a requirement to carry responsibilities beyond their class-teaching duties, and that those in receipt of additional allowances would be expected to carry responsibilities beyond this new basic level. The second factor was the introduction of the National Curriculum, established through the Education Reform Act 1988. This created a uniform curriculum consisting of core and foundation subjects. In order to carry through the changes required to establish this new standard pattern, co-ordinators in each of the subject areas were seen as the main agents of change and development.

Despite enormous variations in primary school size, the model of curriculum leaders or co-ordinators has become firmly established. In small schools, each teacher can have as many as three subjects to manage, whereas in large schools teachers can have as many as twelve teachers to work through and co-ordinate. Notwithstanding these significant anomalies little has been done to address the demands and challenges involved in trying to make such a model work equitably and effectively across all primary schools.

A final reinforcement to the model was made in the OFSTED framework for the inspection of schools, where curriculum co-ordinators are seen as the key element in curriculum management, and inspectors expect to interview each co-ordinator during the course of a primary school inspection. So established has this structure become that the Teacher Training Agency is now working to create a national professional qualification for subject leaders.

This approach to the allocation of management roles and responsibilities has now become established as traditional orthodoxy. We want to challenge this assumption. We do so because we feel the model now prevailing in our primary schools is not sufficiently flexible and robust to cope with present demands, nor with the increasingly complex challenges of the future.

Current realities

Over the past decade or so, we have witnessed an increasing sense of frustration about the management of education. Teachers have absorbed an enormous range of changes to an already complex system, but have also experienced the society they serve to turn on them, blaming them for all the current ills and difficulties of the nation. Schools seem to have become the scapegoat of a society ill at ease with itself, and confused about which direction it needs to take into the future.

Alvin Toffler (1971) warned us a quarter of a century ago that the world was changing faster than ever before, and that the rapid acceleration of changes in all aspects of human activity would create a disorienting condition which he described as *future shock*. He warned that, unless we learn to control the rate of change, in both personal living as well as in social affairs, we are doomed to a massive adaptational breakdown. Many who have been working in the education service over the past few years might claim that such a breakdown has already occurred.

Charles Handy (1989), writing about this world of constant change, suggests that the epoch of intent, brought in with the Industrial Revolution, is now over and that we have entered the *age of unreason* in which the only prediction that will hold true is that no predictions will hold true.

Much change in education has had a reform element about it. It is still the belief of many politicians that changing the structure of schooling is the way to ensure improved learning. While improvement is constantly needed, it is sad that many of the reasons forwarded for wishing to improve are so directly connected with important but essentially tangential issues – to be better than other countries, to prove experts wrong or because standards are different from what they were fifty years ago.

The solutions currently being introduced assume that the only issues to take account of are the ones that have always been taken account of – those which seemed to be appropriate to a world that has passed. Imagination about how to change only stretches to considerations about more or less of what we have already, and the rush to discover panaceas creates a tendency to retrieve discarded orthodoxies from the past.

During the last ten years, schools have been subjected to a range of unprecedented pressures (Whitaker, 1997a). These can be categorized as macro-pressures and micro-pressures.

Macro-pressures

These are pressures affecting the whole world and include:

- rapid advances in science and technology;
- ecological changes – global warming, atmospheric pollution, depletion of natural resources;

- social changes – patterns of family life, drug cultures, unemployment, crime;
- political changes – ethnic conflicts, breakdown of the Soviet system, the emancipation of South Africa; and
- huge developments in information technology.

These macro-pressures impact on schools in two main ways:

1) They demand a curriculum which reflects these enormous trends and changes and which has the capacity to adapt quickly and flexibly to continuously changing situations.
2) They require schools to be a creative part of the change process itself, leading with new ideas and approaches finely tuned to emerging trends and developments.

Micro-pressures

These are closer to home and specific to education:

- devolved budgets to schools – LMS;
- new types of schools – grant-maintained and city technology colleges;
- the National Curriculum;
- new systems of accountability – teacher appraisal, assessment and testing; and
- systematic school inspection – OFSTED.

Not only have these micro-pressures imposed enormous extra demands on an already under-resourced service, but they have also tended to diminish professional authority and create a culture of suspicion and mistrust.

Together these two types of pressure, in their powerful and different ways, have created a range of significant effects on the schools of this country, creating an altogether changed and changing context for the work of teachers and their pupils.

In addition to these varied pressures we also now face a range of psychological challenges which are further testing our capacities to cope in a changed and changing world:

- complexity
- ambiguity
- uncertainty
- confusion
- perplexity
- turbulence

Life is infinitely more complex than it ever has been, with increasing data and phenomena to contend with. Combined with a tendency to social fragmentation, the huge increase in data, regulation and documentation increases the presence of dilemmas, contradictions, quandries and paradoxes in our lives, requiring us to consult with others more in order to seek understanding and meaning. We cannot be certain what the future will bring and so we shorten our timescales, focus on targets and lose sight of the larger picture. The confusions created by these new circumstances lead us to doubt our own abilities and competence, and the turbulence created by a widening gap between what we have to do and what we feel able to do comfortably seems to widen all the time. In addition to all this, teachers have experienced the society they serve turn on them, sometimes with ridicule and contempt. No wonder we suffer stress and breakdown in our schools.

The combination of pressures from increased prescriptions and heightened expectations has brought about some significant effects in schools:

- increase in the weight of individual workloads;
- increase in the complexity of workloads;
- too little time for too many changes;
- the confusion of managing many significant changes simultaneously;
- lack of time for preparation, adjustment and training;
- changes that are changed again either before or during implementation;
- panic to cover the ground with insufficient attention to detail; and
- further erosion of professional time into personal time at the expense of individual well-being and family life.

Management structures built on individual and separated responsibility are placing disproportionate pressure on some teachers, who can feel overwhelmed by the demands placed on them and experience painful feelings of isolation, inadequacy and panic. If left unchecked and unattended to, these can lead to both personal and professional dysfunction. The educational press reports a rapidly developing tendency among teachers (senior staff in particular) to seek early retirement due to breakdowns in health and well-being.

We need to consider whether we have now reached the limit of the usefulness of traditional management structures in our primary schools, and whether constantly changing circumstances demand the development of new systems and structures to handle the ever-increasing workloads that staff in schools are facing.

One response to these demanding challenges is to work towards four kinds of adaptation. A *business as usual* approach simply will not do. Survival depends upon recognizing the threats to well-being and effectiveness, and taking steps, sometimes quite radical and severe ones, to change the habits and patterns hardened over many generations. To survive the challenges to our well-being, four categories of adaptation and change are necessary:

1) conceptual change
2) emotional change
3) aspirational change
4) practical change

Conceptual change

There seems to be an obsession with the past as we move into these challenging times. Strategies like *back to basics* strive to recapture the apparent ease and elegance of earlier times. Such management by nostalgia is bound to be thwarted, since the circumstances that we want to apply previous basics to have changed, and will continue to do so. It is time to stop seeing the future simply as a linear development of the past.

We need to check our attitudes to change. We must not rush always into defensive postures when it becomes necessary to move out of the temporary comfort of the familiar. We are now part of a profession whose *raison d'être* is learning for change. We are perhaps the first generation of educators who cannot predict with any security what the circumstances of our pupils' lives are likely to be in the future. Not only is it dangerous to make forecasts about twenty years ahead, but it is also unwise to risk them for even a few years into the future.

It will be necessary to stop regarding change as an event that will require strenuous efforts from time to time and to appreciate that change is a process of continuous adaptation and modification. Development will become a process of continuously small but significant improvements, rather than occasional all-out efforts. This will require a new alertness to circumstances, and a capacity to change things as and when required.

Emotional change

Over recent years there has developed in the teaching profession an increasing tension between the personal and the professional dimensions of life. As pressure and complexity have increased, there has been a greater tendency than in the past to blur the boundaries between these two important aspects of our lives. Reports about occupational stress note the tendency for many groups of workers to undertake a significant proportion of their work at home, and many teachers find themselves working most evenings and for a significant part of their weekends. While there will need to be practical solutions to this seemingly inexorable invasion of our personal and family lives by our professional activity, it is also important to understand the psychological elements in this emerging tension.

There is an inherited assumption that as we cross the threshold from home to work we must put aside the worries and concerns of our personal lives and concentrate on the job in hand. In the past this was not always easy, but most were able to handle it most of the time. Today, as the boundaries become more ambiguous, and the combined impact of our struggles to lead full and satisfying lives becomes more pronounced and confusing, it is necessary to build new assumptions about the relationship between home and work. It is no longer appropriate to accept that our personal experience of living in a complex, confusing and uncertain world is a matter for lonely and individual struggle. The tensions of school life and the pressures of professional responsibility and accountability need to become legitimate and necessary issues for the organization as a whole. Stress is heightened in significantly changed circumstances, and its presence in our lives is of concern to all, particularly to those with senior responsibility for the organization and management of our work.

We seem to be struggling to keep up appearances in our professional work, while at the same time concealing considerable frustration, confusion, guilt, anger and resentment within ourselves. Breakdowns occur when we can no longer sustain this deception. There is a painful tendency to blame ourselves for the seeming incapacity to keep abreast of ever-increasing workloads. We do not take seriously enough the fact that we are faced with novel situations and unreasonable demands. We have to realize that if we are finding life difficult, then it is because it is (Peck, 1987).

The stress is compounded because we have no proper outlet for these inner pressures and painful emotions. We look at others and they seem to cope, but they too are keeping up appearances and struggling to sustain the approval of those whose good opinions they depend upon for professional self-esteem. A whole new approach to the management of work is required in which an emphasis on professional development is accompanied by a serious concern for personal welfare and well-being. It is in the best interest of any organization to have physically fit, emotionally healthy, as well as professionally competent workers. We are in danger of destroying psychological health and reinforcing emotional disease. The complexities of teaching and managing require us to be at our best – physically, emotionally and intuitively. We can no longer leave an appropriate sense of well-being to individuals to manage for themselves. Stress is created in and by the pressures of organizational life, and it is in organizational setting that it needs to be dealt with.

Aspirational change

Another necessary shift in management development is from obedience to external control, to a proper inner-directed ambition for the school, its pupils and staff. Most teachers are motivated by dearly held beliefs and values about their work and have an enormous commitment to the present and future lives of the pupils they teach. Recent regulations have stolen the driving force of educational development from the profession and placed it in the hands of regulatory bodies whose place and experience is outside schools. If a proper balance of accountability and influence is to be achieved for the educational system, some power and authority needs to be redeemed by those working within schools.

In the future, with faster change and shorter-term plans, greater emphasis will need to be placed on the loftier elements of aspiration and ambition. Underpinning any plans for development need to be dearly held values and beliefs, and clearly articulated principles and visions. These will provide the energy and motivation for a schooling process vital to the creation of optimum conditions for a future society. If we focus on the future only through prosaic and pedantic levels of attainment targets and programmes of work, then we diminish the higher talents of our educators and their pupils. We need to promote greater attention to professional dreams and visions, and engage in the sharing of educational philosophies and beliefs so that we can articulate a set of foundation principles upon which our work in primary schools can be built.

Practical change

All these shifts will require practical adaptation. We will need to stop doing some things we have always done, and start doing other things we have never done before. And we will have to do less of some things in order to do more of others. Nothing less than a thorough overhaul of all our assumptions about teaching and learning, our beliefs about what constitutes a good school and our ideas about what characterizes effective leadership will be enough. Tinkering around produces a repair. What we need is a significant rebuilding.

In their illuminating analysis of the current predicaments faced by staff in schools, Michael Fullan and Andy Hargreaves (1992) emphasize the importance of an inner driving force: 'What is worth fighting for is not to allow our schools to become negative by default but to make them positive by design.'

What this will mean in practice is that security and confidence about what a school does will not depend upon satisfying the somewhat rule-of-thumb criteria of an inspection system that at best expresses personal opinions about practice, but upon the capacity to build the trust, support and confidence of those who have a real stake in the school and its future. Ambitious teachers, involved pupils, supportive parents and committed governors can unite to build that solid confidence and sense of endeavour from which enterprising development can spring. External observation expressed only through such terms as *sound* and *satisfactory* can do little to assist the process of continuous school improvement that the government is so anxious to secure. As the exponents of total quality management proclaim – it is only the customers who can decide whether quality has been achieved.

Activity 1.1

1) Reflect on how change has affected you in recent years. Which changes have you welcomed? Which have you resented? Which have you opposed?
2) In what specific ways have the four categories of change – conceptual, emotional, aspirational, practical – affected your professional roles and responsibilities?

Limitations of the current model

The current model, although notionally creating a management team, in fact tends to reinforce an individualistic tendency in primary school management, allocating separate roles and responsibilities which are conducted by members of staff in isolation from each other. As Fullan and Hargreaves have observed:

> Uncertainty, isolation and individualism are a potent combination. Almost by definition, they sustain educational conservatism, since the opportunity and pressure arising from new ideas are inaccessible. Such narrowness of orientation and experience leads to 'safe', non-risk taking forms of teaching that do little to assist pupil achievement. Where multiple demands are being externally imposed on teachers and their schools, isolated teachers feel powerless in the face of pressures and decisions which they do not often understand and in which they are not involved.

What happens in practice is that responsibilities are spread across all those available to undertake it. Each member of staff carries a responsibility role different from all other members of staff. This means that management work tends to be carried by individuals working alone and separate from each other. Each individual, within the structure of accountability, carries out his or her own planning, operating and reviewing.

As well as tending to build a culture of individualism in management, the current model is also responsibility focused – post-holders accept an ongoing portfolio which tends to be defined in vague terms – *manage, be responsible for, monitor, co-ordinate and oversee*. This can create a lack of precision and an uncertainty about what has to be done.

Each member of staff's management role is defined in terms of responsibility – a requirement to handle a particular aspect of school life. This responsibility is open ended, operating until either the teacher vacates the post or changes are made to the role through mutual agreement. It is also open ended in terms of demand. A subject leader would be expected to deal with all issues arising in that subject area however much or little was in focus at the time.

A further limitation is that of disproportionate workloads. This can occur in three main ways. First, it can occur between posts where an élite subject like English is likely to create a larger workload than a lower-status subject such as music or physical education. Secondly, it occurs between different sizes of schools as described above where in very small schools post-holders can have multiple portfolios and in large schools they can have a large number of colleagues to relate to. Thirdly, it occurs when new initiatives are introduced.

These two factors combine to create a number of serious difficulties with this approach. They

- create a sense of management isolation;
- can lead to significant task overload;
- can result in excessive pressure and stress;
- create inequity across the system in that some teachers can be disproportionately challenged at particular times; and
- create problems of self-motivation.

In their research into the work of primary school co-ordinators, Webb and Vulliamy (1996) note three particular constraints on the role: 'There are three contextual factors which continue to constrain curriculum co-ordinators in their roles. These are: first, coordinator expertise; second, lack of time; third, the nature of power relationships within the school.'

Effective primary school teachers are good all-rounders, and this is the main reason they are recruited. The strength of the primary approach to learning lies in the relationship over a school year between a teacher and a class across the whole curriculum. Despite some pressure in recent years we do not have a tradition of specialist teaching in primary education. This means that some teachers may not be allocated a subject to co-ordinate which is a particular strength, and yet they are expected to influence colleagues in exactly the same way as their more specialist colleagues.

The challenge of time will always be a problem with this model, because as Webb and Vulliamy (1996) point out, increasing the amount of non-contact time for a co-ordinator will not work since other colleagues would almost certainly be teaching, and therefore not available for consultation and collaborative activity.

The problem of power relationships is more complex. While a subject leader can be given delegated authority to initiate staff activity in a particular subject area, he or she may not have the power to exercise this authority. A number of power relationships are significant. First, some co-ordinators may be managing a subject in which they are not the most knowledgeable or capable on the staff. This places the co-ordinator at some disadvantage with some colleagues. Secondly, they may be responsible for a subject in which they have less experience than other colleagues. This applies particularly to recently qualified teachers who are expected to take on curriculum responsibilities early in their career. The challenges of trying to influence colleagues who have significantly more experience have not been sufficiently recognized. Thirdly, there is the general challenge of peer management where colleagues are attempting to influence others, most of whom share the same status and salary levels.

Activity 1.2

What different approaches to management responsibility have you experienced during your career? What have been the particular strengths and weaknesses of these?

The headship collective

The time has come to consider radical alternatives to the traditional model. The phrase 'the headship collective' is used to describe one such alternative. It works from the assumption that headship is too big a job for any one person. In the research referred to earlier, Webb and Vulliamy (1996) found that curriculum leadership was being pushed further down the headship list of priorities, despite the emphasis so often placed on the head's need to be at the forefront of learning and teaching matters.

Hargreaves (1994) aptly depicts the headteacher's dilemma in his characterization of the 'postmodern' school, where 'as the pressures of post modernity are felt, the teacher's role expands to take on new problems and mandates – though little of the old role is cast aside to make room for these changes'. Given this unrealistic and unmanageable workload, headteachers have to make a choice about their priorities based on the size, staffing levels and expertise in their schools.

One impact of the evolutionary crisis – the condition of postmodernity referred to above – is to create an ever-changing diversity to the management and leadership work required in the modern primary school. Yet we attempt to set management structures in concrete which are reinforced by the National Curriculum, OFSTED and the Teacher Training Agency. In times of rapid change and novel circumstances we need the most flexible and adaptable structures it is possible to devise.

The notion of the headship collective also works from the assumption that the tasks of the modern primary school are too varied, complex and numerous to be handled in a structure where everyone holds a unique and separate portfolio of responsibilities. This means that we have to find ways of harnessing the varied skills and abilities of the staff team in a new coalition of endeavour. Management and leadership work must stop being the isolated ploughing of lonely furrows and become the joint and collaborative activity of all staff. This does not mean that there is no place for headteachers; the question rather becomes – what is it that only headteachers can do?

What we need is an arrangement that works to overcome the difficulties outlined above and makes the management and leadership work of a school more geared to school development and management co-operation. And so we propose a way of structuring roles and responsibilities which has more capacity to deal with the complexities and frustrations of modern life in schools. The essential features of this approach are illustrated in Figure 1.1 (Whitaker, 1997b).

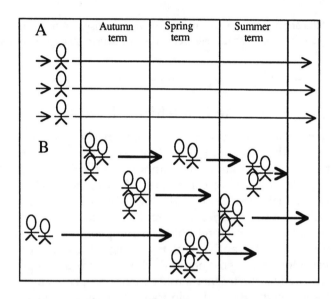

Figure 1.1   Contrasting management structures

The work of the three members of staff in model A in the diagram is driven by an open-ended job description which continues irrespective of the pressures and demands facing a school at any one time. The three colleagues have different roles from each other and carry out much of their management work alone.

In model B of the diagram, the management activity of staff is driven by the school development plan for that particular year, and each member of staff joins a number of temporary teams to carry out the task work specified in the plan.

Instead of conceiving of the management task of the school as a series of functions to be supervised, it is useful to see it as a series of tasks to be undertaken within a specific time period. The school development plan provides an excellent starting point. Part of the school development planning process is to designate a series of development projects for the next academic year. In the responsibility-driven model, some individuals would have significantly large task loads for the following year, whereas others may have no specific projects at all, their roles having more of a maintenance focus. Once a programme of projects and tasks is produced, small teams could then be set up to manage them. By this method, individual management responsibilities would be for specific management tasks and for active membership of temporary task teams. Once a project is completed the team disbands.

Some tasks in a typical school development plan may be quite short lived, perhaps occupying a small task team for a week or two. Others may be more substantial, ranging over a whole academic year and involving some change of team membership as the project develops. Through the regular pattern of staff meetings, teams refer to the staff as a whole, making periodic reports and receiving recommendations, observations, responses and suggestions.

Within the projects teams, status differentials can be minimized, and each member of staff encouraged to contribute according to his or her experience and skill. There are many benefits to be accrued from such a dynamic and highly participative structure. It

- maximizes staff expertise and experience;
- involves all staff in key management and leadership activities;
- achieves a higher work rate;
- removes the frustrations often experienced when decision-making is attempted in too large a group;
- develops new skills and expertise;
- facilitates professional development;
- increases enjoyment and commitment;
- makes better use of time; and
- allows quicker responses to new problems.

Perhaps more than anything, this sort of approach to shared leadership helps a school to move from a red-light mentality – restricting access to action and development – to a green-light mentality – encouraging easy access and involvement in the key tasks of school development. Devolving authority to the task and its team will release heads from too detailed an involvement in development and change, and allow the fuller expression of staff talent and ambition. Teams should be encouraged to set their own detailed targets within the brief designed by the staff as a whole.

In practice some combination of these two approaches is desirable, with individuals carrying some responsibility for receiving information and keeping it flowing, noting developments, identifying projects. When tasks are needed, such as the production of draft policy documents, curriculum plans or reports to governors, these are best tackled in small teams where the process of collaboration reduces isolation, increases motivation and enables work to be completed more effectively and within shorter deadlines.

Such an approach to primary school management creates the conditions for action-focused collective leadership in which there are three main elements:

- *Task*   Identifies specific jobs of work that need to be done.
- *Team*   Allows more power, imagination and creativity to be applied to complex tasks.
- *Support* Creates the working climate in which complexities can be shared and tackled collectively through action of mutual support.

Management structure

This approach to roles and responsibilities allows the staff of a primary school to move out of the traditional thrall of hierarchy with its distinctive status differentials, into a more collaborative and participative arrangement, designed to get the work done in ways that are personally supportive and professionally enriching.

Hierarchies have posed many difficulties in organizations. When management behaviour reinforces status separation, then those lower down the hierarchical triangle can experience a range of painful and inhibiting feelings:

- a sense of inadequacy;
- inability to express oneself;
- inability to influence anyone;
- feelings of being shut out;
- increase in cynicism;
- increase in destructive feelings;
- feelings that one has either to dominate or be dominated;
- feeling that to conform is the best thing;
- feeling that intolerance and oppression have to be accepted;
- feeling that new ideas can only come from the top; and
- feeling that there is no way to communicate with those at the top.

As long ago as 1960, in his pioneering work on organizational behaviour, Chris Argyris coined the phrase *cultural pathologies* to describe such entropic characteristics as dependence, compliance, resistance, complacency, inhibition, depression and resentment. He claimed that when these were constantly present in the members of organizations then their potential to give of their best was significantly reduced.

The model we propose owes much more to heterarchy than it does to hierarchy. We need to recognize the limitations of the hierarchical principle in management, not only from the organizational culture point of view but also in our efforts to create more flexible and involving approaches to leadership. Judi Marshall (1994) notes:

Hierarchies have limitations. They become inflexible. They can create impossible expectations of designated leaders and unproductive dynamics of dependency and abdication of individual responsibility. As we appreciate these problems and seek to honour people's diversity in skills and viewpoints, we need alternative models. Recognizing everyone's equal humanity is an important step, but this can create cosy norms of equal needs, skills, rights and power in all situations. This, too, is limited, denying significant differences. In the notion of heterarchy I see more potential. A heterarchy has no one person or principle in command. Rather, temporary pyramids of authority form as and where appropriate in a system of mutual constraints and influences.

In practice, heterarchical management involves structures which are continuously changing to accommodate new challenges and situations. The management structure would be constantly reconfiguring itself through a variety of teams, often small and temporary, brought into being to tackle the specific tasks and projects of the moment. Leadership roles would be designated according to need rather than seniority, thus involving everyone in the co-management and co-leadership of the school.

This concept helps us to consider some exciting departures from tradition which may help us to deal more effectively with the complexities of the fast changing world and to create new structures which more successfully harness the skills and qualities of all the staff team.

What we are currently witnessing in many future-focused organizations is the attempt to create structures of management and leadership which are characterized more by the acceptance of temporariness than of longevity, by possibility rather than unlikeliness, and integration rather than exclusion. Such approaches reject the idea of singular and simple solutions to problems and proceed on the assumption that compound and complex problems will require compound and complex solutions.

One of the main advantages of this management model is that responsibilities are related to the school development plan. This means that planning for the development of the school includes considerations of how those developments will be tackled and the nature of the tasks required to accomplish them. Staff can see their management responsibilities well ahead, time and resources can be appropriately allocated and realistic deadlines scheduled.

Primary schools have the potential to become genuine heterarchical organizations – reconfiguring the management structure according to the tasks in hand. We need to recognize the inherent flexibility of this approach to leadership, and recognize that in primary schools leadership is a function of the whole team and not the role of one individual. Roland Barth (1988) has coined the phrase *a community of leaders* to capture the potential for shared leadership in primary schools. He contends that nowadays schools need more leadership than the headteacher has time for, and makes the following propositions:

- all teachers have leadership tendencies;
- schools badly need teacher leadership;
- teacher leadership has not been forthcoming; and
- headteacher leadership has been too pivotal.

This suggests that the leadership structure of primary schools has considerable potential for development.

This more fluid and flexible approach makes the school development plan the basis of the leadership structure. If the plan envisages four specific pieces of curriculum development for the year ahead, then the leadership structure needs to be designed with that plan in mind. Four project teams can be created, each with a clear brief to manage the project on behalf of the staff as a whole. Such projects could run consecutively or concurrently. The advantages of this team-focused project approach are to get work done more quickly and efficiently, and to harness the skills and qualities of all staff more equally.

Figure 1.2 (Whitaker, 1997a) shows the leadership structure of a one-form entry primary school with eight members of staff. The school development plan has established four development projects together with a review task and a community development initiative.

In this particular structure, the head (A) provides support and encouragement to all projects, and takes an active part in two, but not in

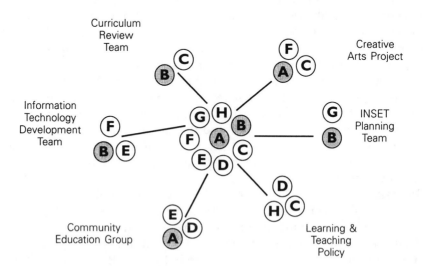

Figure 1.2 Team-focused leadership

the chairing role. The deputy head (B) works in three teams, as does the senior allowance holder (C). All other colleagues work in two teams, apart from (H), who is newly qualified and recently appointed. This particular configuration is temporary. When a project is completed, there is a planned gap before a new one is taken up, but individuals are available to join the *ad hoc* team, which can be convened when urgent and unexpected tasks descend.

Activity 1.3

1) What are your responses to the collective approach to management work in primary schools?
2) What advantages are there in a team approach? What difficulties can you foresee?

Role definitions and job descriptions

A more democratic, egalitarian and supportive approach to leadership demands new thinking on job descriptions and role definitions. Far too often job descriptions for management roles, such as curriculum co-ordination, are couched in eternal terms – referring to quite general areas of activity over the years ahead. They usually define areas of responsibility, rather than tasks to be managed. Such job descriptions can create considerable difficulties. They

- tend to encourage rigidity – *it's not my job*;
- stifle initiative, when what is required is flexibility, and enterprise; and
- tend to define professional activity rather than inspire energy and imagination.

Flexible leadership in primary schools will need more imaginative and motivating job descriptions. In one school, after a period of considerable struggle for tighter and tighter definitions of role, the staff realized that the secret lay in freedom rather than description, and came up with a small post-it sized statement for everyone consisting of only three words – DO YOUR BEST! It was the trusting assumption behind this that the staff found so invigorating, encouraging them to see beyond the somewhat pedestrian demands of their traditional and often restricting job definitions.

In considering how job descriptions might be devised to help in the creation of the sorts of interesting and stimulating jobs most of us want, it is useful to consider the following, all of which have featured in some radical examples of primary school job descriptions:

- enjoy your work;

- pursue your interests and enthusiasms;
- connect with colleagues constantly;
- announce all successes and achievements;
- keep asking questions;
- allocate time for thinking and reflection;
- take some risks; and
- have a dream that we can all buy into.

In determining the membership of projects teams one school has developed a set of criteria:

- How can we make this project special?
- What can we learn from it?
- How can we have fun with it?

In defining leadership roles and responsibilities there are a number of ways that whole-staff involvement can be harnessed:

- Set up a development project on team-focused leadership, job descriptions and appropriate management training. Plan a pilot project and report back on options for action.
- Circulate everyone's job descriptions to all members of staff with the request – *how can this job help you to carry out your own role more effectively?*
- Send a memo to colleagues asking – *in my specialist area, what particular sorts of help will be of most support to you?*
- Plan an INSET day on issues of leadership and support. Invite an external facilitator so all members of staff can participate fully.
- Plan a short course on leadership skills for pupils. Run it as an optional activity and find out what the children think of leadership, and what sort they like best.

Professional development

One of the distinct benefits of this heterarchical approach to primary school management lies in its capacity to facilitate and encourage professional development. One of the most powerful sources of professional learning is watching capable colleagues exercising their roles and responsibilities. Working alongside colleagues in a variety of temporary task teams is an ideal way to learn and to develop management skills and qualities.

A number of important principles of professional development are implicit in the approach described above:

- It fosters continous professional learning; none of us has nothing to learn.
- Learning with and through our colleagues enables examples to be

followed, feedback to be sought and received, and new skills to be supported.

• Collaborative work enables and encourages the important learning processes of reflection and dialogue.

• The professional learning objectives colleagues bring with them into a team task become a vital part of the task itself.

One of the most important developments in organization management over recent years has been the concept of *the learning organization*. In the face of rapid and accelerating change it is increasingly necessary to see learning in the organizational context as well as at the individual level. Garratt (1987) argues that learning has become the key development commodity of an organization:

> Generating and and selling know-how and know-why, the learning of the organization and its people, is becoming the core of any organization which has the chance of surviving in the longer term. We already know a lot about organizational learning processes. When this is added to the new ideas on the generation of vision, the refinement of thinking processes, the development of policy and strategy, the notion of managing as a 'holistic' process, and the acquisition of new managerial skills from outside the traditional boundaries, then there is a powerful mix available.

Learning organizations have recognized for some time that collaboration together with a proper individualism is the key source of dynamic strength for development. An increasing tendency to tackle work through task groups and temporary teams requires attention to the processes of collaboration as well as to the work itself. This requires a focus on collective learning if the potential of participants is to be harnessed effectively. There will need to be an enhanced capacity to use conflict creatively, to use dialogue rather than discussion to root out defective thinking habits and defensive routines. The process of action learning defined by Revans (1980), involving team members using the experience of the work itself as the chief source for improvement, will need to become a way of life.

The learning organization is one that is geared to change and determined to develop and refine its capacities to move into the future with confidence, curiosity and commitment.

In the increasingly high-pressured world of complex tasks and insufficient time it will no longer be possible to separate training and learning from the work itself. Action learning will become the key imperative of professional development. Schools will need to become their own research institutions accompanying every major development task they undertake with a research element, and all members of staff will need to have their own lines of inquiry. Sometimes learning outcomes will be as important as the task outcomes, providing valuable insights and understandings that will enable the school to function more effectively in the future.

Membership of teams will need to reflect not only the expertise available on the staff but also the learning needs of individuals. Appraisal targets may be one of the key determinants of team membership. Heterarchical management allows a much earlier and powerful involvement in key management and leadership activity than the individualistic approach can ever achieve. Having the support of more skilful and experienced colleagues as we try out our skills for the first time creates a culture conducive to shared endeavour and collaborative learning. We can receive support and feedback about our efforts instantly, rather than having to work it out for ourselves.

As we move into a new century and a new millennium, the management of primary schools will be tested as never before. Education is now a high political priority for most governments as they grapple with the issues created by accelerating change, increasing complexity and profound uncertainty. These are severe challenges for educators who now find themselves in the survival business. As Joanna Macy (1995) observes:

> Until the late twentieth century, every generation throughout history lived with the tacit certainty that there would be generations to follow. Each assumed, without questioning, that its children and children's children would walk the same earth, under the same sky. Hardships, failures and personal death were encompassed in that vaster assurance of continuity. That certainty is now lost to us, whatever our politics. That loss, unmeasured and immeasurable, is the pivotal psychological reality of our time.

While the struggle for standards of literacy and numeracy currently preoccupies us, it will be wider considerations that will increasingly challenge the need for primary schools to provide a substantially more comprehensive and life-focusing foundation for the children who attend them. We must work towards these future tasks with management structures designed to meet them, structures which are inherently flexible and which optimize the creative resourcefulness of staff. In the future it will be our capacity to work with and through each other rather than our individual talents and abilities which will hold the key to success.

ISSUES FOR DISCUSSION

1) Only through a combining of talents can the staff of a primary school provide the flexibility of management required in the modern primary school.
2) All our traditions of management and leadership have to be challenged

and re-examined if primary schools are to live effectively with constant change.
3) Schools will need to become their own research institutions if they are to learn faster than the world around them is changing.

Further reading

Dalin, P. and Rust, V. (1996) *Towards Schooling for the Twenty-First Century*, Cassell, London.
Fullan, M. and Hargreaves, A. (1992) *What's Worth Fighting For In Your School*, Open University Press, Milton Keynes.
Webb, R. and Vulliamy, G. (1996) *Roles and Responsibilities in the Primary School*, Open University Press, Buckingham.

2

Managing the learning lives of children

The learning process • Learners and learning • The curriculum • Teachers and teaching • Teaching as leadership • The organizational setting

The learning process

As we move inexorably closer to a new century and a new millennium, it is important to consider the framework for learning that both the children and adults of the future will need. While our traditional framework of subjects provided security drawn from long experience, it is dangerous to assume that what seemed useful in the past will necessarily serve the changing needs of the future. In their study of schools for the twenty-first century, Per Dalin and Val Rust (1996) consider this issue of curriculum design:

> It will become increasingly difficult to define a comprehensive curriculum, both because the knowledge revolution will bring new and important knowledge into the school arena, and because the students' needs will constantly be changing. In all likelihood educational officials will likely move away from detailed teaching plans and focus more on general and thematic goals. They will attempt to define what is fundamental and exemplary.

The task of detailed curriculum design, they suggest, will again become the responsibility of educators themselves, working together within their schools. It will involve the identification of those areas where detailed knowledge and deep understanding will become increasingly important as the next century unfolds. Whatever happens, we need to accept the necessity for continuous modification and change. The essence of the curriculum will be its temporary focus, and its adaptability to new circumstances and situations. We will need to resist the temptation for a big reform movement that will attempt, once again, to write the curriculum in stone.

However, it will be unwise to discard all that we have learnt about subject disciplines and crosscurricular dimensions until we are clear that a more useful and manageable framework has emerged. We certainly need imagination and debate. What is required is a new synthesis of the factors which have traditionally been separated and kept apart – what we learn, how we learn it, how it is taught, who teaches it and how we will be able to use it. The National Curriculum is a subject-specific and content-based framework for education in schools. It ignores issues of teaching and learning, and the future uses to which the knowledge acquired through it might profitable be used. We would argue that it is time to bring these powerfully related factors into a new synthesis. Appreciating the inevitable connectedness of all the parts is long overdue. This is illustrated in Figure 2.1 (Whitaker, 1997a).

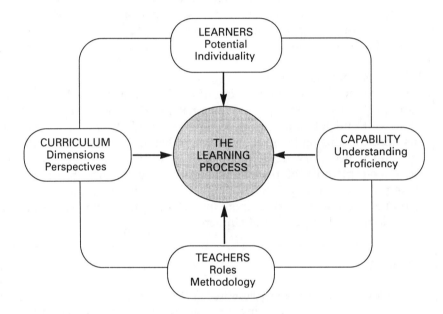

Figure 2.1 A framework for learning and teaching

At the heart of this framework is the learning process – what actually happens when learners and teachers work together to achieve understanding and proficiency. Three very distinct but powerfully connected factors feed into this process – the curriculum itself, the learners for whom it is devised and the teachers who strive to bring it to life. The outcome is not a set canon of knowledge, but a whole variety of understandings and proficiencies which provide a rich resource for the management of human life on the planet. This framework does not claim to be the model which we should adopt, but is offered as a model to stimulate thinking and professional discussion.

While we have one of the most detailed content specifications for our professional work in schools, we have one of the least documented explanations of the learning process. Much of our pedagogy is a collection of rules of thumb handed down over the generations. As yet, we have no professional council which can provide descriptions of good practice, and the business of trying to make any sense of the enormous complexities of learning and teaching is left to academics who publish their ideas, and to the practitioners, who get on as best they can. It seems to be generally accepted that we already know enough about learning and pedagogy to guide us into the future. This may be a dangerously arrogant view. It is more likely that we have significantly underestimated the intricate and complex nature of learning and teaching, traditionally viewing it from an instrumental and mechanistic perspective as imparting known information to passive pupils in lecture halls and classrooms. Any departure from this tradition tends to be labelled as *progressivism* and dismissed as pernicious dogma.

Primary schools have always taken the learning process seriously and much of what we do know about the ways to manage learning in classrooms has been developed by imaginative practitioners supported by insights and understandings from academic research. School development plans need to focus on learning much more than on curriculum, for this is where much necessary development needs to take place. Few schools, amidst their plethora of policy statements, have documents about the learning process and yet what happens moment by moment in the classrooms of our schools is far more important than elegant classifications of knowledge and targets for attainment.

Activity 2.1

Use the framework for learning illustrated in Figure 2.1 to reflect on and review your own approach to the management of learning. What particular factors would you emphasize in your own model of the learning process?

Learners and learning

There has been a tendency to perceive learning as something that others do to us rather than as something we do for ourselves. Many definitions of learning point to a process of acquisition – the child as an empty repository dependent on inputs from the adult world, gradually filling up during the processes of socialization and schooling. Success is measured in terms of how quickly and how completely this filling-up process is completed. The education system is desperately in need of new definitions and understandings if it is to succeed in liberating learning from the stranglehold of traditional orthodoxies and the limitations of too narrow an understanding of its complex processes.

Plutarch said that a child's mind is not a vessel to be filled but a fire to be kindled. Sylvia Ashton Warner (1980) notes: 'What a dangerous activity teaching is. All this plastering on of foreign stuff. Why plaster on at all when there is so much inside already?' In the struggle to improve the quality of our educational system we need to adopt an altogether more life-enhancing and optimistic appreciation of the learning process and of the enormous potential of young children to make their own way in the world.

Alternative and more life-enhancing definitions of learning abound and it is important to note some of the elements that go to make up such a vital but complex process in the development and well-being of people (Whitaker, 1995). Diana Whitmore (1986) emphasizes the awakening aspect: 'Learning should be a living process of awakening – a series of creative steps in unfoldment.' Joseph Zinker (1977) points to the creative contribution of the human spirit and suggests that learning involves '. . . releasing oneself, heart and soul into the world'. He also highlights the importance of the individual learner's will and determination: '. . . developing the courage to push against boundaries and test new behaviours.' Jack Mezzirow (1983) sees learning as a process of adjusting and acclimatizing to the world. For him, learning is 'The means by which people come to perceive, interpret, criticise and transform the worlds in which they live'.

One of the keys to understanding the learning process, and of being able to contribute to it successfully as an educator, is the appreciation that all the resources for learning are already within us; they are not acquired through teaching. Theodore Roszak (1981) emphasizes the central importance of this potential: 'We all bring into school a wholly unexplored, radically unpredictable identity. To educate is to unfold that identity – to unfold it with the utmost delicacy, recognizing that it is the most precious resource of our species, the true wealth of the human nation.'

Good teaching can awaken and direct this potential while at the same time encouraging and supporting the unfolding of identity and destiny. We need to appreciate that virtually all of us are born as *going concerns* – with all the resources for successful growth and development available to us at birth. Successful learners are those who are able to activate those resources in relation to circumstance and need.

Violet Oaklander (1978) captures the wealth of these resources and many of the essential qualities of learning that children bring with them to school:

> Children are our finest teachers. They already know how to grow, how to develop, how to learn, how to expand and discover, how to feel, laugh and cry and get mad, what is right for them and what is not right for them, what they need. They already know how to love and be joyful and live life to its fullest, to work and to be strong and full of energy. All they need is the space to do it.

Strongly associated with many traditional concepts of education is the assumption that learning demands a dependence on the teacher. Many of us come to believe that to succeed at learning we inevitably require the directing and controlling presence of a teacher or instructor. This obsession with the primacy of teaching and instruction has stolen from the individual the awareness that one of our most significant genetic features is an awesome capacity for self-development, intellectual growth and self-directed learning. Natural learning, as Seymour Papert (1980) has observed, requires neither teacher nor curriculum, and by the time most children start school they have exercised their huge learning potential in myriad ways to become sturdy individuals with the skills of adaptation, self-management and communication well established.

In her study of children's thinking Margaret Donaldson (1978) concludes: '. . . there exists a fundamental human urge to make sense of the world and bring it under deliberate control.'

Christian Schiller (1984) puts it another way:

> To young children the world is one. They are active, they are curious, they want to explore and experience. They run from one part of the field of experience to another, quite regardless of the fences we put round what we call subjects. They do not regard them because they do not see them, and if we insist on recognition we simply impede their progress and retard their learning.

It is this essential urge that humanistic psychologists have referred to as the *actualizing tendency* – that basic directional force within people to strive for understanding and fulfilment. The role of the educator is to stimulate and encourage this awesome potential and provide the conditions and resources for its healthy growth and development.

Perhaps more than anything learning is a creative process, a bringing into being. Joseph Zinker (1977) expresses something of its enormous complexity and tantalizing intricacy:

> Creativity is a celebration of one's grandeur, one's sense of making anything possible. Creativity is a celebration of life – my celebration of life. It is a bold statement: I am here! I love life! I love me! I can be anything! I can do anything!
>
> Creativity is not merely the conception, but the act itself, the fruition of that which is urgent, which demands to be stated.
>
> Creativity is an act of bravery. It states: I am willing to risk ridicule and failure so that I can experience this day with newness and freshness. The person who dares to create, to break boundaries, not only partakes of a miracle, but also comes to realize that in the process of being . . . is a miracle.

Teaching style has long been regarded as one of the keys to successful classroom practice. Less attention has been paid to the styles and stances adopted by pupils in their learning. This is surprising, since questions about how and why we are able to manage to learn are fundamental in attempting to formulate an effective framework for classroom management.

Valuable insights into learning behaviour have been provided by the ORACLE Project (Galton and Simon, 1980) which undertook detailed observation of pupils in primary school classrooms. As well as identifying a range of teaching styles the research describes four distinct types of learner:

1) *Attention seekers*   Pupils who spend considerable amounts of time out of their place, moving round the classroom and waiting to gain the teacher's attention.
2) *Intermittent workers*   Pupils who are frequently distracted from their work but do not draw the teacher's attention to themselves, flitting from one conversation to another without getting on with their work.
3) *Solitary workers*   Pupils who receive less teacher attention than others but listen and watch when other pupils receive attention. They tend to be reluctant to interact with other pupils and remain relatively static.
4) *Quiet collaborators*   Pupils who appear busy and co-operative but do rely heavily on the support of teacher for which they are prepared to wait.

While all these learner types could be identified in all the classrooms observed, their proportions varied according to the teaching style adopted. Learner behaviour can change according to needs and circumstances – an attention seeker in one teacher's classroom may become an intermittent worker in another's.

Of significance in this research are the insights into the inner needs that learners exercise in classrooms – the need for attention, the yearning for friendship and interaction, the fear of failure, the longing for approval and the dread of embarrassment or humiliation. Many pupils spend much energy gaining and avoiding contact with teachers and other pupils. Sensitive teacher attention and friendly pupil dialogue seem to be prerequisites for comfortable learning in classrooms, and an awareness of the differing degrees of confidence and insecurity children experience in the classroom setting is vital to pupil welfare and progress. What many pupils are struggling for, perhaps instinctively, through dialogue with other pupils and with the teacher are the reflective processes outlined above. They strive in often awkward and sometimes apparently deviant ways to seek understanding and insight into what is expected of them and how they can deliver.

Traditionally, the world of the classroom has honoured the brain and denied the heart. Careful observation of pupil behaviour seems to suggest that learning involves a lot more than a cognitive tussle. It is often an overwhelming struggle to cope with and survive the collection of demands, expectations and pressures that are activated moment by moment in classrooms throughout the land. That most of us survive has become the sole justification for traditional practice – *it didn't do me any harm!* Perhaps unwittingly we have allowed our horizons to be lowered. Learning should be a glorious affair, not a struggle to survive.

Something of the complexity of the learning process is revealed in the work of Honey and Mumford (1986). Building on the pioneering work of David Kolb and associates they have suggested that in the process of learning we incorporate four specific stances:

1) Learning by feeling.
2) Learning by watching.
3) Learning by thinking.
4) Learning by doing.

As we build and develop the skills of learning we draw on all four of theses elements, but often, in the light of circumstance and experience, develop a preference for one or two and a relative disinclination towards the others. Since each of us will incorporate and utilize these elements in different ways and in different combinations we each acquire a distinctive and unique learning style. Our success in formal learning will depend to what extent these four elements are catered for in school and the extent to which individuality of style is supported sensitively and creatively by teachers.

Honey and Mumford (1986) acknowledged that all learners incorporate each of the four elements in their learning but found that they also develop a preponderance for one or two. Four distinct styles are defined:

1) *Reflector*   Reflecting on concrete experience and drawing conclusions.
2) *Theorist*   Reflecting on data and information and developing ideas.
3) *Pragmatist*   Thinking about problems and trying out possibilities.
4) *Activist*   Trying out ideas, responding to challenges and taking risks.

In a similar vein, Denis Postle (1989) points to the work of John Heron who has suggested four modes of learning which provide an insight into what is going on in the psyche when we learn:

- *Action*   Learning by doing.
- *Conceptual*   Learning about a subject.
- *Imaginal*   The use of the imagination.
- *Emotional*   Learning by encounter and direct experience.

Heron suggests that while each mode depends upon each of the others, the capacity to learn at an emotional level is the nourishment for the whole learning process, providing a foundation for the involvement of the imagination which in turn acts as a spring for the conceptual stage which then pushes through into learning action.

Since the traditional assumption is that there is a single proper way to learn and that is how we have to train children, we have not paid attention to the burgeoning skills of learning that pupils have been developing for themselves since birth. Teaching styles need to be designed to acknowledge and support the different styles that learners adopt when faced with learning challenges and as teachers we need to build on the preferred elements pupils have evolved while encouraging and nourishing the neglected and avoided ones.

Perhaps one of the most frustrating challenges for educators is that while we can isolate many of the elements that contribute to effective and successful learning and point to some of the problems and difficulties that inhibit and frustrate it, the learning process itself is largely unpredictable, confusing, haphazard and messy. Perhaps what we need to learn more than anything else is to trust the learners to do more of it for themselves. It is worth recalling the observations about good learners made by Postman and Weingartner (1971). They

- enjoy solving problems;
- know what is relevant for their survival;
- rely on their own judgement;
- are not afraid of being wrong and can change their minds when necessary;
- are not fast answerers – they think first;
- are flexible and adapt according to situation and challenge;
- have a high degree of respect for facts;
- are skilled in inquiry;
- do not need to have an absolute, final, irrevocable solution to every problem; and
- do not get depressed by the prospect of saying *I don't know*.

As teachers we need to be guided by the learners themselves. We have to create opportunities for them to talk about themselves as learners – about what excites them, frustrates them, challenges them and inspires them in their learning. We need to recognize that our single most important contribution to their future well-being is to help them to develop into effective and capable learners. Noting the new educational challenges created by fast and accelerating change, Alvin Toffler (1971) notes that pupils will need skills in three crucial areas. First, they will need skills in learning itself. Schools must not only present data and information but also help pupils to develop the skills of handling it. Pupils must learn how to discard old ideas and how to replace them. Secondly, they must learn about relating to others. Increasing pressures in society and faster change will increase the difficulties in maintaining human ties. Education must help pupils to accept the absence of deep friendships, to accept loneliness and mistrust, or it must find new ways to accelerate friendship formation. Thirdly, rapid change will multiply the kinds and complexities of decision-making facing individuals. Therefore education must address the issue of overchoice directly.

The protracted and disputatious debate about the detail of the National Curriculum has revealed the tendency to see success as lying in making the right choices – whether knowledge is more important than skill, design of the curriculum more important than its delivery or structure more relevant than process. The problem lies in the creating of false dichotomies and the posing of dilemmas. These vital issues affecting the management and development of formal learning in schools cannot be reduced to questions of either/or. What is needed is an acceptance that all are important and that each has an appropriate and significant contribution to make to the whole. What is equally vital is that we learn to appreciate that it is the relationships between these necessary contributory parts that holds the key to change and improvement. Until we realize that the key to understanding human affairs and activities lies more in making connections between the various factors than in struggling to define a pecking order of relative importance, we are unlikely to satisfy our desperate need to raise the quality of learning in schools.

In further attempting to create a more synthesizing definition of learning, it is useful to consider three specific and interdependent elements. These are set out in Figure 2.2. This interpretation of learning suggests that a

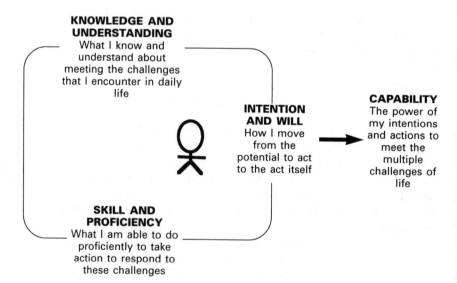

KNOWLEDGE AND UNDERSTANDING
What I know and understand about meeting the challenges that I encounter in daily life

INTENTION AND WILL
How I move from the potential to act to the act itself

CAPABILITY
The power of my intentions and actions to meet the multiple challenges of life

SKILL AND PROFICIENCY
What I am able to do proficiently to take action to respond to these challenges

Figure 2.2 The integrated learner

preoccupation with determining a single correct balance between knowledge and skill, a key feature in the debate about the National Curriculum, fails to give attention to a missing third element – the will and determination of the learner. It is not enough to be concerned only with the capacity to learn; we have to give more concerted attention to the learner's inclination and determination to learn – to those factors which create learning commitment in pupils. In the race to articulate the smartest target and the most rigorous programme of study we are in danger of avoiding the most vital of factors – the learner's own relationship to these prescriptions. Theodore Roszak (1981) observes:

> Everybody has an interest in education, but what is the child's interest – independent of all adult intervention and influence? Does that seem an impossible question to answer? Very likely it does. As impossible as it once seemed to say what a woman's interest was in life independent of her husband or her father. As impossible as it once seemed to say what the interest of slaves might be in life independent of their masters. There are those who live in such ingrained, seemingly 'natural' conditions of subjugation that we cannot begin to imagine what autonomous interests they have in the world. Children are in that category, more so than any other social dependant. Yet, they have their own interest, it is the interest that each of us discovers, if only in moments of unaccustomed exhilaration or strange absorption, when we become our own person, caught up in our own work, our own salvation. In such moments, we find an autonomy and an adventure that alone deserves to be called life. That is the child's interest, and it needs to be defended from nothing so much as the terrible 'practicalities' that are always foremost in the adult mind.

The art and skill of the educator lie in an ability to relate deeply and powerfully to this dimension of learning. It stems from an unshakeable belief in the awesome learning potential of pupils and their innate capacity to release it. It also requires a persistent curiosity about the conditions needed for learners to release this talent with vigour and determination. Unless pupils bring a desire and a commitment to learn with them into the classroom, their achievements are likely to be partial or incomplete. Learning is a complex act of creation which requires a reaching beyond perceived boundaries to something as yet unknowable. It requires courage but it also needs support. Teaching is a process of engaging day by day with these aspects of learners and nourishing them into full expression.

At the heart of educational management lies a deep concern for, and fascination with, learners and the intricacies of their learning. A driving curiosity to understand the inner process of each child's learning is the hallmark of the truly effective teacher. Over the past decade an obsession with the design of the curriculum has tended to stifle attention to this crucial area of school management. No amount of curriculum tinkering will raise standards if the teachers who have to teach it have insufficient command of the complexities of learning, and of the enormous variations that exist in each learner's management of it.

Issues of learning must be at the centre of educational decision-making and, at the very least, a primary school should have a document which declares its current beliefs and shared understandings about the nature of learning and of the significant factors that contribute to it. Such a developing understanding is a chief characteristic of professionalism.

The curriculum

In specifying the planned outcomes from the learning process, we need to look beyond that which can be simply measured. The model outlined in Figure 2.2 suggests three aspects to the outcomes of learning. First, we need to think in terms of capability, rather than knowing. Knowledge is highly desirable and vital to our survival and well-being, but it is incomplete. Education needs to produce people capable of acting in their own and the world's best interests. Two states of being become vital to this – understanding and proficiency. Schools have been instructed to concentrate on knowledge and skill performance. Capability goes well beyond this, envisaging the practical uses to which understanding and proficiency will need to be put. Such an enhanced view of learning enables us to help pupils to prepare for an active and creative role in the world. It recognizes that learning is for living, not just for knowing, and it helps us to build the life-centred curriculum that our future citizens so desperately need.

If the education system is to find its way out of its current dilemmas and difficulties it will need to depart from its traditional reliance on permanency, and the perpetuation of traditional assumptions about learning and learners. Reforms to education have tended to focus on two key areas – the structure of schooling and the content of the curriculum.

A catalogue of structural changes – selective secondary education, comprehensive schools, an increased span of compulsory attendance, the expansion of nursery provision and more recently the introduction of city technology colleges and grant-maintained schools – have all been attempts to create structures designed to improve standards. But attention to structures, without an equal consideration for the social and psychological dynamics they create, is unlikely to achieve the changes that are most necessary if schooling is to satisfy the considerable hopes raised for it.

Compared with modifications to the structure of schooling, those directed at the curriculum have been immense. Over the past thirty years, vast resources have been allocated to curriculum research and development. First, the Schools Council, and later the School Curriculum Development Committee, were formed to co-ordinate development and dissemination of new ideas in the fields of curriculum and examinations.

Now with these bodies long gone, there is little evidence that the prestigious projects of the early 1970s have radically modified the curriculum in either primary or secondary schools. The plethora of reports by HMI, DES and government committees of inquiry remains largely unread by the majority of those involved in the day-to-day teaching in our schools.

The Education Reform Act 1988 has radically changed the process of curriculum development and reform, imposing on schools a national programme of content based on core and foundations subjects, four key stages of learning, programmes of study and attainment targets. In addition a national system of assessment and testing has been introduced with external examinations being conducted at the ages of 7, 11, 14 and 16. Some of the most significant features of this change have been the difficulty of imposing an untested model on pupils and the challenge of producing a definitive set of targets relevant in a fast changing world. Major changes to the core subjects have had to be made even before the foundation subject curriculum has been agreed. New bureaucracies have been created to devise, implement, monitor and evaluate this new system but it is difficult to make a case that they will succeed in helping the process of schooling become the liberating and deeply satisfying experience it should be for its participants.

We need to bring to our considerations of learning a much greater attention to the participants in the whole process. It is our pupils who will manage the world when their time comes, and they need to be involved in the means by which they are prepared for that awesome responsibility. Not one official document has been produced explaining the National Curriculum to the children for whom it was designed. This gives some indication of the low expectations of understanding held about our pupils, and a measure of the disregard held for their own hopes and aspirations.

The continuing development of information technologies will enable children to undertake for themselves at home, through CD-Rom and allied technologies, a good deal of the basic work currently done by schools. Within the first decade or so of the next century this will present schools with a fundamental question about the role of schools in what John Abbot (1996) describes as the *learning society*. The law insists that our children receive an appropriate education, not that they attend school. It is likely that we will see a fragmenting of full-time attendance in schools, and a greater incidence of part-time contracts, where children use local schools for those parts of the learning they cannot do better for themselves. This, rather than competition for full-time places, currently the panacea for improving standards, will bring real market forces into the schooling system. Methods of teaching will have to change to accommodate these shifting patterns. We need to attend to our own professional methodologies and practices quickly, before events force us into crisis action.

Capability

The goals our society currently sets for its learners are subject specific and tied to detailed objectives which can be measured on a ten-point scale. Such is our ambition for the children in our schools. It is interesting to see how other countries express their educational ambitions. In 1994 the Norwegian Department of Education produced a new curriculum framework (Dalin and Rust, 1996). Among its declarations are a set of six goals for schooling:

1) A person searching for meaning.
2) A creative person.
3) A working person.
4) An enlightened person.
5) A co-operating person.
6) An environmentally friendly person.

What a stunning contrast between this and our own statements of intent. What is interesting is that statements like this adorn the brochures produced by many primary schools for parents. Such an approach to learning is central to their philosophy of education and schooling, but sadly it has been held up to ridicule and contempt.

While the National Curriculum currently dominates the timetables of most primary schools, it is likely that we will see continuing development in its pattern and design in the years to come. What is important is that schools themselves have their own clear view about what it is they intend for their learners. Most primary schoolteachers are enormously ambitious for their pupils, and look to qualities and capabilities well beyond the somewhat life-limiting and instrumental targets set within the National Curriculum.

Managing a primary school is an act of optimism guided by clear visions and high ideals. While the government has moved towards target-driven school management in the battle for raised standards, we must not confuse targets with ambitions and intentions. A vital part of effective primary school management lies in the articulation and explanation of bold visions for the future lives of its pupils.

Teachers and teaching

Perhaps one of the reasons why teachers have been disparaged so readily lies in a false and dangerously limited perception of the nature of the work they do. Regarded at best as the skilful transmission of subject knowledge, teaching has been reduced to a basic formula by those who have driven the legislation. It has been difficult and stressful for teachers to be dictated to by those who hold such a simplistic and limited model of the schooling process. Over the past twenty years, the teaching profession has moved

---

Activity 2.2

Consider the classification of skills and qualities outlined in Figure 2.3. Use each of the five categories to reflect on your own teaching style. What are the key elements of your own approach? What are the principles upon which this approach is based?

---

away from simple, formulaic approaches to teaching. A great many teachers, aware of the restrictive and dispiriting effects on pupils of simplistic nostrums, have engaged in a search for more life-enhancing and effective programmes of study.

Many of the notions currently put forward by politicians seem to reaffirm those inhibiting and restrictive notions of schooling that teachers have been trying to move on from. These are summarized well by Carl Rogers (1980):

1) Teachers are the sole possessors of knowledge: pupils the expected recipients.
2) Teaching is the means of getting the knowledge into the recipients. Tests and examinations measure how much the pupil has received.
3) Teachers alone possess power, pupils obey.
4) Rule by authority is the accepted policy in the classroom.
5) Pupils are to be distrusted, they cannot be expected to work satisfactorily without the teacher constantly controlling and checking them.
6) Pupils are best controlled by being kept in a constant state of fear.
7) Democracy is taught about but not practised in the classroom. Pupils do not play a part in the formulation of their individual goals, these are determined for them.
8) There is no room for whole persons in the education system, only their intellects. Emotional development is not regarded as a necessary area for learning.

One of the ways we can help to bring about a more informed approach to educational decision-making is to articulate a more comprehensive analysis of the work that teachers actually do. The current perception of teaching is dangerously limiting. Even in some initial training institutions teaching is still regarded as pedagogy – the science of teaching children. Very little attention seems to be given to the fact that in addition to a wealth of cognitive and curriculum considerations, teaching also encompasses a whole range of organizational issues that are generated when purposeful activity is conducted in a collective setting. Issues of institutional management, organizational psychology, culture, climate and personal welfare are major concerns for classroom teachers, demanding knowledge, skills and qualities beyond those traditionally associated with pedagogy. It is time that teachers in schools were afforded the same understanding and respect as those who occupy positions as managers in other kinds of organization.

If we adopt the frequently used definition of management as getting things done with and through other people, we can see the relevance. Teachers are charged with tasks to do with organizing learning in a pupil community. The complexities of this responsibility are certainly equal to those experienced by senior managers in industrial and commercial organizations. But we still conceive of teaching as a discrete, specialized activity somehow devoid of organizational and management implications. Educational management has tended to focus only on the non-educational elements of organizational life and has concerned itself largely with the roles and responsibilities of senior staff. The essence of management in schools is the transaction of classroom learning. The co-ordination of a subject or department, while challenging and complex, is less significant by comparison. Perhaps the key contribution that management training and development can make to education is to focus on the complexities of classroom life and the challenges to teachers of managing learning in a large group of pupils with differing abilities, needs, behaviour and self-awareness.

One way to create a more complete understanding of teaching as managing is to examine the range of elements which combine to describe and explain it. These are set out in Figure 2.3.

OCCUPATIONAL
SKILLS AND QUALITIES
• subject specialization
• teaching methods
• child development
• history of education
• curriculum design
• assessment

RELATIONAL
SKILLS AND QUALITIES
• courtesy and
  consideration
• warmth
• listening
• empathy
• responsiveness
• respect, etc.

MOTIVATIONAL
SKILLS AND QUALITIES
• ambition
• aspiration
• inspiration
• encouragement
• feedback
• support

MANAGERIAL
SKILLS AND QUALITIES
• creating
• planning
• communicating
• motivating
• organizing
• evaluating

SITUATIONAL SKILLS AND
QUALITIES
• simultaneity
• variability
• change
• serendipity
• unpredictability
• chaos

Figure 2.3 Professional skills and qualities

Occupational skills and qualities

These are the skills and qualities that are developed through training and experience. They are of a specialist and technical nature and specific to particular occupations and professions. Teachers have different occupational skills from nurses, lawyers or engineers, for example. They are often the key focus of job-related training within organizations.

Relational skills and qualities

These are the skills and qualities acquired and developed through the process of socialization. Their purpose is to develop and sustain relationships and enable social living. They determine our capacity to get on well with other people in both professional and social settings. A complete list of personal skills and qualities would be very long indeed.

Until fairly recently, these skills rarely featured in the formal educational process although they are constantly referred to by adults in the socializing of the young. Whilst they are crucially important in teaching, they have rarely been the subject of training and development. It is often our relationships with others that cause our most difficult and emotionally painful moments. It is not surprising, then, that the additional pressures that work involves can increase the challenge and stress in our own relationships.

Success in teaching requires us not only to be aware of this but also to improve our own skills in order to manage our relationships effectively and sensitively.

Managerial skills and qualities

These are the skills and qualities needed to work with and through other people. Teaching has not traditionally been associated with that professional activity known as *management*, but even a cursory glance at the following analysis will demonstrate that teaching is indeed a management activity *par excellence*. The following classification of managerial skills provides a useful starting point for consideration (Whitaker, 1983):

Creating
- having good ideas
- finding original solutions to common problems
- anticipating the consequences of decisions and actions
- employing lateral thinking
- using imagination and intuition

Planning
- relating present to future needs
- recognizing what is important and what merely urgent
- anticipating future trends
- analysing

Communicating
- understanding people

- listening
- explaining
- written communication
- getting others to talk
- tact
- tolerance of other's mistakes
- giving thanks and encouragement
- keeping everyone informed
- using information technology

Motivating
- inspiring others
- providing realistic challenges
- helping others to set goals and targets
- helping others to value their own contributions and achievements

Organizing
- making fair demands on others
- making rapid decisions
- being in front when it counts
- staying calm when the going is difficult
- recognizing when the job is done

Evaluating
- comparing outcomes with intentions
- self-evaluation
- helping to appraise the work of others
- taking corrective action where necessary

Far too little attention seems to be given to a managerial approach in initial teacher education and if we are to succeed in raising standards of teaching then a more comprehensive taxonomy of teaching skills and qualities will be needed.

Motivational skills and qualities

Although referred to in the managerial category, the motivational aspects of teaching require special reference. Teaching is one of the very few professions where one of the key processes of operation is also one of its significant products. Teachers engage with their pupils in ways that can bring the variables of needs, experiences and desires into a powerful combination. Teachers have their own ambitions and aspirations for their pupils but are also concerned to arouse, support and respect the sometimes tentative ambitions and aspirations pupils have for themselves. One of the aims held by most schools is to inculcate a love of learning in their pupils which will be life long. This category is one of the most crucial in the professional repertoire and yet it seems to be afforded insufficient attention in the initial and continuing education of teachers.

Situational skills and qualities

This category refers to the skills and qualities that arise out of the infinitely varied, complex and changing circumstances in which teachers operate. No two minutes in teaching are ever the same. Pupils perceptions, understanding and confusions are in a continuous state of development and it is never easy for a teacher to understand the state of the learning variables for a class of learners at any specific moment. Learning is not a straightforward, predictable and easily manageable process and any number of unplanned and unpredictable factors can arise to enhance or inhibit it. It is often the sensitive awareness of complexity that teachers apply at crucial moments that makes the difference between confusion and understanding. The skills of good teachers are geared to serendipitous moments and unexpected opportunities and a key element in their approach is a subtle capacity to operate on the edge of chaos – that fine dividing line between order and disorder. These are elusive skills, difficult to train and impossible to plan for. In good teachers they seem to be part of a vital set of predispositions that distinguish excellent practitioners from the rest.

One of the most frustrating aspects of management work is realizing at the end of the day that although you have been exceedingly busy, many planned tasks and activities remain neglected and unattended to. Over recent years time management has become something of a preoccupation as we struggle to pack more and more into the same amount of time.

Part of the desperation about time and workload arises out of a basic misperception about the nature of managerial work. Most of us see our roles as requiring us to attend to those tasks and activities designated in our job descriptions. We make plans and organize our time to deal with these requirements. What we find, however, as we set out to conduct these tasks is that we are constantly interrupted. During the course of most days we find ourselves engaged in a series of interactions, few of which had been planned. People approach us and make requests. Often these approaches seem friendly and undemanding, prefaced by such phrases as *Can I have a word? Have you got a minute?* or *Are you busy?* The modesty of these requests usually belie their importance. Few of us turn down these requests; in fact we tend to respond to them with willingness and sensitivity. Taken individually, these interactions are usually very brief, seldom longer than a few minutes and often very much less, but they do create a diversion in our already tightly planned schedule. It is not uncommon to find that a succession of short interruptions has placed our whole schedule in jeopardy. The tendency is to blame ourselves for giving more attention to the apparently urgent than to the important tasks we have set ourselves. We seem to find ourselves preoccupied with incidents and events that conspire to divert us from the real tasks and challenges of our roles. One of the consequences is that we can feel out of control, reacting to events rather than directing them. We can feel guilty because we are so driven by events and worried that perhaps we lack the skills for the job.

What we have here is a classic management dilemma. We have tended to think that good managers are always in control of their destiny and are only effective when they operate in a proactive way, demonstrating supreme control over their actions and the situations in which they find themselves. The reality is quite different. Far from dealing with trivia and apparently minor incidents, these interruptions are crucial to the well-being of the organization, enabling if to function effectively, to deal with its temporary difficulties and problems and to engage in the essential daily work. Research has shown (Mintzberg, 1973) that management by interruption is a highly effective way of operating, creating countless opportunities for real issues to be dealt with, policies to be highlighted, values to be demonstrated and visions pursued. It is because managers are so good in this incidental mode that so many schools are well run, and are able to deal with their crises and satisfy the demands made on them. Figure 2.4 (Whitaker, 1995) suggests that teachers, as indeed most managers, operate in two distinct but related modes – fixed and flexible.

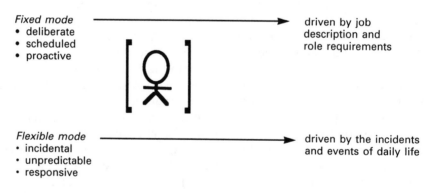

Figure 2.4 Operational modes

It is often in the flexible mode that managers do their most effective work. In the spontaneity of the moment they are able to deal with the urgent issues, creatively helping others to gain the information they need, resolve their dilemmas and difficulties and receive the encouragement and reassurance that is so often necessary to function effectively.

One of the challenges of management work lies in placing these two modes in a realistic balance. Since the flexible mode tends not to be referred to in job descriptions we do not afford it the importance it deserves, nor allocate time for it by not scheduling our deliberate work too tightly. We need to appreciate that being interrupted presents opportunities to lead and manage, to advance the work of the organization by responding to the needs others are facing and by helping them to manage their work more effectively.

Activity 2.3

What is your response to the curriculum statement (on p. 34) issued by the Norwegian Department of Education? Make a list of your own goals for schooling.

Teaching as leadership

Another useful way to examine the nature of the teacher's role is through the concept of leadership. Teachers can be regarded as exercising one of the most demanding leadership challenges devised by society – the education of the next generation. Leadership can be regarded as that part of a manager's work concerned with helping people to tackle prescribed tasks to the optimum of their ability. It is concerned more with effectiveness than with efficiency and more with quality than with attainment.

As well as considering leadership from the leader's own perspective, it is important to have regard for the needs we have of our leaders. Good leaders seem have an infinite capacity not only to satisfy vital needs but also to anticipate them. Such a capacity grows out of four key qualities:

1) Genuine interpersonal behaviour.
2) Warmth, care and respect for those we work with.
3) Empathy.
4) A strong and unshifting belief in the potential of others to grow, develop and change.

All of us are needy, and failure to get some very specific needs satisfied, particularly those that contribute to our pattern of motivation, can result in loss of confidence and enthusiasm; a sense of not being involved and a part of things; a feeling of being unappreciated and undervalued and a reduction of job commitment and energy. These are expensive losses which few organizations can afford. Good leadership is the delicate process of anticipating these needs in others and striving to satisfy them. This is as true for learners in classrooms as it is for workers in factories or offices. Teaching is an act of discovering what the felt needs of the pupil are and the growth needs they invariably conceal. Figure 2.5 indicates a range of needs we are likely to experience quite frequently by pupils during the process of learning (Whitaker, 1993).

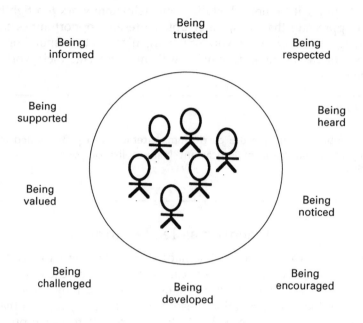

Figure 2.5   Leadership and needs

Effective teachers are those who are able to reach out to pupils, to appreciate and understand their needs and seek specific and individual ways of satisfying them. Diana Whitmore (1986) asserts: 'If children were to experience adults as welcoming, guiding and supportive, they would discover the wonder of life, the joy of exploring, the beauty of understanding.'

As teachers we can help to create these felt experiences in pupils if we seize opportunities, usually in the flexible operational mode described above, to respond to some basic needs:

- *Trusting*   Conveying to pupils a belief in their abilities. Resisting the temptation to increase control when things are difficult. Expressing delight at successes and achievements.
- *Listening*   Constantly seeking opportunities to listen to pupils' current experiences. Asking questions, seeking information, eliciting opinions, delving into details and showing genuine interest and concern.
- *Noticing*   Taking note of contributions and providing regular positive feedback on successes and achievements.

- *Encouraging* Empathizing with the demands and challenges of the learning process. Providing support for problem-solving and action planning.
- *Developing* Offering practical help for those striving to make breakthroughs in knowledge and skill. Working to create new learning opportunities
- *Challenging* Building a climate of systematic and continuous improvement. Constantly helping others to seek new angles, new possibilities and new ideas.
- *Valuing* Providing detailed and specific feedback so that all pupils feel a deep sense that their contributions and efforts are valued.
- *Informing* Keeping information flowing freely through the classroom. Checking that pupils know what is going on.
- *Supporting* Offering practical help as well as moral support. Getting alongside pupils as often as possible. Providing a helping hand and a listening ear.

In the world of fast and accelerating change the skills of effective leadership are developed in and through experience. Warren Bennis (1989) notes: 'Leaders learn by leading and they learn best by leading in the face of obstacles. As weather shapes mountains, so problems make leaders. Difficult bosses, lack of vision in the executive suite, circumstances beyond their control, have been the leader's basic curriculum.' This suggests a radical revision of the way that leadership has traditionally been conceived. Teachers, like those in other leadership positions, must no longer assume they are where they are because of what they have learnt, but because they have a capacity to learn faster than the rate of change in the surrounding environment.

Eric Hoffer (1985) also emphasizes the importance of learning in the basic approach of effective leaders: 'In times of drastic change it is the learners who inherit the future, the learned find themselves equipped to live in a world that no longer exists.' This suggests a new vision of the pupil–teacher relationship, one that helps to destroy the idea that teaching is an élite and specialist occupation. Theodore Roszak (1981) suggests that in every educational exchange it is first of all the teacher who has something to learn. In approaching pupils there are vital questions to consider:

- Who is this child?
- What does he or she bring to this situation?
- What is there here for me to discover that no one else has ever known before?

It is through interactions with pupils, what Roszak describes as *glad encounters with the unexpected*, that we can engage in discovering and empowering each child's learning destiny.

Teaching and leadership are both concerned with helping others to see that something is possible, and supporting them in the process of removing the blocks which prevent them standing on their own feet. It is what Daniel Rosenblatt (1975) describes as '. . . offering a kind of hope that change is possible'.

Leadership, as teaching, creates an atmosphere that promotes the taking of small steps towards change, change that is free of shame, fear, guilt, humiliation and degradation:

> There has to be some kind of educational process bringing the art of living into day to day management. There has always been a complete difference between the way individuals relate to their colleagues and the way they relate to their friends and family. In the latter area, kindness, tolerance etc are not regarded as sentimental and wet, but as making the relationship work. Can one parallel this in business now? The difference between the two sets of attitudes is beginning to narrow and that may be the answer to tomorrow's problems.

This quotation from Francis Kinsman (1991) highlights a key challenge for teachers and leaders – to counter the traditional and unnecessary separation in organizations of the personal and the professional. People are whole beings and are at their best when they feel complete and integrated. The separation into parts of ourselves is one of the most damaging tendencies in human activity.

There are no simple solutions in management because there are no simple problems. If problems were simple and straightforward there would be no need of management in the first place. Leadership is an active response to complexity, an ambitious striving towards achievement in awkward situations. It is a journey of belief and hope and downright determination.

The organizational setting

When people participate in organizational life, they are significantly affected by the dynamics they encounter and contribute to, and behave in ways designed to protect and advance appropriate self-interest. Some of the dynamics that arise in organizational settings can seriously impede and inhibit our capacity to be effective and to realize and utilize the full range of our skills and abilities. In successful organizations the impact of these dynamics is quite different – they activate and enhance personal effectiveness.

Just as in the organization of work in factories and offices, so in schools we have tended not to appreciate the powerful effect that organizational dynamics have on learners. Many of the causes of serious underachievement can be attributed to organizational factors rather than cognitive ones. These elements can inhibit the capacity of pupils to realize their potential for learning. Teachers, too, can find themselves deflected from the primary function of managing pupil learning by the pressures and demands of purely organizational issues.

In recent years, with an ever-accelerating rate of change, there has been a concerted struggle to discover and define new organizational structures and to create a new deal for the individuals who participate in them. There is a new concern to replace many of the inherited organizational traditions that exploit the individual and diminish human dignity with practices that are altogether more life enhancing and more successful in bringing the best out of people.

From a traditional preoccupation with product, we are discovering the importance of attending also to process. In the new management paradigm, the key question becomes – how can we help people to be as effective as they are capable of being and to be as successful as they want to be? The following observations apply as much to classrooms as they do to schools.

Organizational life

When we enter an organization, we cease to be free agents, and subject ourselves to a range of contractual requirements and institutional obligations. We accept defined roles with boundaries that specify the functions we are expected to perform, and become part of an elaborate hierarchy of dependent relationships. This involves a considerable challenge to our powers of adjustment and accommodation, often requiring us to accept things we feel uncomfortable about or uncommitted to. What we often experience in organizations, whether as employee or pupil, is a severe challenge to our directional tendency as we encounter impediments to our hopes and aspirations, lack of interest in our needs and disregard for our anxieties and concerns.

A key function of those with senior responsibility in organizations is to manage the match between the needs and requirements of the institution with the needs and aspirations of each of its individual participants. Perhaps it is because this is so difficult that so little concern has been shown for it. But since organizational life is inevitably complex, difficult and frustrating there is all the more reason to apply energy and imagination to its management. When serious mismatches occur we create dissonances and dysfunction, and the organization fails to optimize its available potential.

The struggle for match needs to be considered in relation to a set of key factors:

- purposes and intentions
- values and attitudes
- roles and relationships
- practices and behaviours
- power and authority.

Purposes and intentions

People tend to work best when they feel a strong sense of commitment to clearly defined purposes. A sense of ownership is sometimes used to describe a powerful association between individual and organizational goals. When organizational aims are defined by a minority of senior staff and imposed on the others as a requirement, then there is often a weak sense of association, and compliance rather than commitment is the likely outcome. Therefore, the deliberate management of intentions becomes a major management task requiring the active, if sometimes disputatious, involvement of all those who will be required to serve them. Because this process can be messy, involving the compromising of cherished ideals, it is often avoided. A poorer end product is traded for a quieter and more prescribed life.

Values and attitudes

While an individual teacher's work will be conditioned by the attitudes, beliefs and ideas that are brought to bear upon it, so the work of the school as a whole will be conditioned by the ways that individual value systems relate and interact with each other. Each participant in organizational life can be considered as having a personal value system consisting of

- *values*: specified and prized opinions;
- *attitudes*: more or less settled modes of thinking;
- *assumptions*: taken-for-granted ideas and opinions;
- *ideals*: high personal concepts and visions;
- *beliefs*: ideas accepted as truths; and
- *prejudices*: preconceived opinions.

This value system has a powerful effect. Not only does it determine how an individual thinks and feels but it also affects behaviour particularly in relationships. New relationships are very much about testing out interpersonal value systems for similarities and differences. Clashes of values may inhibit the development of the relationship while similarities of attitude may serve to extend or deepen it. The decision to end or continue an interaction will often be determined by the sense of comfort or discomfort that is experienced as the two value systems interact. Extended across a wider pattern of relationships in an organization this process becomes complex and frequently confusing.

Roles and relationships

It is through the exercising of roles and the building of relationships that the management of an organization is done. In countless daily interactions, some exceedingly brief, decisions are made, ideas exchanged, possibilities explored, problems dealt with and concerns expressed. The extent to which we can successfully perform our roles and responsibilities will depend on how well we feel we can transact business with others – colleagues on the staff or pupils in the classroom. We prefer to engage with those colleagues with whom there is a high degree of commonality, and disengage from those whose values threaten us or cause discomfort and anxiety. When we are new to an organization we are prepared to negotiate and adjust as we strive to build effective working relationships, and to compromise values if necessary to maintain politeness and a comfortable interpersonal climate. In long-established situations, in the staffroom or classroom, relationships are more likely to settle into a number of patterns:

• intimate and enjoyable relationships;
• diffident but polite relationships;
• strained and difficult relationships; and
• hostile relationships.

In a large organization all these combinations are likely. These profiles will condition relationships and determine interpersonal behaviours at both the personal and the professional level.

Practices and behaviours

In organizations where work functions are complex, requiring some degree of personal autonomy about style and operation – learning and teaching would both fall within this category – issues of conformity and nonconformity sometimes arise. Where a particular house style of practice is developed by the participants themselves, then there is often a high degree of attention to methodology and technique. In professional organizations such as schools, styles and practices in teaching are often regarded as the concern of the individual, although the same is not true about learning. Approval or disapproval of practice by senior staff often depends on whether the practice is in tune with their preferred method. Far too often there is a conspiracy to avoid attention to practice, creating awkward tensions among colleagues who work in contrasting ways.

Power and authority

A major determinant of personal behaviour in organizations is the way that those placed in the upper levels of the organizational hierarchy behave to those placed lower. In schools this applies to the relationships between senior staff and their colleagues and between teachers and pupils in classrooms. Research has demonstrated (Rowan, 1988) that when people are overcontrolled and oversupervised they feel mistrusted, and this produces a withholding of energy, enthusiasm and commitment to the task in hand. Hierarchies have been found to produce a range of inhibiting effects on those in the middle and lower levels:

- feelings of inadequacy;
- inability to express oneself;
- inability to influence anyone;
- feelings of being shut out;
- increase in cynicism;
- increase in destructive feelings;
- feelings that one has either to dominate or be dominated;
- feeling that to conform is the safest way forward;
- feeling that intolerance and exploitation has to be accepted;
- feeling that new ideas must only come from the top; and
- feeling that those at the top are not interested in these feelings and that there are no easy ways of communicating with them.

Primary schools are one of the most familiar organizations in our society. Like the local shop or parish church, there is one in most villages and neighbourhoods, and almost all of us have spent some years as a member of one. It is sad, therefore, that they have featured hardly at all in the literature of organizations. Indeed there seems to be a view that schools lie outside the boundaries of organizational theory and therefore do not need managing. The tendency to think of schools as separate from the general community of organizations says something about our social attitudes to learning, as well as our values about the role of children and teachers in society. It is as if their predominantly child population debars primary schools from serious attention; that anything to do with the pre-adult world is somehow frivolous, is best left to women and does not need to be taken seriously. How sad it is that most people working in the non-educational mainstream of organizations would regard as ridiculous the idea that primary schools have much to demonstrate about effective management and leadership.

This tendency to ignore, or at least to marginalize, the pre-adult world is dangerously negligent in a society which needs all the good ideas it can get. If we want to understand more about how and why people behave as they do when they are adults, it is sensible to note what happens to them when they are children. Primary schools are ideal places in which to study the concept of organization, to observe how young children react to their first experiences of institutional life, how they respond to controlling forces other than those provided by their parents, and how they make the decisions about how to manage their personal needs, their developing relationships and their educational potential.

Not only is it in primary schools that children undergo their first experience of planned and organized education but it is also the first time they encounter that most powerful of social structures – organizational life. The transition from home to school is one of the most significant rites of passage in early childhood – for the 4- or 5-year-old often more significant and traumatic than later ones will be. That children manage it so well is a tribute to their frequently underestimated powers of understanding and adaptation, and their capacity for sensible self-direction. By lunchtime on their first day at school, most children have sorted out a whole of range of regulations and requirements, gained a sense of the sources of power in the organization, learnt about possible danger points to be avoided and made some new friends with whom to share all these new experiences.

To dismiss primary schools as simplistic and straightforward is to make a significant error of perception and understanding. In contrast with primary schools, most manufacturing organizations manage a reasonably clear and identifiable set of systems and procedures. Most products have a finite design and can be produced within a set of accurate tolerances. Raw materials can be specified, machine processes set up and the production process conducted to a high degree of predictability. Primary schools on the other hand operate exclusively as human systems within which the variables are both incalculable and enormously complex. Pupils and their teachers work in close proximity to each other but are differentiated by a whole set of constantly changing elements – previous experience, present mood, intelligence, aptitude, proficiency, personality, attitudes, values, prejudices, hopes, aspirations, fears, frailties, will, determination, thoughts, feelings and self-esteem. The product that primary education is concerned with is nothing less than constant and continuous change in human perception, knowledge, understanding, skill and capability. Few other organizations in our society could claim such an awesome and demanding challenge.

This is not to suggest that manufacturing or commercial organizations are simple and straightforward to manage, but that primary schools involve management and leadership factors that have have been significantly underestimated and consistently ignored. Teachers begin their professional lives by taking charge of a significant organization of their own. A class of thirty or so young learners is a sizeable organization in any context and the teacher takes on a range of complex management tasks – the strategic leadership of thirty hearts and minds, all at different stages of growth and development; the building and developing of a social and moral culture within which the work of the class can be safely managed; the devising and designing of learning experiences to enable each child to advance in knowledge, skill and understanding; and the monitoring of the constantly shifting dynamics of the learning process in cramped conditions with barely adequate resources. In addition to all this there is the enormous bureaucracy of paperwork to manage, parental concerns to be dealt with, social and emotional concerns of children to be responded to and the constant public scrutiny of politicians and media to be coped with.

Those who run our primary schools – the heads, deputies, curriculum co-ordinators and classroom teachers – are among the most skilful and imaginative exponents of management and leadership in our society. Such is the complexity of school life that few of their functions can ever be carried out one at a time. They have developed what can only be described as the art of skilful simultaneity – that capacity to operate in a variety of management modes at the same time. Theirs is a complex and undefinable world, packed with intensity and unpredictability. That the vast majority of our primary schools are havens of calmness, purposefulness, endeavour, joy, visual brightness and stimulation is a tribute to those who manage them.

What sensitive and alert observers of good primary schools will discern is a whole range of subtle and effective forms of leadership at work – leadership that helps the children themselves to consider big ideas and relate them to their developing world view, that encourages rather than cajoles, that arouses rather than imposes and that kindles rather than enforces. What we rarely see in these places is leadership which arbitrarily imposes its own will, that underestimates the potentialities and aspirations of its participants and which patronizes the small size and short age of its young members. What we also see in the good primary school is something even more enterprising and exciting – pupils as managers, exercising levels of self-direction, responsibility and accountability that they may never experience in their later careers.

If we wish to help our schools to develop effectively in the fast changing world, then we need to realize and appreciate their significance as complex organizations, faced with the most formidable of tasks – the bringing of young people to a relevant and appropriate state of readiness to take on the awesome responsibilities of adult life. We will need to take a more lively interest in the power of primary schools to inform us about the skills of building safe and nourishing organizations, and to reveal the sorts of management and leadership expertise that many business organizations would be proud to possess.

Activity 2.4

1) Reflect on your own experiences as a pupil. What factors helped or hindered your own learning?
2) In what specific ways can the culture of the classroom affect a pupil's capacity to learn effectively at school?

ISSUES FOR DISCUSSION

1) One of the key challenges for the teaching profession is to address the issue of pedagogy and to produce documented descriptions of methodology and practice to guide teachers in their complex and demanding work.

2) As a society we have to consider whether the traditions subject-based approach to primary school learning has the best potential to prepare young children for the complex, uncertain and constantly changing world they will live in as adults.

3) Until we understand the complex dynamics and variables of classroom life and their impact on children's learning, we will not be in a position to deal with the issue of educational standards effectively.

Further reading

Abbott, J. (1996) Chaos and Complexity: or just Education? In *Education 2000 News*, March, Education 2000, Letchworth.

Dalin P. and Rust, V. (1996) *Towards Schooling for the Twenty-First Century*, Cassell, London.

Whitaker, P. (1997) *Primary Schools and the Future*, Open University Press, Buckingham.

3

Leadership: principles and practices

Purposeful leadership • Being an expert • Action-centred leadership • Trans-formational leadership: the moral imperative • Professional relationships and motivation • Intervention: constraints, purposes and processes • Leading the team • Investing in the school's culture: principles of leadership

> The effectiveness of the school improvement approach is dependent on the growth of what might be termed collaborative professionality whereby heads and teachers increasingly adopt a problem-solving approach.
>
> (Hoyle, 1992)

Purposeful leadership

Leaders today operate in a context of increasingly detailed answerability to parents, governors, LEAs, the DfEE and the world of business for the quality of education in their schools. The late 1980s and 1990s brought major legislation – the culmination of Callaghan's (1976) Ruskin speech calling for more accountability – that resulted in a great number of externally imposed innovations. All these have to be 'managed'. Leaders must ensure that their schools have annually reviewed, publicly available school development plans, systematic teacher appraisal, a school marketing policy, efficient monitoring and assessment procedures for the National Curriculum – and all this whilst managing directed time, professional development days, SATs and a 'real' school budget. It is not just that headteachers and others need to possess a clearer vision and wider range of skills and qualities than ever before but also that they will be called upon to articulate, communicate and apply them more frequently, and in more complex and stressful situations, not least in their own schools amongst staff whose morale is not always high. Yet in the ever-increasing number of texts concerned with leadership (of people) and management of the curriculum and organization, the most neglected area is often the process of being a leader. There seems to be an assumption that once aims, objectives and means of assessment have been clarified and placed in a plan all that has to be done is to follow rationally a series of prescribed steps or to complete a checklist; or, at another extreme, that leaders (or managers) must already possess the necessary qualities and skills or they would not be leaders! Those who have experienced leadership roles will know that prescribed checklists for action are fallible and that opportunities for teachers (as distinct from headteachers) to develop leadership and management skills are even now few and far between.

Recent developments of a national qualification for new and aspiring headteachers, subject leaders and serving headteachers by the Teacher Training Agency (TTA) are to be welcomed, although it is too early to judge the quality or impact of these.

In an investigation into primary heads' perspectives of their work in the 1990s, Geoff Southworth (1995) found that their jobs had become more complex and stressful, involving longer hours of work which was often concerned more with administrative and organizational tasks and less with involvement with colleagues. He found that headship was about continuing reconciliation of 'dualities and dilemmas' between, for example: 'the tension between being a head and/or being a teacher; the need to manage the organization and to provide professional leadership; the exercise of one's own power and authority alongside the need to empower others; maintaining the school and also developing it.'

The management of uncertainty and change is likely to be achieved most effectively if the leader has a clear sense of vision which is shared by staff and is able to articulate this and communicate it through the myriad of interactions in and without school that occur on a daily basis, and through the rituals, signs and symbols which represent the ethos and direction of the school. Most important of all, though, are self-knowledge and the ability to preserve and foster a personal–professional life balance.

Management style is the biggest single factor in making quality improvements in school. It will be the headteacher who ensures collegiality internally – so necessary if progress in and continuity within and beyond the National Curriculum are to be achieved. It will be he or she who ensures that the staff gain skills of communication and collaboration needed for working more closely with parents and governors. This kind of facilitating leadership places an emphasis upon 'consultation, team-work and participation' identified long ago as contributing to effective leadership (DES, 1977a). In 1983, the DES reiterated their view of the importance of effective leadership:

> Head teachers, and other senior staff with management responsibilities within the schools, are of crucial importance. Only if they are effective managers of their teaching staffs and have the material resources available to them, as well as possessing the qualities needed for educational leadership, can schools offer their pupils the quality of education which they have a right to expect.

Yet effective leadership is the result of complex interactions between style, prevailing staffroom learning cultures, uses and perceptions of power and authority, and individual and group relationships as applied to particular tasks. An increasing number of teachers who are not heads or deputies have become 'leaders' within curriculum and pastoral areas of school life. Indeed, the recommendation in ILEA's *Improving Primary Schools* (1985) that 'Primary school teachers, except possibly in their probationary year, should take responsibility for advising the rest of the staff on major aspects of the curriculum or associated matters, for example assessment', is now enshrined in legislation (DES, 1988).

ILEA's Junior School Project's (1986) findings confirmed the move from a concept of the headteacher as leader to a concept of the head as 'leader among leaders', who works to facilitate leadership and encourage it among the whole staff. Three of the twelve key factors in effective schooling concerned leadership:

Purposeful leadership of the staff by the headteacher
'Purposeful leadership' occurred where the headteacher understood the needs of the school and was actively involved in the school's work, without exerting total control over the rest of the staff. In effective schools, headteachers were involved in curriculum discussions and influenced the content of guidelines drawn up within the school, without taking total control. They also influenced teaching strategies of teachers, but only selectively, where they judged it necessary ... a systematic policy of record keeping was important. With regard to in-service training, those heads exhibiting purposeful leadership did not allow teachers total freedom to attend any course: attendance was encouraged for a good reason ... Thus, effective headteachers were sufficiently involved in, and knowledgeable about, what went on in the classrooms and about progress of individual pupils. They were more able to feel confident about their teaching staff and did not need to intervene constantly. At the same time, however, they were not afraid to assert their leadership where appropriate.

The involvement of the deputy head
Where the head generally involved the deputy in policy decisions, it was beneficial to the pupils ...

Thus it appeared that a certain amount of delegation by the headteacher, and a sharing of responsibilities, promoted effectiveness.

The involvement of teachers
In successful schools, the teachers were involved in curriculum planning and played a major role in developing their own curriculum guidelines. As with the deputy head, teacher involvement in decisions

concerning which class they were to teach, was important. Similarly, consultation with teachers about decisions on spending was important. It appears that schools in which teachers were consulted on issues affecting school policy, as well as those affecting them directly, were more likely to be successful.

The Primary School Staff Relationships (PSSR) project (Nias, Southworth and Yeomans, 1989) indicated that the heads of schools that offered a 'positive' model of such relationships *lived* the beliefs underlying 'their' schools' culture. Thus, these heads were able to operate at two different levels: a high level of abstraction (e.g. defining their beliefs about the social and moral purposes of education) and at the level of their day-to-day actions, even those at the most mundane and detailed level (Southworth, 1988). From his review of literature on effective leadership, Southworth (1990) derived a list of characteristics of an effective headteacher. An effective headteacher

- emphasizes the centrality of teaching and learning: via his or her teaching commitment; persistent interest in the children's work and development; through attention to teachers' plans, practice, reflections and evaluations;
- ensures that there are explicit curriculum aims, guidelines and pupil record-keeping systems and that all of these are utilized by teachers and other staff in order to establish some consistency, continuity and coherence;
- acts as an exemplar: regularly teaches; leads assemblies; works long and hard for the school;
- ensures that the teachers have some non-contact time;
- sets high expectations for self, children and staff;
- encourages and develops others to lead and accept positions of responsibility;
- involves the deputy head in policy decision-making; head and deputy operate as partners;
- is conscious of the school's and individual teacher's needs with regard to teacher attendance on in-service training courses; is aware of own professional development needs;
- is considerate towards staff: offers psychological support; takes an interest in staff as people; is willing (on occasions) to help reconcile and make allowance for personal/professional role conflicts (health problems, domestic crises, clash of evening commitments);
- constantly inquires into many aspects of the school as an organization: tours the school before, during and after school; visits staff in their classroom and workplaces; perceives the school from different perspectives; observes and listens; manages 'by wandering about';

- develops and sustains a whole-school perspective in so far as there is a shared and agreed vision of effective practice which is adopted by and becomes the staff's collective mission;
- nurtures and maintains a school culture which is inclusive of the school's staff and which facilitates professional and social collaboration;
- is personally tolerant of ambiguity;
- ensures that the school has an explicit and understood development plan: has a sense of direction; anticipates future developments; and
- involves parents and governors in the work and life of the school; is an effective communicator of the school's successes and challenges, presents a positive image of the school, staff and children.

An interesting elaboration of this view emerged from the PSSR project (Nias, 1987b). One of its members gave four examples of how effective heads worked:

First, these primary heads devoted time nearly each day, certainly every week, to touring the school. They walked the corridors, visited all areas of the school, met and talked with colleagues and co-workers. If they were free from teaching duties they did this during the school day, if they were a teaching head they did it either when released from teaching or before and after school.

Literally, the heads were out and about and, in common with many other managers, they were, as Peters and Austin say, doing MBWA – Managing By Wandering About!

Second, MBWA embraced a range of key skills. The heads in the PSSR project, for example, were constantly listening to the school. Their tours allowed them to hear how colleagues thought the school was doing, to talk about successes and difficulties, to share problems and anticipate developments.

In a sense the heads were not so much monitoring the school as enquiring into the school: How are we doing? What are we thinking? What do we need to be doing? The heads were forever finding out about their schools. MBWA thus involves curiosity, the capacity to listen, and the ability to seek out or anticipate challenges before they become problems which ambush . . .

Third, the heads were also skilled negotiators. They met staff face-to-face and, moreover, they met staff very frequently. They kept times between seeing staff to a minimum. Consequently, it did not take long to up-date one another, nor was there much time for difficulties to develop, let alone fester and infect other parts of the school.

Simultaneously, if they suspected there was someone who was unhappy, discomforted or displeased their tours not only kept them in-touch but also created opportunities for the 'problem' to be aired, and shared and provided a context whereby the two could resolve, say, some disagreement, on a one-to-one basis.

Fourth, all of these activities enabled the heads to manage the school as an organism rather than as an organization. Whether it was cause or effect I do not know but the heads' close and constant involvement with people, their problems, aspirations, successes and *feelings* certainly made it impossible for them to remain insensitive to the emotional side of the school in terms of the staff and the children.

These heads did not regard their schools as mechanisms controlled by lines of command and driven purely by instructions and systems. Rather, they accepted that their schools were densely populated places loaded with feelings and values.

(Southworth, 1988)

It is clear that the preferred management culture for effective schooling – paradoxically given more emphasis by the introduction of a National Curriculum – is *interdependence* rather than dependence or independence. Jennifer Nias (1987a), in another paper outlining the 'culture of collaboration' that characterized some of the schools in the PSSR project, claimed that

To work effectively together, people must share three understandings about their work (that is, in schools, about education). They must agree on what they are trying to achieve (aims and purposes), on how to achieve it (so, they must hold similar beliefs about cause and effect) and on how hard they will work and to what standard. Teachers are aware of the need for agreement on these dimensions.

Research in America identified two categories of schools as 'learning enriched' and 'learning impoverished'. The characteristics of 'learning enriched' schools were

- Collaborative goals at the building level
- Minimum uncertainty
- Positive attitudes of teachers
- Principals supported teachers and removed barriers for them
- Principals fostered collaboration as opposed to competition.

(Rosenholtz, 1989)

Characteristics of 'learning impoverished' schools were

- No clear goals or shared values
- Teachers rarely talked to one another
- Teacher perceived the school to be routine
- Norms of self-reliance flourished, as did isolation.

(Rosenholtz, 1989)

The same work identified 'stuck' and 'moving' schools. Headteachers must be people centred as well as task centred and they must be skilled in managing uncertainty themselves so that they can assist others. They must be able to mediate in situations of conflict or potential conflict, and they must be able to manage themselves.

Being an expert

The national initiative by the TTA through which training programmes for new heads and aspiring heads were established has also spawned a set of national draft standards for different groups of teachers. One of these is the school leader, and it is likely that these standards will become national 'benchmarks' by which successful leadership in schools will be judged. It is worth, therefore, considering these. The group of professionals from LEAs, schools, higher education and others who advised on this defined the *core purpose* as being: 'To provide professional leadership which creates and maintains a clear educational vision, which secures pupils' learning and achievement and the continuous improvement of the school.'

From this, it developed a number of key tasks relating to strategic direction and development, teaching and learning, people and relationships, resources, and accountability (Figure 3.1). It is worth noting that almost all these demand high levels of personal and interpersonal qualities and skills allied to considerable self-knowledge and a clear focus upon creating and maintaining conditions which provide optimum opportunities for good teaching, learning and achievement – and that they recognize explicitly the importance of the motivation and commitment of staff and pupils, parents and governors to achieve this.

The difficulty with this approach, though its intentions are admirable, is that it may oversimplify and 'rationalize' the essential qualities needed by leaders through assessment, which will only measure that which is easily measurable.

Tim Brighouse (1991) proposes seven leadership qualities:

1. be cheerful and optimistic . . . those who follow need to feel the leader has seen the other side of the mountain . . . the need for vision;
2. be welcoming and ready to be enthusiastic;
3. be a good listener – when listening, give people your individual attention;
4. be considered an effective user of time;
5. celebrate others and blame themselves;
6. manage change;
7. have a clear educational philosophy and set a personal example.

Strategic direction and development
- Building an ethos and providing an educational vision and direction that promotes continuous improvement and secures pupils' learning achievement, their spiritual, moral, cultural and social development.
- Ensuring the school development plan identifies appropriate priorities and targets for increased teacher effectiveness and school improvement and relates to overall financial planning.
- Ensuring there is commitment, motivation and involvement in meeting long, medium and short term aims, objectives and targets which secure the educational success of the school.
- Ensuring that the management, finance, organization and administration of the school supports its vision, values and objectives for good teaching, learning and improved standards of achievement.
- Monitoring, evaluating and reviewing policies, priorities and targets of the school and taking the necessary action for improvement.

Learning and teaching
- Creating and maintaining an environment for effective learning, teaching, good behaviour and discipline.
- Establishing a clear moral code where cultural, social and religious differences are respected and spiritual growth is encouraged.
- Monitoring and evaluating the quality of teaching and the quality of pupils' learning and achievements in order to set and meet targets to secure improvement.
- Monitoring, evaluating and reviewing the curriculum and its associated assessment in order to identify areas for improvement.

People and relationships
- Creating a positive climate focused on improving standards of achievement which values all staff and ensures their commitment to personal and professional development.
- Ensuring professional development activities for all staff are linked to improving pupils' standards of achievement and to individual and to school needs and the school development plan through target setting and appraisal.
- Planning, allocating, supporting and evaluating work undertaken by groups, teams and individuals, with clear roles and responsibilities for all participants.
- Developing and maintaining effective working relationships with pupils, parents, staff and governors.
- Developing effective relations with the wider community.

Resources
- Working with governors and senior colleagues to recruit and select the highest possible quality of staff.
- Working with senior colleagues and team leaders to deploy, develop and retain staff.
- Ensuring the effective and efficient management and organization of accommodation and learning resources within the school budget.
- Monitoring, controlling and reviewing the use of all resources in order to raise pupil achievements.

Accountability
- Providing information, advice and support to the governing body so that it can meet its accountabilities for securing effective teaching and learning, raising standards of achievement and meet its statutory responsibilities.
- Creating and developing an organization in which all staff recognize their accountability for the success of the school.
- Presenting a coherent account of the school's performance in a form appropriate to a range of audiences e.g. governors, parents, teachers, OFSTED, the LEA etc.
- Fulfilling professional duties as specified in the Terms and Conditions of Service of Teachers.

Figure 3.1 Key tasks of the 'expert' leader
Source: Teacher Training Agency (1996)

He proposes eight principles for behaviour which are consistent with achieving success:

1. Keep it simple!
2. Do not transfer the blame to actions beyond your control. Otherwise, 'we become paralysed, reinforce dependence, and waste time in our need to give urgent attention to raising the aspirations and achievements in the next generation'.
3. Reinforce the professional culture of the school.
4. Practise being brave.
5. Empower others.
6. Build visions.
7. Prioritize – decide what not to do, prioritize.
8. Find allies.

This provides an interesting complement to the more clinical competency categories of the TTA. Teaching is an art as well as a craft. Good teachers 'aren't just well-oiled machines. They are emotional, passionate beings who fill their work and their classes with pleasure, creativity, challenge and joy. Teaching involves immense amounts of emotional labour' (Hargreaves, 1997). Headteachers must be able to create and sustain a climate in which there is room for planned personal, professional and institutional growth and development of rational and non-rational kinds – and this means being able to manage the reasoning and emotional selves of the individual and the team in order to succeed in the task.

In the case of primary school headteachers, the people they must influence are the staff, the children, the parents, the school governors and the LEA. Although each of these groups will influence the headteacher, only he or she is in a position to have an overview that takes into account each of the needs expressed but that is more than their sum. This is expected of a leader and is variously called a policy, an ideal, a set of aspirations or a vision for the school the head holds and is expected to communicate to all the interested groups that make up a school community. Figure 3.2 is a simple representation of the head at the centre of a very complex communications network.

The network is complex because between groups and within each group there will be expectations, demands and abilities that may conflict. The head will need to identify and balance these interests before decisions are made, wherever possible taking into account the different influences at work and the consequences of accepting one at the expense of another. How effectively and efficiently this network operates depends on the head's ability to receive and interpret signals accurately, to ensure communication within and between groups and to influence one or more of the groups. The head is regarded by all groups as the focal point of school life – with the possible exception of the pupils, who may regard their class teacher in this way.

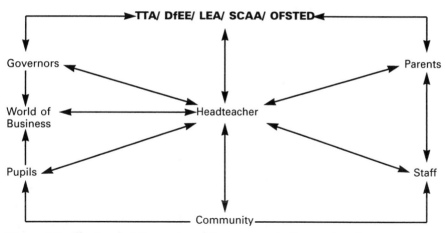

Figure 3.2 The head at the centre of the communications network

Indeed, a useful analogy may be drawn here for, like the class teacher, the head has to ensure that his or her 'audience' feels secure (through good organization and an environment conducive to learning); feels able to contribute (to their own learning and, hence, feeling of self-worth); feels able to communicate (through the building of satisfactory working/professional relationships); and feels a sense of continuity, progression and achievement (through the head's ability to monitor and assess progress). So it is the way in which the head intervenes in the lives of these groups that is crucial to his or her success in influencing them.

There may be fears among headteachers that changes in structural relationships both externally and internally (which have been caused by the increased powers of governors, the introduction of the local financial management of schools, increased parental choice over school selection, the implementation and monitoring of the National Curriculum and teacher appraisal) will *of necessity* cause their role to become more administrative and less professional. Given that the abiding functions of leaders in schools will remain the achievement of task, individual and group maintenance and development and 'boundary' management, the roles of *leading professional* and *chief executive* (or professional-as-administrator – Hughes, 1988) will need to continue to be combined. In this sense, heads of primary schools will become more like their secondary school counterparts:

> The innovating head, it appears, relies partly on exerting influence on staff colleagues as a fellow professional; equally, however, he accepts his position as chief executive, and uses the organizational controls which are available to him to get things moving. Professional and executive considerations reinforce each other as complementary aspects of a coherent and unified strategy.
>
> (Hughes, 1976)

Roles	Description	Representative activities
Decisional		
Entrepreneur	Searches school and its environment for opportunities to initiate change through 'improvement projects'	Reviews of curriculum and policy involving initiation of 'improvement projects'
Disturbance handler	Responsible for corrective action when school faces unexpected disturbances	*Ad hoc* coping with breakdown of school facilities, unwelcome visitors; discipline
Resources	Responsible for the allocation of school resources of all kinds – in effect the making or approval of all significant decisions	Distribution of human and material resources in accordance with head's 'philosophy' and scale of priorities; timetabling; budgeting
Negotiator	Representing the school at negotiations	Promoting or defending the interests of the school
Leading professional roles		
Goal-setter and evaluator	Determining the overall character of the school and overseeing progress towards this as a goal	Shaping curriculum and organization; formulating statements of aims (e.g. in-school prospectus); school self-evaluation
Curriculum co-ordinator and developer	Making final decisions on emphases to be given among curriculum subjects and materials	Keeping informed of curriculum developments; chairing meetings; allocating posts of responsibility for curriculum areas; choice and purchase of materials; classroom supervision of teachers
Teacher	The head's time in classrooms:	Scheduled teaching of classes or

		...concern for children and teachers; solidarity with teachers' interests
	...and seen by them as exemplifying 'professionalism'	
Chief executive roles		
Interpersonal		
Figure-head	Symbolic head, performing routine legal or social duties	Assembly; signing reports and authorizations
Leader/supervisor	Responsible for the motivation and co-ordination of subordinates' work	Embodied in virtually all managerial activities involving subordinates: classroom visits, discussions, etc.
Liaison	Maintenance of network of outside contacts	Correspondence; external committee work; links with LEA people and governors
Informational		
Monitor	Seeks and receives wide variety of information to develop understanding of organization and environment; emerges as nerve centre of internal and external information	Handling mail and contacts concerned primarily with receiving information (e.g. observational tours of school; LEA and government circulars and memoranda)
Disseminator	Transmits information to members of staff: some information factual, some involving interpretation and integration of diverse value positions from outsiders	Directing mail and other material to teachers for informational purposes; verbal contacts involving information flow to subordinates
Spokesperson	Transmits information to outsiders on school's plans, policies, actions, results, etc.: serves as education 'expert' to general public	Governors' meetings; handling contacts involving transmission of information to outsiders

Figure 3.3 Summary of the head's managerial roles
Source: Coulson (1987)

Many heads will continue to activate and integrate contrasting and potentially conflicting aspects of their total role successfully (Hughes, 1976). Figure 3.3 provides a summary of the primary head's managerial roles.

Action-centred leadership

Given that most learning about management will continue to take place 'on the job', it may be helpful to identify a number of categories that, despite overlap and interdependency, constitute the kinds of knowledge necessary for leaders. These have been conceptualized as follows:

- *Knowledge of people*   This will play an important part in interpersonal relationships and the decisions taken in initiating and responding to colleagues.
- *Situational knowledge*   This is concerned with how managers interpret the information they receive about school life, how they assess its status and significance and how they communicate it.
- *Knowledge of educational practice*   This covers the extent to which managers keep themselves informed about new and existing practices in teaching, learning, organization, staff development, external relationships, etc.
- *Conceptual knowledge*   Usually at an implicit level, this is defined as 'that set of concepts, theories and ideas that a person has consciously stored in memory' that is an aid to 'analysing issues or problems, or debating policies and practices' (Eraut, 1988).
- *Process knowledge*   this is commonly known as 'know-how'. It is partly a matter of knowing all the things one has to do and making sensible plans for doing them; and partly a matter of possessing and using practical, routinized skills.
- *Control knowledge*   This covers self-awareness, and sensitivity; self-knowledge about one's strengths and weaknesses, the gap between what one says and what one does, and what one knows and does not know; self-management in such matters as the use of time, prioritization and delegation; self-development in its broadest sense; and generalized intellectual skills like strategic thinking and policy analysis (Eraut, 1988).

Anyone who has been involved in leadership will know that there can be enormous discrepancies between what has been called the logic of planning and the logic of action (Stake, 1967). In the action of managing even the best-laid plans may go astray.

Below is a fine example, from an industrial context, of the logic of rational planning for action-centred leadership. It is suggested that there are inter-related purposes for the action-centred leader – developing individuals, achieving the task and building the team – and it is implied that there are 'action points' for putting these purposes into practice (The Industrial Society, 1983):

1. Set the task of the team. Put it across with enthusiasm and remind people of it often.
2. Make leaders accountable for 4–15 people. Instruct them in leadership actions.
3. Plan the work, check its progress, design jobs and arrange work to encourage the commitment of individuals and the team.
4. Set individual targets after consulting. Discuss progress with each person regularly, but at least once a year.
5. Delegate decisions to individuals. If not, consult those affected before you decide.
6. Communicate the importance of everyone's job. Explain decisions to help people apply them. Brief the team together monthly on progress, policy, people and points of action.
7. Train and develop people, especially the young. Gain support for rules and procedures, set an example and 'have a go' at those who break them.
8. Where unions are recognized, encourage joining, attendance at meetings, standing for office and speaking up for what each person believes is in the interest of the organization and all who work in it.
9. Serve people in the team and care for their well-being. Improve working conditions and safety. Work alongside people. Deal with grievances promptly and attend social functions.
10. Monitor action. Learn from success and mistakes. Regularly walk round each person's place of work to observe, listen and praise.

These stages of action are clearly relevant to leaders in primary schools in their planning, but in considering their actions it is necessary to uncover the value system and attitudes upon which this planning and action are based.

McGregor (1960) proposed two perspectives on management. He devised a 'Theory X' and 'Theory Y' view of human enterprise. McGregor postulates that workers become passive as a result of Theory X. Theory X

> is a conventional management perspective, which views people as needing to be directed, controlled and motivated, with their behaviour moulded to fit the needs of the organization. It reflects paternalistic and mechanistic approaches to management, which emphasize man's need for external pressures to 'keep him in shape' and combat his natural laziness and irresponsibility. Like a donkey, man works best with a conditioning mixture of the carrot (bribes) and the stick (threats). In practice, Theory X is exemplified in individual incentive schemes, clocking on, emphasis on discipline, and promotion based on length of service.

Theory Y, on the other hand, conceives a humanity as naturally active. Everyone has the potential for development, the capacity for responsibility and the readiness to direct his or her behaviour towards the goals of the organization. This is the participative approach in which work is seen as potentially satisfying in itself, because it is as natural an activity as playing. People only become passive and unco-operative because of their experiences, and it is a manager's job to remove obstacles and release potential. In practice, Theory Y is exemplified by agreeing targets, good delegation and job enrichment.

This book, whilst recognizing that there are occasions for adopting a Theory X approach, asserts that more effective leadership will occur through the use of a Theory Y view of management. We argue, for example, that in the case of the checklists and prescribed steps associated with Theory X, no account is taken of the attitudes to development held by the people with whom you have to work, nor to their expectations, abilities, feelings and different processes of working. These will tend to get in the way of the appreciation of the 'grand plan' devised in the tranquillity of home or office. Theory X also implies that leaders or managers have acquired the necessary expertise to 'manage' adults. This is by no means necessarily so, since almost all headteachers and deputies will have spent most of their professional lives working with children, and not with the adults who now claim the major part of their time and attention.

Transformational leadership: the moral imperative

The 'culture' or 'ethos' of a school is directly related to the development of quality relationships (i.e. those which foster positive regard and confidence within a professional learning ethos which provides challenge and support) that exist within it. Leaders have a special responsibility to ensure, as far as possible, that staff relationships are positive. This is not to suggest that there will be no disagreement or conflict, for it is not possible to mandate good relationships.

One theory which meets the uncertain demands of schooling in the twentieth century is 'transformational leadership'. In this kind of leadership, leaders and followers are united in pursuit of higher-level goals that are common to both.

Sergiovanni developed this theory because he found that previous theories did not apply to the new 'non-linear' conditions and loose structuring which characterize schools now. He believes that to succeed, school leaders need to engage, above all, in processes of socialization, shared values and collegiality: 'Using a values-based approach for defining the role of [the headteacher] . . . not only ensures that what [headteachers] decide to do meets acceptable standards, but also provides the school with a set of indicators that defines its educational and moral health' (Sergiovanni, 1995).

The theory suggests that leaders' work should reflect *six organizing principles*: '1) co-operation (among teachers); 2) empowerment (ownership by teachers); 3) responsibility (encouraged in teachers); 4) accountability (by teachers for decisions and achievements); 5) meaningfulness (of work to teachers); 6) ability–authority (delegated authority based upon ability of teachers to act in the forefront of decision-making)' (Sergiovanni, 1995). Sergiovanni sees leadership as embodying a

> *a set of forces* available for improving and maintaining quality schooling. These are technical (the use of sound management techniques); human (harnessing the school's social and interpersonal potential); educational (derived from expert knowledge about education and schooling matters); symbolic (derived from focusing the attention of others on matters of importance to the school); and cultural (building a unique school culture).

Leadership of schools is not simply an applied science. It represents more than the possession and application of a set of knowledge, skills or predispositions to be reflective or collaborative. It involves both 'doing right things' and 'doing things right'; it involves a combination of the heart, the head and the hand:

> The *heart* of leadership has to do with what a person believes, values, dreams about, and is committed to ... The *head* of leadership has to do with the theories of practice each one of us has developed over time, and our ability to reflect on ... [and act appropriately in] ... the situations we face in the light of those theories ... the *hand* of leadership has to do with the actions we take, the decisions we make, the leadership and management behaviours we use as our strategies become institutionalized.
>
> (Sergiovanni, 1995)

It becomes moral because it raises the level of human conduct and ethical aspiration of both the leader and the led. The challenge of leadership is to balance the four competing sources of authority – the bureaucratic (management), personal, professional and moral – in such a way that all those in the school bond and bind together to sustain and develop both achievement and the commitment to a shared set of values which are underpinned by principles of social justice and democracy:

* What kind of leader are you?
* How would you define your values?
* What strategies do you use to empower staff?
* How do staff respond? (Ask for feedback.)

Professional relationships and motivation

What most influences teachers in schools? Below are a number of vignettes provided by headteachers in answer to this question. Each has been selected because it provides an example of a different quality of leadership in action, and of how teachers were motivated by processes of social influence. In particular, each teacher was helped by the head in processes of internalization rather than in compliance or identification with authority or charisma. Change based on such compliance or identification is less likely to be long term than change that accords with or may be adapted to the person's own value system.

Example 1: timing (knowing when to help and when to let staff get on)

In my first year of teaching I had a problem with teaching mathematics. I knew what I wanted to teach but my organization was letting me down and producing a negative effect with my class. My headteacher noticed this without me having to go to him, showing an awareness of things going on in school and an awareness of the problems confronting new teachers. He suggested that he took my class for mathematics for a period of three week while I stayed in the classroom and watched.

From this I gained a good deal of knowledge about organization not only of mathematics but also of other subjects. His was a practical help which the situation needed initially and from then on he gave advice when asked for or when he felt it necessary.

Example 2: clear communication

The head in question was an excellent organizer. She knew what she wanted within the school and she made sure all the staff knew what was happening down to the last detail. This covered all aspects of school life, from organization of the curriculum to ordinary everyday events and the social life of the school. No member of staff likes to know they are being left in the dark; if they know what to expect they will respond positively.

Example 3: practical empathy

A few years ago I was teaching in a large primary school where three teachers were serving a probationary year. These were young female teachers, all with quiet personalities. On the staff at the time were some rather forceful characters. The three young teachers were afraid to enter the staffroom at playtime (and admitted this). The headteacher concerned dealt with this by having small weekly meetings with them to discuss their problems and the progress they were making. (As deputy head I was also involved.) This was in addition to helping them individually in classrooms, or with lesson plans and evaluation.

By being together, they felt more confident expressing opinions about their work. The sympathy shown by the head, by placing himself in their position, encouraged them to contribute in full staff meetings.

Example 4: leading by example

The headteacher was very enthusiastic about the countryside and 'environmental studies'. He inspired others. A Bird and Tree Festival was held annually at which an invited speaker talked to the children. A tree or shrub was planted in the school grounds. All the classes prepared for the day by studying some aspect of the environment and a prize was awarded for the best class project. There was music, dance, verse, writing and creative activities. The headteacher worked hard to build up to the day and he, throughout the year, kept the school garden attractive and productive of fruits, vegetables and flowers. The school benefited tremendously from the interest radiated by the headteacher without whom none of this would have taken place.

Example 5: supporting staff against external pressures

Several years ago, the school where I worked as a language consultant had a particularly obnoxious chairman of governors who thought a great deal of himself and very little of teachers. His manner towards teachers was hectoring and loud and he and I fell foul of each other during a course I was running in my own time. He made loud comments and suggestions and his presence and attitude were undermining my work.

The head arrived on the scene and summed it up. His choices were to support me and incur the displeasure of the chairman and its consequences, or to laugh it off and let me down. He spoke very coldly to the man, saying, 'If you feel you can do this better, then please go ahead. That will give Mrs X the chance to go home and rest; she's done a full day's work already. Otherwise I'd suggest you leave the premises.' He left, clearly furious. At the next governors' meeting the head tackled the man and gained the support of the other governors.

The head had shown his integrity by supporting me, who would make little trouble for him, at the risk of offending someone who was likely to make a lot – and subsequently tried to.

Example 6: caring about personal and professional needs

The head for whom I worked the longest was a fatherly, old-fashioned gentlemanly style of headteacher. I willingly served on his staff and loyally supported almost everything he did. In analysing why this was so, I've decided that it was because he genuinely cared about me as a person. He expressed interest, not only in my professional work, but also in the members of my family and in all my out-of-school activities. He always had time to listen. This concern, which applied equally to all members of staff, caused me to feel valued, and I gave my very best in response.

If effective leadership means the ability to achieve such a response from members of staff, that was an instance of it. Not perhaps a very dramatic situation but an 'effective' one.

Example 7: setting standards

As a newly qualified teacher my head was seldom too busy to talk to me and would continue to discuss the matter in hand even when I was on playground duty, by doing the duty with me. He always displayed a sympathetic approach and was ready with encouragement and praise when he visited the classroom. If he thought I was doing something which didn't quite measure up to his requirements or standards, he would say so – but always in a friendly fashion. I never felt that I was being put down and I respected that. He wouldn't suffer fools gladly, but he did it in a pleasant fashion. He was rather of the 'old school' and valued scholarship and 'standards'. He urged me to continue my own education, night-school courses, etc., in order to become better qualified. Although formal himself he accepted that teachers would try new ideas and methods, which he tolerated rather than really enthused over. This head was respected in the community and was liked by parents, children and staff.

As a new teacher I appreciated his listening ear and his readiness to devote time to me. I respected his judgements and I found his advice to be wise and practical. I valued him greatly as a colleague and, later, as a friend.

Example 8: supporting change

When first appointed as a deputy head I wanted to introduce a new maths approach throughout the school. I was given the opportunity by the headteacher of first of all going round other classes to see what they were doing currently in maths (he took my class during these times). Next, staff meetings were arranged where I could talk about the new maths approach to the head and the staff.

Once general approval had been gained, the head agreed that the approach should be introduced. The head had encouraged me in this venture throughout by enabling me to see what was needed and by backing the need for change (and taking the final decision to introduce the new approach).

These examples show how teachers were *motivated* by various leadership styles and strategies. The main purpose of intervention by the leader is motivation. The heads of the schools concerned intervened in various ways in the teachers' professional development, and this motivated them. In work concerned with questioning the teacher's self-image, the nature of professional relationships is of prime importance. For example, changing one's teaching style may involve a temporary 'burden of incompetence' (MacDonald, 1973), so that there will be a considerable need for psychological and moral support. Change must take into account such matters as anxiety, status and identity (Day, 1981). Successful development requires more than rational planning and action. It requires a knowledge of, and allowance for, the way people feel. This 'affective' area is rarely made explicit in preparation for developmental work, yet the attitudes of teachers to the head or other person who intervenes in their professional lives are clearly vital to the success of the intervention.

How is the leader who intervenes perceived? Is he or she an authority or a threat? A 'process helper' or a judge with alien values? The answers to these questions will depend largely on the interpersonal relationships formed with colleagues, and these will in turn be determined by how much the leader is seen to take into account personal individual factors in his or her management of people.

In a survey conducted with sixty headteachers, the most commonly cited qualities of a good head were in the 'affective' area of the work, in other words:

1) sympathy towards the ideas of others:
2) appreciation of others' points of view;
3) understanding of and concern for others;
4) compassion;
5) approachability by staff, parents and children;
6) the ability to deal with problems as they arise and 'still have a smile';
7) the ability to inspire trust and confidence;
8) tolerance, especially of opposing ideas;
9) tact;
10) willingness to praise, and be seen to praise;
11) humour;
12) the quality of being a good listener;
13) the ability to cope with opposition and unpopularity; as well as with support and encouragement;
14) the ability to know when to pressurize and when to stand off;
15) the capacity to be fair and just, and to be seen to be fair and just; and
16) the ability to lead, to guide, to cajole when necessary, to be loyal and supportive of the staff, and to maintain enthusiasm despite any problems.

Few who read this list will be surprised. Yet we must ask, how do heads gain and refine these qualities? There are still relatively few training opportunities in the field of interpersonal skills and helping others to increase professional effectiveness.

Intervention: constraints, purposes and processes

Most of the time, in working with children, teachers are not able to spend much time reflecting on why they do what they do. The main reasons for this are the number of children involved, and the time and energy available. Classroom decisions have to be made, and problems resolved, relatively quickly. Because of the nature of their work, teachers become socialized into acting in this way, with the theory that underlies each action almost always at an implicit level. This may be part of the reason for teachers' common mistrust of 'theory' as they understand it, i.e. not related to practice. Given that this is so, it would not be surprising if leaders who are or have been part of this apparently 'theoryless' environment, in which decisions are taken on the spot and solutions quickly found to 'cope' with emerging problems, behaved in a similar way in their work with other teachers. After all, they have rarely received any in-service preparation for their new roles. And yet, because the head will be dealing with fewer 'clients', and because often decisions about development or change do not need to be taken on the spot, the leader has more opportunity to reflect and evaluate.

Since much teaching behaviour is at an intuitive and implicit level (we all have a 'filter system' in order to cope with the masses of information with which we have to deal), from time to time teachers need the help of a colleague or 'critical friend' from outside in identifying both areas of strength and areas for improvement. Often the headteacher fulfils this role, by means of the following:

1) Taking an 'overview' of the needs of the school as a whole.
2) Observing and working alongside individual teachers.
3) Providing the means by which the practice of individuals and the school may be monitored and reviewed.
4) Ensuring commitment of staff through participation in decision-taking.

The headteacher who observes his or her teachers at work in their classrooms, who encourages them to discuss their work with each other and him or herself at regular meetings with groups and individuals, will soon get to know the various stages of professional development reached by each of the teachers. Thus, having established a context for the learning, the head will be in a position to plan for the most effective means of motivating through a series of purposeful intervention strategies – purposeful in the sense that his or her perceptions of institutional need, which may be in potential conflict with those of the staff, can be modified in the light of systematically collected evidence of perceived staff need. So desired results may be achieved by thinking of the intervention strategies not only in terms of the task but also in terms of human motivation and learning factors. (A detailed discussion of these is contained in Chapter 4.)

Sergiovanni (1995) identifies *four leadership strategies* associated with the principles and forces of 'transformational leadership':

1. *Bartering*: the leader gives to those led something they want in exchange for what the leader wants. (This approach works best when the head and teachers do not share common goals and interests.);
2. *Building*: the leader provides the climate and interpersonal support that enhances teachers' opportunities for fulfilment of individual needs for achievement, responsibility, competence, and esteem. (Once a minimum level of common effort is achieved, this approach is recommended to shift the emphasis from extrinsic to intrinsic rewards.);
3. *Bonding*: heads and teachers develop together a set of shared values about the relationships they want to share and the ties they want to create to become a community of colleagues. (This approach attempts to shift the emphasis from what the head provides to obligations and commitments teachers feel toward each other.);
4. *Binding*: heads and teachers together commit themselves to a set of shared values and ideas that ties them together as a 'we'. (This is a means of establishing the moral authority that enables people to become self-managing.)

Stage	Leadership by	Results
1) Initiation (getting started)	Bartering (push)	Has value (helps achieve competence)
2) Uncertainty (muddling through)	Building (support)	Adds value (increases readiness for excellence)
3) Transformative (breakthrough)	Bonding (inspire)	Adds value (helps achieve excellence)
4) Routinization (promoting self-management)	Binding (sustain)	Adds value (promotes self-management)

Figure 3.4   Four leadership strategies
Source: Sergiovanni, 1990

One way to help teachers is by identifying how and why they learn. It has been suggested that teachers are motivated to learn when they (rather than others) identify a need or problem. Havelock (1973) presented problem-solving as a rational process (Figure 3.5). It is clear from this model that identifying and solving problems is a complex business. For example, the initial disturbance may come from a self-generated or from an externally generated source (e.g. a new headteacher, a missive from the LEA, a visit by a colleague to the classroom or simply a knowledge that all is not well). The feeling of need that arises may or may not be strong enough to warrant a decision to act. Indeed, the teacher may feel unable or unworthy to do

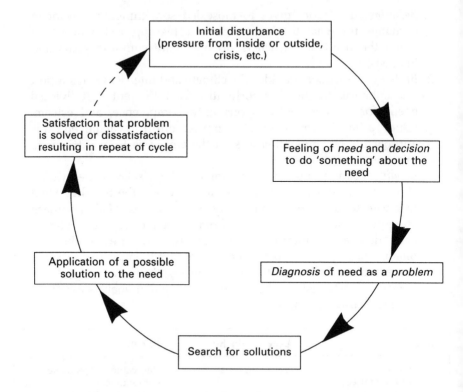

Figure 3.5   Rational problem-solving model
Source: Havelock (1973)

something about the need, until and unless it is diagnosed as a problem. Even if the need is diagnosed as a problem, teachers may be inhibited in their search for solutions by lack of time, energy, ability, resources or skills. Clearly, the leader has a responsibility to ensure that teachers do have opportunities to reflect on their work, as well as to help them in identifying problems by providing alternative perspectives on their work.

It should not be assumed, however, that *all* adults have a need to be self-directing at all times. Some teachers, like some children, may need to be 'told' things on occasion, or may expect that they should be told (a 'felt incompetence' formed by such factors as role, expectation, socialization or psychological needs – McGregor's 'Theory X'). Indeed, when teachers are participants in their own learning, problems may arise because their inquiry skills are either underdeveloped or undeveloped. The leader will need to take this into account. Among teachers, as among children, the need and ability to be self-directing will vary. 'Need', for example, depends upon factors such as cognitive and personality development, motivation, social development and role expectation.

The assumptions about professional learning and the nature of change that underpin the thinking expressed in this book are as follows:

1) Professional development is not something that can be forced, because it is the teacher who develops (active), and not the teacher who is developed (passive) (Eraut, 1977).
2) Change that is not internalized is likely to be distorted and temporary. Hence, power-coercive strategies or external initiatives that rely on authority rather than on encouraging development may seem to work, but usually result in 'token' changes at surface level only. The head will often be the one responsible for ensuring a transfer of ownership of an innovation from agencies outside the institution to those inside.
3) Change at deeper levels involves the modification of perceptions and attitudes, and this is unlikely to occur unless there is participation in the decision-making and planning of the in-service activity.
4) The leader's role is consultative and collaborative.

Many people have suggested that teachers in schools will work most happily and effectively in an environment to which they feel they belong (how many times do we hear the teacher talk of 'my class' and the head talk of 'my school'!), with which they can identify and in which they feel accepted and esteemed – not only by their pupils but also by colleagues and their heads. Perhaps the prime task of the consultant/leader concerned with motivating staff is to provide the right conditions for motivation.

Leading the team

Like an individual, a team must be led in ways that take account of its stage of development as well as the purposes of the leader. The 'leader' needs to be able to

1) identify the team's stage of development;
2) be aware of the range of approaches available to him or her;
3) select the appropriate approach, according to the team's stage of development and the leader's purposes;
4) possess and be able to use the ability to put this approach into practice; and
5) monitor the effectiveness of the approach, and modify where necessary.

In the ideal and most effective model of leadership, the head's role is collaborative and he or she will operate according to principles of participation, negotiation, trust and responsibility. The more the head 'tells' (makes the decisions and announces them) or 'sells' (through persuasion) the more he or she will demonstrate his or her use of authority and the less will be the personal investment of colleagues in the enterprise. The more the head 'consults' (e.g. presents a problem, gets suggestions, makes decisions) or 'shares' (defines limits, asks group to make decisions), the greater will be the area of freedom felt by colleagues, and the stronger their investment. Whatever the question to be dealt with – whether it is to agree on a policy for staff development, or to review curriculum, or roles and responsibilities – it is crucial that the focus has been agreed through consultation so that all agree to commit themselves to the task in hand. The way in which this agreement occurs depends on the leadership roles adopted and the skills that can be applied.

In practice, the head who then operates any of the above models (with the possible exception of 'telling') will do so by means of talking, observing and listening. He or she will therefore need to possess and use a variety of skills necessary to the leading of effective discussion, and these will include the following:

1) Negotiating skills (contract-making).
2) Summarizing skills (to form links between different ideas, where appropriate).
3) Questioning skills (to open rather than close discussions).
4) Selection skills (of key points in arguments).
5) Focusing skills (to concentrate and clarify discussion points).
6) Synthesizing and evaluation skills (to 'sharpen' issues).
7) Timing skills (to know when, and when not, to intervene in discussion).
8) Listening skills (to listen actively in order to respond to what is really being said – the hidden agenda).
9) Non-verbal skills (to identify people's attitudes and feelings, through observing posture, gesture, facial expression, etc.).

To summarize, in meeting with colleagues, either individually or collectively, the leader will need to demonstrate his or her ability to

1) negotiate sympathetically;
2) listen (actively), note and act;
3) account for individual needs;
4) ensure continuity and support; and
5) send colleagues away with a sense of achievement.

Let us now consider four crucial factors in the process of management.

The needs of the individual and the needs of the institution

These needs may be different, and sometimes conflicting. Colleagues need to perceive the need for development (and thus change), and feel a responsibility for implementing and sharing in this. Individuals like to have responsibility and be trusted, but they also need to see benefits for themselves as well as for 'the school', for example. How may this be achieved? One way is by making social contracts with staff through negotiation. By these means, colleagues accept that they may, at times and in the interests of others, contribute part of their autonomy. For example, the development of particular schemes of work may have to wait until there has been an appraisal of classroom teaching approaches. This 'contract-making' is often linked with the agreement to set different kinds of objectives according to agreed priorities.

Short, medium and long-term tasks

There may be some tasks better left until a later date because other tasks are more urgent, or because it is desirable for the staff to feel an immediate sense of achievement. So it is the head's responsibility to ensure that tasks are assigned different priorities. This is not to say that all three kinds of tasks are not being pursued at the same time, but simply that there is an agreement to place more emphasis at any given time on one rather than another.

Timing and containable time

Closely linked to these two factors is the concept of 'containable time'. Changes must be manageable, and the time and energy teachers have available to devote to change are limited. It is counterproductive to stretch people beyond their personal limits. Through initial contract-making, agreements can be reached concerning the amount of time to be spent on any given task or project. The knowledge that a meeting or other event will end at a given time will provide security for staff with other commitments.

A personal sense of timing is also important. Friday afternoon three or four weeks into term, or a wet and windy day that has unsettled the pupils in the school, may not be the best time to introduce a new idea!

Handling confrontation

Inevitably tensions will occur from time to time, and the leader will be expected to handle them. There is no formula for success, but here are some notes drawn from the experiences of sixty deputy headteachers:

1) Provide support and guidance, i.e. identify the causes and try to eliminate or alleviate the problem through discussion/practical help and support.
2) Praise strengths and improvements.
3) Avoid open confrontation.
4) Offer positive 'professional' criticism.
5) Minimize feelings of being threatened.
6) Be prepared to accept modifications/compromise.

7) Avoid showing prejudice in open staff meetings if personal opinions are put forward.
8) Where you cannot handle confrontation, be willing to use arbitration.

To these may be added a ninth:

9) Know which battles to fight, which to avoid, and which to lose!

Investing in the school's culture: principles of leadership

What qualities, then, do you need to possess in order to be an effective leader? First you have to recognize that you are involved in the management of human and physical resources. You have to help individuals to develop, while at the same time maintain the team. You must also ensure that the task, whatever it may be, is achieved. This will only happen if you can motivate and support others. *Management is getting things done with and by other people.* In order to do this well, you will need skills of planning and organization, in particular: identifying opportunities by being knowledgeable about the needs of staff and children, setting targets, the art of delegation and using your time to the best advantage; communication – formal and informal; and assessment and evaluation – through monitoring, observing and synthesizing. Most important, then, are the skills of working with people. No amount of forward planning, careful budgeting or efficient administration can substitute for this.

One of the first principles-in-action is participation by staff. This is based on the assumption that if people are involved in making the decisions that shape their activities, then they are likely to be more committed to their work. It is important to remember, though, that collectivity does not abolish the ultimate responsibility for the headteacher for the work of the school. The nine major areas of responsibility for the headteacher (each of which is dealt with in more detail in the other chapters) are as follows.

The school climate or ethos

It will be the head's policies regarding, for example, access to classrooms by parents, team teaching, a policy of professional development that is school focused, the use of reward and punishment systems, the collegiality of school decision-making, that will determine whether the school is perceived as 'open' or 'closed' by staff and parents.

Organizational health: teaching and learning processes

What does the way in which school and classrooms are organized 'say' about the school? Is there a predominance of class teaching or individual work? Are the classroom doors usually open or closed?

The framework/expectations (standards of behaviour and achievement)

What are the standards of the school? Is there a high level of commitment by staff and children to providing a stimulating environment for learning? Is there an effective monitoring system for children's work? Is there a regular monitoring of staff's work? Are there regular head–staff, staff–staff, staff–parent, head–parent consultations?

Routines (morale)

Are there frameworks of routines for staff and children in school? Are the regularly organized staff seminars, appraisal interviews, meetings with parents, professional development opportunities valued?

Management of relationships

Leadership is a process, not a style. Constraints upon the processes are likely to be brought about by a number of factors. Some are outside the leader's control, i.e. national and local educational policy. Some, however, are within the power of the head to influence.

Self

It is essential to have a strong professional philosophy. However, forceful expression of this may inhibit staff (who may not be so strong, clear thinking or forthright), alienate staff or inhibit the leader from acting in a collegial/democratic/consultative way with staff. Instead, the leader may resort to 'devious' manipulation that may, in itself, be counterproductive. Another problem for the leader is his or her isolation by status. It is difficult to share one's weaknesses, for example, with the person who is to write your reference!

Staff

It is unlikely that all the staff of a school will teach in the same way. Indeed, it is questionable whether this should be so, except in the most general terms. However, it will be necessary to establish a unanimity of purpose for the school and to lead by example, avoiding the temptation to 'force feed'. The head should, therefore,

1) create opportunities to develop unanimity from early success in an easy, non-controversial area, and limit change to single manageable areas but initiate changes fairly rapidly after initial assessment of needs;
2) establish consensus on problems – their recognition, analysis and

resolution. Changes in management structure, for example, require a consensus of opinion in favour if they are to work;

3) give more thought to the operation to maximize contributions from all – this means plenty of preparation. Summarize discussion and record by written precis, ensuring continuous feedback to participants;

4) ensure acceptance by all team members that they may at times contribute best by surrendering part of their own autonomy, e.g. by accepting house rules in discussion and holding back criticism or interruption until the appropriate time;

5) identify motivation factors of each member of the team as individuals;

6) be aware of possible insecurities of staff (it is possible you may be carried away by your own enthusiasm);

7) ensure a commitment to the process rather than to the product of development; and

8) establish a communication system that ensures truthful, honest and open assessment and evaluation.

The curriculum

The curriculum represents the knowledge the school regards as important that the students gain. It includes the National Curriculum but is more than the sum of its parts. In practice it is a mixture of tradition (the culture passed down by society), innovation (ideas developed by educationists) and basic skills development (numeracy and literacy). The curriculum is now under public scrutiny and there is more public participation in its content. It is no longer enough to say that the head/leader must be aware of all major developments and ensure that the staff are aware of them. It is the effective management of the curriculum in relation to these developments that is vital, and this involves planning, monitoring and evaluating the content, the processes and the outcomes, and ensuring that all are communicated and understood by a variety of audiences.

Evaluation and assessment

Whereas assessment of the pupils' work is an essential of every teacher's job, evaluation of the work of individual teachers and the school as a whole is a prime responsibility of the headteacher. The purposes and practices of evaluation are considered in detail in Chapter 6 but they run implicitly through all aspects of management practice. For example, evaluation will involve a regular review of

1) staff progress;
2) the effectiveness of internal and external communications;
3) the roles and responsibilities of staff; and
4) the curriculum.

How the head manages these evaluations determines his or her effectiveness.

Conclusion

Some recent literature, whilst admitting to the complexity of leadership, nevertheless remains within the old paradigm of leading from the front: 'The new manager . . . will not be a classical, hierarchically oriented bureaucrat but a customized version of Indiana Jones; proactive; entrepreneurial; communicating in various languages; able to inspire, motivate and persuade subordinates, superiors, colleagues and outside constituents' (Gerding and Screnbuijseur, cited in Beare and Slaughter, 1993).

It is our view that leaders must now operate within a *changing context* in which the traditional dominant relationship between headteachers and teachers, schools and the public is moving to one of more equal partnerships. As schools move towards a more decentralized situation, independence and isolation (called by some, 'autonomy') are being replaced by co-operation, with an emphasis on school as community. The 'new' successful leader is more likely to be a 'steward' than a comic-book hero figure.

The leader within these roles is one who by skilled intervention, clear vision, the application of principles of social justice and a pragmatic recognition that the best way of learning is through motivation and commitment, influences others to achieve mutually agreed upon purposes for the organization:

> The principal for the next decade must remember that he or she is a person whose work as an educational leader is, first, foremost, and always with persons – persons who are physical, intellectual, spiritual, emotional, and sound beings . . . As a person in a community, the principal of the 1990s and beyond will be concerned with several things. Recognizing that communities and their occupants flourish in caring, nurturing environments, these principals will seek to utilize a caring ethic to guide their decisions and actions . . . They will view teachers, students, parents, and others as colleagues, partners, co-learners, and (where possible) friends. And they will relish the challenge of working with these groups to [build] a community of learners in which all persons can flourish.
>
> (Beck and Murphy, 1993)

Further reading

Beare, H. and Slaughter, R. (1993) *Education for the Twenty-First Century*, Routledge, London.

Brighouse, T. (1991) *What Makes a Good School?* Network Educational Press, Stafford.

Sergiovanni, T.J. (1995) *The Principalship: A Reflective Practice Perspective*, Allyn & Bacon, London.

4

Change processes

Professional learning • Promoting change • Resistance to change • Force-field analysis • The management task • Leadership roles • The head and the heart of change • The helping process: entitlements, contracting and action planning

There is nothing more difficult to carry out, nor more doubtful of success, nor more dangerous to handle, than to initiate a new order of things. For the reformer has enemies in all who profit by the old order, and only lukewarm defenders in all those who would profit by the new order. The lukewarmness arises partly from fear of their adversaries who have law in their favour, and partly from the incredulity of mankind who do not truly believe in anything new until they have had actual experience of it.

(Machiavelli, 1513)

'Innovation' as used in this chapter refers to ideas or practices that are new or different from those that exist in the school and classroom. The introduction and use of anything that is new also imply change. So the focus for this chapter is school-centred change, planned as a deliberate and collaborative process involving a change agent (who may be any member of the school staff) and client, or group of clients, in solving a problem in order to increase the effectiveness of children's education. Change itself, whether major or minor, requires time, energy, skill and, most importantly, the commitment of the person who is being expected or encouraged to make the change. Problems of commitment especially arise where the need for change has been identified by someone other than the person expected to change.

Leaders need to understand the implications that changes, for example, in the culture of teaching and learning in their schools, have for their staff and pupils. As the National Curriculum, SATs and the effects of OFSTED inspections become 'institutionalized', it will not be simply a matter of management through monitoring. The ability and willingness of teachers to offer enthusiastically a broad range of teaching and learning approaches, rather than being seduced into 'teaching to the test', will be paramount if the quality of learning experiences is to be maintained. As information technology, too, becomes more widely available, the teacher's role as expert 'mediator' of knowledge and trustworthy 'negotiator' of meanings will become increasingly important. Collaboration and interdependency will need to complement the effects of the independent learning which accompanies the global information explosion. To nurture life-long learning habits in children requires teachers themselves to be life-long learners; and they will look to school leaders to model this, to provide appropriate challenge, and to support professional development opportunities for all in their schools. Leaders themselves, therefore, need to understand and respond dynamically to new situational demands through an understanding of their context and a clearly articulated vision of the future. Too much reliance on advance planning – even 'flexible' planning – may be a mistake. Change leaders need to be both 'light on their feet' and attentive to the development of authentic shared understandings and vision. This is the evolutionary perspective described by Louis and Miles (1990):

> The evolutionary perspective rests on the assumption that the environment both inside and outside organizations is often chaotic. No specific plan can last for very long, because it will either become outmoded due to changing external pressures, or because disagreement over priorities arises within the organization. Yet, there is no reason to assume that the best response is to plan passively, relying on incremental decisions. Instead, the organization can cycle back and forth between efforts to gain normative consensus about what it may become, to plan strategies for getting there, and to carry out decentralized incremental experimentation that harnesses the creativity of all members to the change effort . . . Strategy is viewed as a flexible tool, rather than a semi-permanent expansion of the mission.

The problem for the head, deputy head or any other member of staff who may take a leadership role is how to achieve and support a commitment to change that will be more than 'token'. Rather than beginning, in this chapter, by describing various approaches or models that might be adopted or examining the well documented innovation overload of the late 1980s and 1990s, it is necessary first to investigate the likely psychological and social contexts that influence the attitudes of the teachers involved.

Professional learning

If we assume that professional development is a normal rather than an exceptional process, and that most teachers are capable of reflecting on their performances and improving them in the light of such reflection, then it follows that they are no strangers to innovation. Indeed, they are constantly having to take decisions about teaching that involve change. Many are immediate 'on-the-spot' decisions taken in the classroom when there is no time for reflection; others are the result of a conscious thought process that occurs outside the classroom. These are 'reflective' decisions (Sutcliffe and Whitfield, 1976).

It may be argued, however, that while these decisions are based on the teachers' identification of need, and while development of this kind occurs naturally and without intervention, such development is limited by the physical and social environment or context in which the teachers work and by their perceptions. For example, the classroom in which they work contains much more 'information' than they can handle, and their decisions about practice are concerned with finding ways in which they can survive, cope and teach effectively in a world that is stable. Thus practices are, in a sense, rules of action that allow them both to maintain a stable view of, for example, the classroom or the school, and to give priority to certain kinds of information while ignoring others. They are theories of control. A new teacher very quickly develops assumptions about practices that allow him or her to cope with the complexities of teaching and being a member of staff. However, since it is rare for these to be made explicit or tested, the possibilities for evaluating these assumptions which underpin his or her teaching are minimal.

To survive in a school it will be necessary for a teacher to accept the often unstated norms and expectations of the school and wider community. In the staffroom setting, for example, talk about teaching is governed by assumptions about the nature of talk about teaching. Thus, what happens in the classroom and what is said to happen in the classroom may be quite different, and it may not be surprising if the 'doctrine' of teacher as educationist is contradicted by the 'commitments' arising in the classroom situation of teacher as practitioner (Keddie, 1971). The imperatives of the National Curriculum may provide help in minimizing these contradictions but they will not remove them.

So there are both perceptual and contextual constraints that may militate against teachers exercising their capacities to be self-critical. Indeed, all but the newest teachers are likely to have found their own personal solutions to problems shortly after entering the school. These enable them to strike a balance between opposing forces of teacher personality factors, ideological factors, the curriculum and its presentation, external requirements and the characteristics of pupils (Lacey, 1977). It is only when the teacher perceives that this personal solution is itself inadequate that he or she will be moved to search for means by which he or she can change, e.g. reaching an agreed target or implementing, in the best possible way, aspects of the National Curriculum or agreed school policy. The responsibility of the headteacher is crucial both in creating a climate for examination of thinking and practice by ensuring regular opportunities for teachers to review their personal solutions and by providing appropriate support.

Promoting change

Finally, the importance of the teacher as the implementer cannot be overemphasized. How (s)he perceives the innovation, its effectiveness, its fit, and the importance that gets attached to implementation, and continued use, determines whether or not something new gets used.

(Lewis, 1987)

Genuine innovation is unlikely to occur unless the teacher him or herself feels a great sense of ownership of the innovation, is committed to its value for the pupils in his or her classroom and can call upon support for its implementation, particularly in terms of training and resources. In the world of the 1990s, teachers are expected to implement a curriculum designed by others and, at first sight, this may appear to be a repeat of centre-periphery innovation models of the 1960s that failed to permeate the majority of schools. However, innovation of the late 1980s and 1990s is legislated and monitored so that the issue of choice of implementation is no longer appropriate. Nevertheless, those who promote legislated change at grass-roots level will still have to be convinced of its value in order to assimilate, accommodate and, where necessary, transform practices. Knowing how to manage the individual and group involved in innovation is the key to successful change.

In one sense, changes in conditions of service imposed in the 1980s have, at least in theory, assisted the headteacher in promoting change. The practice of 'directed time' within teachers' designated 1265 hours, the five 'professional development' days each year, the annual school development plan and teacher appraisal, all provide potentially rich opportunities for institutional and personal review and target-setting. The local management of schools (LMS) has, for most schools, provided finance that may be used to release teachers from classroom duties. All provide potentially rich opportunities for teachers to engage in reflective curriculum and professional development. Most heads, however, have received little or no training in the management of these opportunities (DES, 1989b). Indeed, few training opportunities exist that focus upon the knowledge that educational change agents need to exercise in managing change (Figure 4.1) The initiatives by the Teacher Training Agency (TTA) in providing in-service opportunities for new, aspiring and serving headteachers through approved programmes and the development of national competency-based standards, provide new opportunities for systematic training, though their effectiveness is yet to be established.

1) Assess the situation (people, resources, constraints). For example, you may approach or be approached informally by individuals, or formally through your appraisal system, or 'hear' a need voiced during a staff meeting, or initiate a staff meeting yourself.

2. Identify an area of concern (general or specific). The realization that there is a need for change may come through listening to staff and being aware of their thoughts, needs and relationships. If not, the ground has to be prepared for change. This will include planning how and when to implement change.

3) Communicate the concern formally to
   a)   headteacher/deputy headteacher;
   b)   staff colleagues; and
   c)   other involved people, e.g. parents/ancillaries.

4) Meet formally with colleagues to
   a)   identify the specifics of the problem(s);   Negotiations of
   b)   clarify issues;   meanings
   c)   generate discussion of new ideas;   and contracting
   d)   decide on group aims and specific strategies: consensus seeking; joint formulation of valid alternative strategies, leading to establishment of priorities and agreed deadlines; and
   e)   decide on ways of monitoring the implementation of the plan.

5) Implementation of the plan (with back-up provided, e.g. time and resources).

6) Revision of plan in the light of experience   Flexibility
   a)   recognition that the logic of planning   as a criterion and the logic of action may not match).   of action

7) Reflective monitoring and appraisal of the effectiveness and new planning if appropriate.

8) Consolidation of new pattern/plan.

9) Long-term 'after-care' support and evaluation.

Figure 4.1   Procedures in the management of change

Resistance to change

There is no assumption here that all innovation or change is for the better, nor that what is right for one teacher is necessarily right for another. Teachers, like children, will be at different stages of development and have different needs. These needs may be expressed through an apparent or real aversion to new ideas that involve them in change. There may be three types of response by teachers who are 'invited' to change:

1) The rational adopter – someone who might be said to adopt a step-by-step approach to solving problems. This person will

   a) clarify goals and problems;
   b) collect information about how the problems arise;
   c) consider ways to resolve the problems;
   d) implement these; and
   e) evaluate the success of the strategies implemented.

2) The Stone Age obstructionist – who neither accepts the need for change, nor responds to 'invitations' to be involved.
3) The pragmatic sceptic – who expresses 'a concern for immediate contingencies and consequences'. This person will evaluate change proposals in terms of their validity for him or her in his or her classroom. The pragmatic sceptic will ask three questions:

   a) What do I/my pupils get out of it?
   b) Can I relate it to what I do/how I teach?
   c) What is its cost (in time, energy and finance)?

The pragmatic sceptic wants to see a return on the investment.

There may be connections between these responses and those of teachers influenced by their own career expectations and the broader political context of education. For example, schools may continue to be faced with changing pupil populations, increasing behavioural problems among pupils and diminishing financial resources. Staff may find increasing difficulties in achieving promotion. The increased 'intervention' in school life by parents, LEAs and central government through the National Curriculum, governing bodies, OFSTED inspections, curriculum monitoring, appraisal, greater central control of the teaching process itself and negative media coverage may reinforce perceptions by teachers that there is less trust in their 'professionalism'. The head may, therefore, have to help motivate some teachers who are frustrated, apathetic, resentful or 'burnt out'. Hand (1981) divided the teaching force of the 1980s into three categories:

1) Those who are frustrated in their ambitions.
2) Those who are happy to be in their final school posts.
3) Those likely to gain (further) promotion.

A fourth category has been added to the teaching force of the 1990s and beyond:

4) Those who are happy to be in their present posts but who find it difficult to cope with the stresses caused by externally imposed innovation.

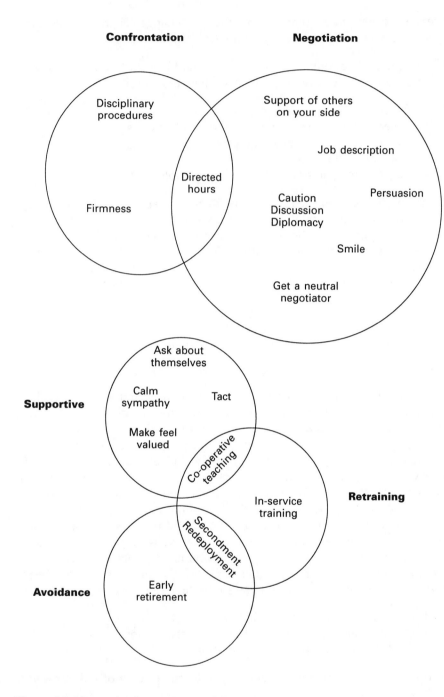

Figure 4.2   Strategies for managing difficult people

Not all schools will contain all these clear-cut categories of teacher and, indeed, these categories are not in reality mutually exclusive – people and contexts can and do change. However, they do serve to draw the attention of headteachers and others concerned with innovation to the complex web of role expectations, institutional constraints, professional experiences, teaching attitudes and approaches and personality factors that may influence the responses of teachers to change.

A group of headteachers attending a management training programme identified the strategies in Figure 4.2 for managing difficult people. It is as well to remember that apparently 'difficult' colleagues may not be simply 'pig-headed' in their resistance to change. They may, for example, distrust their own ability to change, have a preference for current, well tried and tested practice or lack the extra energy necessary to begin and sustain something new. They need to be approached in different ways. One way of planning for work that is more likely to involve controversy is to use a technique called 'force-field analysis'.

Force-field analysis

Force-field analysis is a conceptually simple yet powerful method of planning programmes of action. It may be undertaken alone or, preferably, with a critical friend. Its purpose is to identify facilitating and restraining forces associated with a particular planned task as a means of developing action strategies. Ultimately the balance between them might be adjusted so that it is shifted towards success or the achievement of a stated goal. Figure 4.3 shows the forces as arrows. The arrows can be made long or short, thick or thin to indicate the perceived strength of the forces.

One partner in a pair assists the other to identify restraining and facilitating forces, which are then shown diagrammatically. The use of simple and open-questioning techniques enables that person to focus on those forces that seem critical in relation to success of the achievement of the goal. Finally, and again by appropriate questioning, one member of the pair supports the other in finding methods of minimizing the restraining forces and maximizing the facilitating forces. These methods form the basis of an action plan for the achievement of the stated goal. Roles are then reversed if both members of the pair are planning programmes jointly.

It is important, then, to move with care, particularly when new (innovative) practices are being suggested. Figure 4.4 illustrates the affective dimensions of leading change. It cannot be assumed that rational discussion will convince 'Stone Age obstructionists', who neither accept the need for change nor respond to the invitation to be involved. However, there are a number of dimensions of morale in organizations that, when linked to assumptions that professionals wish to increase their effectiveness, may be used as guiding principles for motivation. Most teachers would wish to have (Miller and Fom, 1966)

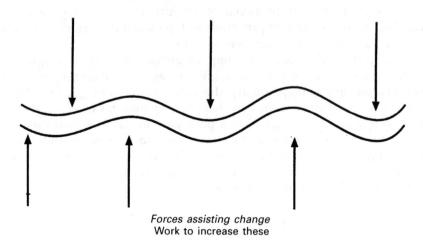

Restraining forces

Forces resisting change
Work to decrease these

Forces assisting change
Work to increase these

Facilitating forces

4.3   Force-field analysis
Source: Egan (1982)

1) intrinsic job satisfaction;
2) involvement in the immediate work of the group that constitutes the school;
3) identification with the organization;
4) satisfying interpersonal relationships with 'superiors' and immediate colleagues in the organization; and
5) satisfaction from work status.

The management task

Developing learning cultures for staff as well as children

Although a great deal of importance seems to be attached to the nature of the human environment in which change takes place it has not traditionally been the subject for much deliberate attention. A number of writers have used the notion of culture in relation to the work of schools. Fullan and Hargreaves (1992) describe it as: '... the guiding beliefs and expectations evident in the way a school operates, particularly in reference to how

1) The staff need to perceive the needs for and purpose of change; and feel a responsibility for sharing in decisions about its implementation and timing, under sustained visible leadership
2) There must be good two-way communication with staff who are directly and indirectly involved.
3) There is a need for a positive climate for change, and this will depend largely upon the ability of the headteacher to create and work with a learning culture.
4) There is a need for time to implement change. It is a process, not an event.
5) There is a need for those involved to see benefits for themselves in addition to 'the school' and pupils.

Figure 4.4 Interpersonal relationships in change: motivation

people relate (or fail to relate) to each other. In simple terms culture is "the way we do things and relate to each other around here" '.

Nias, Southworth and Yeomans (1989) use the term to describe the multiple social realities that people construct for themselves. Westoby (1988) refers to organizational culture as 'social habitat', including the informal, ephemeral and covert as well as the visible and official. Essentially then, culture is about people in the organizational setting and is characterized by behaviour – what people say and do; relationships – how they work with and through each other; attitudes and values – how assumptions, beliefs and prejudices affect the formal and informal workings of the organization.

One of the keys to successful whole-school development is a sensitive attention to what affects culture. Essentially this means trying to make sense of why people behave as they do; the extent to which their behaviour is culturally determined and the ways in which culture can be deliberately built and developed in ways that optimize the organizational purposes: 'the only thing of real importance that leaders do is create and manage culture . . . the unique talent of leaders is their ability to work with culture' (Schein, 1985). Some cultures struggle to maintain the status quo in the face of demand and expectation – for change. Others are anxious to avoid any sense for sameness or complacency. Most organizations live a life somewhere between these two extremes.

The quality of leadership of adults in schools is as important as the quality of leadership by teachers in classrooms, so attitudes of leaders are important in enabling the full potential of staff to be recognized and enhanced. It is a prime management task to plan, support and monitor the innovation process though not necessarily always to initiate it. The head should provide environments that minimize constraints on learning, and in which a variety of concrete personal experiences may be reflected upon, talked about and assimilated or accommodated – in short, to promote reflection on, as well as reflection in, practice (Schon, 1983). Teachers need time for planning and this may involve (temporary) changes in teaching or lesson organization only heads are in a position to support – by, for example, taking a class in order to release a teacher who wishes to visit other learning environments.

In organizational terms, this implies that the headteacher will ensure that regular opportunities exist for individuals and groups of individuals to

1) reflect on practice;
2) share practice;
3) identify issues for change that may arise from (1) and (2);
4) generate alternative strategies for change;
5) acquire the appropriate help to achieve this (human and material);
6) apply the strategies; and
7) monitor and evaluate the processes and outcomes.

Equally, factors which may constrain success, for example, should be taken into account:

- *Innovation overload* Don't involve yourself or others in too many changes simultaneously. Change (the act) and changing (the process of implementing the act) take time and emotional as well as intellectual energy. Already complex management tasks can be compounded by the number of innovations that have to be handled simultaneously.
- *Multiple-role pressures* Teachers play a variety of life roles. For example, a teacher may also carry the role of parent, partner, nurse (to an aged relative). It is necessary to consider the stress these may cause when promoting innovation.
- *Disclosure and feedback sensitivities* All change involves disclosure (e.g. of present practice through review) and feedback – whether these occur privately or, as is more likely with school development planning, target-setting and appraisal/review, publicly. The act of disclosure will create initial turbulence for many teachers if only because it is not a part of the traditional professional culture that ensures many teachers plan, carry out and evaluate their work in the relative isolation of their own classrooms. For successful sharing, for self or peer confrontation, a school climate of trust, confidence and confidentiality is essential.
- *Transformation* The most fundamental form of innovation involves the transformation of teachers' attitudes and values. Resistance to change imposed from the outside may be an act of strength rather than weakness by teachers who are reluctant to move out of their spheres of competence because they are not committed to the values of what is proposed. This is a particularly difficult dilemma for heads who wish to support teacher autonomy and ownership of change so that teachers will internalize rather than comply with it.
- *Time* The amount of time needed to innovate successfully is frequently underestimated. Too many of those who determine policy assume, incorrectly, that teachers can assimilate and implement new ideas with a minimum of planning time. Temporary 'burdens of incompetence',

and the discomfort and dismay that are the defining characteristics of innovation (MacDonald, 1973), are not always considered. Day-to-day 'system maintenance' demands on a teacher's time and energy are often underestimated.

There is a tendency among teachers themselves and those outside the profession to assume that teachers, as 'trained professionals', will be in possession of skills that might be called for. This assumption, if not tested, may hinder the implementation of innovation. On the one hand, teachers may be slow to admit they need help; on the other hand, innovation managers may resort to claiming that it is the responsibility of the individual teacher to use his or her professional judgement or skills at the implementation stage. Some of the factors likely to discourage pedagogical innovations are:

A sense of inadequacy and low self-esteem in staff;
Lack of relevant skills;
Failure of authorities to provide advisory and specialist consultancy service;
Lack of interest or conviction in staff, particularly in sustaining change processes over a period of time;
Inadequate allocation of resources (time and personnel as well as money);
Failure to appreciate the subtleties of group interactions when the balance of power in an existing institution is threatened;
Tendency for institutions to revert to earlier forms of organization and control if the pressure for change is not continuous.

(Skilbeck, 1982)

The emphasis so far has been on the teachers' felt needs, whether these involve them as individuals in classrooms, in the wider needs of the school or a combination of both. Figure 4.5 illustrates the importance of these by suggesting reasons for participation in change.

---

1) Individuals like to have responsibility and be trusted (ownership).
2) To create a feeling of belonging in the school (collegiality).
3) Support and encouragement to staff boost morale (colleagueship).
4) It eases one's workload (in the short term) (practicality)!

(NB Where responsibility is given, so must authority be.)

Figure 4.5 Reasons for participation in change

This is not to suggest that the head's needs are any less legitimate but that, like children, teachers may be best motivated when following their own interests and where the work is based on their own experiences. Eraut (1977) suggests that 'The best way to promote teacher development may be to expect it, or at least be careful that one's actions do not implicitly suggest that one does not expect it'. These principles have clear links with problem-solving models of innovation which place the client's needs at the centre of the learning process. The client is thus an active causal agent and participant at every stage of his or her learning. Our point, then, is that where work is able to be related to personal experience and perceived needs, and occurs in the context in which this experience and these needs occur (i.e. the classroom or school), the teacher will feel more involved and learn more.

It follows that the primary function of headteachers and 'leaders' in schools is not to identify need for others, *but to involve others in identifying needs*. This indicates a recognition that change based on the teachers' perceived need is of prime importance. The steps towards successful leadership in Chapter 3, are relevant here.

Leadership roles

The general leadership stance taken by headteachers who achieve success in promoting change will be consultative rather than directive or prescriptive, authoritative rather than authoritarian. The former is built on agreement through stature whereas the latter is built on the use of status alone.

Although writing in a different context – that of evaluation – MacDonald's (1974) description of three 'ideal types' of evaluation study might equally apply to styles of leadership and intervention in schools:

1) *Bureaucratic* In which the key concepts are service, utility and efficiency, and in which the key justificatory concept is 'the reality of power'.
2) *Autocratic* In which the key concepts are 'principle' and 'objectivity', and in which the key justificatory concept is 'the responsibility of office'.
3) *Democratic* In which the key concepts are confidentiality, negotiation and accessibility, and in which the key justificatory concept is 'the right to know'.

There are clearly in-built difficulties of role definition for the headteacher who embarks on a 'democratic' style of leadership. Schools are not democracies since, albeit through the governing body, the head and not the teachers has responsibility for the curriculum and standards of the school. The head writes references on the staff so that there will inevitably be a power and authority gap. In cases where the head is non-teaching, there may also be a 'credibility' problem. Without denying the existence of these problems it is, nevertheless, possible for them to be minimized rather than emphasized by the way in which heads approach their leadership role. Research suggests that the 'participative' style of leadership is most effective in leading staff development (see Chapter 3). It would involve the head in playing any one or a combination of the following three roles:

1) *Catalyst* Who prods and pressures the system to be less complacent and to start reviewing its work.
2) *Solution-giver* Who knows when and how to offer a solution appropriate to colleagues' needs.
3) *Process helper* Who can help colleagues in the 'how to' of change.

---

1) Is the change short term, with a quickly achieved goal?
2) Is the change long term, involving continuity and spread through the school?
3) What is your estimated timescale? If a lengthy period, then be aware of the need for continuity and progression through staff meetings, discussions, priorities and choices.
4) Do you lead by example?
5) Enthusiasm – are you aware of possible insecurity of staff?
6) Are you able to offer the support needed to all staff and especially to those who feel unsure? Is there a colleague on the staff who could do this?
7) Can you make sufficient resources available – are you aware whether additional resources will be needed next year, and whether this will mean a reduction in cash for other areas of the curriculum?
8) Will you offer the advantage of school time to allow staff to implement change (i.e. head teaches their class or takes on a group/supply cover)?
9) Do you use external help where appropriate? For example,
   a)   visits – in pairs to other schools, workshops;
   b)   INSET days and 'directed time' as an integral part of a curriculum and staff-development programme; and
   c)   use of external consultants (from local university).

Figure 4.6   Thinking and planning questions

Whatever the starting point for change, the head will need to pose the following questions:

1) What challenge and support do individuals need from me? Can this be made available?
2) What challenge and support does the teacher/group of teachers need from
   a)   inside
   b)   outside the school?

   Can this be made available?
3) What are the priorities for action? (What is appropriate at this time, at this stage of development?) What are the most appropriate strategies?
4) Is the activity practical in terms of time, energy and resources?
5) What will the teachers gain from the activity?
6) What knowledge, understanding and skills do I have?

In effect, the asking of these questions and those posed in Figure 4.6 is the beginning of the formulation of a process-orientated policy for staff development within which innovation may occur.

The head and the heart of change

Michael Fullan (1993) sees productive change as the constant 'search for understanding, knowing that there is no ultimate answer' (Stacey, 1992). He suggests a set of eight inter-related basic lessons:

CHART 1:   The Eight Basic Lessons of the New Paradigm of Change

Lesson One: You Can't Mandate What Matters
               (The more complex the change the less you can force it)

Lesson Two: Change is a Journey not a Blueprint
               (Change is non-linear, loaded with uncertainty and excitement and sometimes perverse)

Lesson Three: Problems are Our Friends
               (Problems are inevitable and you can't learn without them)

Lesson Four: Vision and Strategic Planning Come Later
               (Premature visions and planning blind)

Lesson Five: Individualism and Collectivism Must Have Equal Power
               (There are no one-sided solutions to isolation and group think)

Lesson Six: Neither Centralization Nor Decentralization Works
               (Both top-down and bottom-up strategies are necessary)

Lesson Seven: Connection with the Wider Environment is Critical for Success
               (The best organizations learn externally as well as internally)

Lesson Eight: Every Person is a Change Agent
               (Change is too important to leave to the experts, personal mind set and mastery is the ultimate protection)

(Fullan, 1993)

Clear implications may be drawn from these for the kind of leadership which can be most effective. First, change is a process rather than a series of events, and as such cannot be forced; secondly, managing problems is a way of learning; thirdly, no single change strategy or 'blueprint' will apply to all change situations; fourthly, every member of staff is a change agent. Teaching is, after all, a 'moral' enterprise aimed at the betterment of pupils. As such it is about change and so teachers must be involved in decisions about change; and, fifthly, leaders must take account of external as well as internal environmental climates. There must be a culture of purposeful dialogue:

> People do not provoke new insights when their discussions are characterized by orderly equilibrium, conformity, and dependence. Neither do they do so when their discussions enter the explosively unstable equilibrium of all-out conflict or complete avoidance of the issues . . . People spark new ideas off each other when they argue and disagree – when they are conflicting, confused, and searching for new meaning – yet remain willing to discuss and listen to each other.
>
> (Stacey, 1992)

All those involved in promoting change must be concerned with the manner as well as the matter of change. Many programmes of professional development are based on what we believe to be a myth, that one can simply sit down with others, work out policies, aims, strategies, and so on and implement them according to rational procedures based on apparently rational agreements. This does not take account of the fact that there may be conflicts over, for example, values, power and practicalities, an increase in workload or a desire for old certainties.

In work concerned with questioning the teacher's self-image, the affective relationship is of prime importance if one is to take into account such concerns as anxiety, status and identity. The affective area is rarely made explicit, yet the attitudes of teachers are clearly crucial to the success, not only of the process of innovation but also of the interventionist. How is the headteacher perceived? Is he or she an authority or a threat? Is he or she a process helper or a judge with alien values? During the process of devising a policy and carrying it through, it is likely that the head, far from being non-directive, will play a variety of supportive roles. After all, he or she is as committed to the professional development enterprise as anyone, and so cannot hope to be a 'neutral' figure – except when playing a role of 'procedural neutrality' that '. . . expresses a teacher's commitment not to use his authority to promote judgements which go beyond impartial criteria of rationality' (Elliott, 1975).

While it is important to build mutually supportive relationships with teachers based on the commitment of both to enhancing the quality of education in the school, headteachers must be prepared to donate their experience and responsibilities in ways that are both appropriate to their role as head (with accountability to LEA and parents, as well as teachers) and to their role as a member of a team (with accountability to children and teachers). There will be times when some teachers may need to be 'told' or have an expectation that they should be 'told' or 'directed'; others when they should have some say in what and how they learn. Their perceptions may be formed by such factors as role expectation, socialization or psychological needs. Indeed, when adults are participants in their own learning, problems may arise because their inquiry skills are either underdeveloped or undeveloped. Among adults as among children, then, the need and ability to be self-directing will vary, and depend on factors such as cognitive and personality development, motivation, social development and role expectation (Day and Baskett, 1982). It follows that *the head will need to be able to adopt a variety of roles*: he or she will at various times be acting as an appraiser (of staff and pupil work); an adviser/counsellor (to staff and pupils); an organizer (of timetable, curriculum, resources); a linking agent (between staff within the school, between staff and other teachers, between staff and pupils, and staff and parents); an expert (on curriculum content or teaching techniques); a promoter (of an idea, and so on); a legitimator; or a devil's advocate (to test out commitment to a process or the logic of an idea). In effect the one individual is expected to be an innovator, a change agent, an evaluator and a friend!

American research (Miles, Saxl and Lieberman, 1988) has revealed six skills needed by educational change agents which remain relevant today. Whilst the relative importance of each of these skills will vary according to time and social contexts, the list provides an interesting repertoire upon which to reflect. Of the eighteen skills, six were classified as general skills. These were interpersonal ease, group functioning, training/doing workshops, master teacher, educational content and administrative/organizational ability (see Figure 4.7). Regardless, however, of a change agent's knowledge, skills and organizational abilities, there will still be those in the school who, for a variety of reasons, will be resistant.

Skill and description	Examples
Interpersonal ease Relating simply and directly to others	Very open person . . . can deal with people . . . nice manner . . . has always been able to deal with staff . . . you have to be able to work with people, know when to stroke, when to hold back, when to assert, know 'which buttons to push' . . . gives individuals time to vent feelings, lets them know her interest in them . . . She can talk to anyone . . .
Group functioning Understanding group dynamics, able to facilitate team work	Has ability to get a group moving . . . He started with nothing and then made us come together as a united body . . . good group facilitator . . . lets the discussion flow
Training/doing workshops Direct instruction, teaching adults in systematic ways	Gave workshops on how to develop plans . . . taught us consensus method with 5-finger game . . . He prepares a great deal and enjoys it. He has the right chemistry and can impart knowledge at the peer level . . .
Educational general (master teacher) Wide educational experience, able to impart skills to others	Excellent teaching skills . . . taught all the grades, grade leader work, resource teacher have done staff development with teachers . . . Title I programs where I was always assisting, supporting, being resource person to teachers . . . a real master teacher, much teacher training work
Educational content	Demonstrating expertise in a subject area . . . Parents

Knowledge of school subject matter	thought kindergarten would be all academic. She showed them the value of play, of trips ... knows a great deal about teaching, especially reading. What she doesn't know she finds out ...
Administrative/organizational Defining and structuring work, activities, time	Highly organized, has everything prepared in advance ... I could take an idea and turn it into a program ... Well organized, good at prioritizing, scheduling, knows how to set things up ...
Initiative-taking Starting or pushing activities, moving directly toward action	Assertive, clear sense of what he wanted to do ...ability to poke and prod where needed to get things done ... I had to assert myself so he didn't step on me
Trust/rapport-building Developing a sense of safety, openness, reduced threat on part of clients; good relationship-building	A breath of fresh air. In two weeks he had gained confidence of staff ... She had to become one of the gang, eat lunch with them. A skilled seducer (knows how to get people to ask for help) ... I have not repeated what they said so trust was built ... Even those who knew everything before, now let her help because they are not threatened ... She was so open and understanding that I stopped feeling funny
Support Providing nurturant relationship, positive affective relationship	Able to accept harsh things teachers say. 'It's OK, everyone has these feelings.' ... A certain compassion for others. Always patient, never critical, very enthusiastic
Confrontation Direct expression of negative information, without generating negative effect	Can challenge in a positive way ... She will lay it on the line about what works and what won't ... He is talkative and factual. His strength is being outspoken ... He can point out things and get away with being blunt ... Able to tell people they were wrong, and they accept it
Conflict mediation Resolving or improving situations where multiple incompatible interests are in play	Effected a compromise between upper and lower grade teachers on use of a checklist ... Teachers resented the chair's autocratic behaviour. So she spoke openly to him about it. Things have been considerably better ... The principal is very vindictive. He was constantly mediating, getting her to soften her attitude ... Can handle people who are terribly angry, unreasonable, keeps cool
Collaboration Creating relationships where influence is mutually shared	Deals on same level we do, puts in his ideas ... I've never seen a time where teachers felt they were told to do something ... Leads and directs us, but not in a way like professors and students, but as peers. Doesn't judge us or put us down ... Has ideas of her own, like in maths, but flexible enough to maintain the teachers' way of doing things too
Confidence-building Strengthening client's sense of efficacy, belief in self	She makes all feel confident and competent. Doesn't patronize ... 'You can do it.' She'll help ... He has a way of drawing out teachers' ideas. He injects a great deal, but you feel powerful ... She makes people feel like a million in themselves. Like a shot of adrenaline boosting your mind, ego, talents and professional expertise ... Her attitude: 'try it, you'll like it.'

Diagnosing individuals Forming a valid picture of the needs/problems of an individual teacher or administrator as a basis for action	You need to realize that when a teacher says she has the worst class, that means 'I need help' . . . He has an ability to focus in on problems and get rid of the verbiage . . . picking up the real message . . . sensitive, looks at teacher priorities first . . . knows when an off-hand joke is a signal for help
Diagnosing organizations Forming a valid picture of the needs/problems of a school as an organization (including its culture) as a basis for action	Analysing situation, recognizing problems, jumping ahead of where you are to where you want to go . . . when I analysed beyond the surface, I saw the principal was using meetings for administrative purposes . . . Anticipates problems schools face when they enter the program . . . brought in report on reading/maths and attendance, helped us know where we should be going . . . helped team look at the data in the assessment package
Managing/controlling Orchestrating the improvement process; coordinating activities, time and people; direct influence on others	She filled all the gaps in terms of legwork, preparing materials and coordination of our contact with admin. and district . . . a task master and keeps the process going . . . makes people do things rather than doing them himself . . . He sets a pace, like the bouncing ball on songs . . .
Resource-bringing Locating and providing information, materials, practices, equipment useful to clients	If it's broken he fixes it. He uses his network to get us supplies . . . Brings ideas that she has seen work elsewhere . . . Had the newest research, methods, articles, ideas, waters it down for our needs . . . Brought manipulative materials for help with multiplication . . .
Demonstration Modelling new behaviour in classrooms or meetings	He's a great story teller – gets the kids very interested . . . willing to go into classrooms and take risks . . . modelling . . . was real, did demos with their classes . . . Watching someone else teach my class makes me reflect on what I am doing . . . showed the chair by his own behaviour how to be more open . . .

Figure 4.7   Skills needed by change agents
Source: Miles, Saxl and Lieberman (1988)

The two main principles that seem to be fundamental to the intervention practices of the headteacher are

1) the perceived needs of the teacher(s) are of paramount (though not sole) importance; and
2) the interventionist's role is collaborative and co-equal, but not necessarily neutral or non-directive.

Interdependence rather than dependence or independence is thus a central feature in this process regardless of whether the change is focused on classroom teaching and organization, curriculum content, or school management and organizational structures.

The helping process: entitlements, contracting and action planning

The implication throughout this chapter has been that for innovation and change to have long-term success, relationships between colleagues need to be open, there needs to be an ethos of trust and sharing in activities that involve disclosure and feedback and that those in leadership roles need to be sensitive to a variety of learning needs among colleagues. It is also important to recognize that

> it is not always easy to receive help;
> it is difficult to commit oneself to change;
> it is difficult to submit to the influence of a helper; help is a threat to esteem, integrity and independence;
> it is not easy to trust a stranger and be open with him or her;
> it is not easy to see one's problems clearly at first; and
> sometimes problems seem too large, too overwhelming, or too unique to share easily.
>
> (Egan, 1982)

The message for leaders is that it is not enough to propose or make organizational or other changes without taking into account the amount of support those involved in implementing the changes will need – for change of this kind 'will not persist if some individual changes do not occur; and changes in the way professionals think and work will soon regress without supporting organizational change' (Schmuck, 1980).

The notion of formal 'entitlements' and contracts for and between staff may appear to be alienating to the essentially non-legalistic tradition of primary schools. Yet there is a sense in which, in the same way that pupils are entitled to a National Curriculum, all governors to annual school development plans and all teachers to appraisal, all teachers may be 'entitled' to support in the processes of change. Whilst some 'entitlements' may be context and task specific, there may be others that are more general and that, along with job specifications, should be made explicit, for example, the following:

- Consultation in the formulation of school development planning.
- Time to reflect on and participate in the monitoring and evaluation of curriculum.
- Quality support appropriate to training and development needs raised by the processes of change.
- Equal rights in judgements made of the outcomes of change.
- Ownership of the change process.

The curriculum reform movements of the 1960s and 1970s were largely unsuccessful because they were often initiated outside the school community, did not involve classroom teachers in the curriculum design and ignored the user context. Teachers were, by inference, passive receivers of curriculum packages. They had no sense of 'ownership' in what was largely a top-down process of innovation. The curriculum reform movements of the late 1980s and 1990s are ensured of adoption at the initial stage of implementation because they are the products of legislation. External monitoring, assessment and inspection will, however, only ensure that the letter (not the spirit) of the law is enacted. The fact remains that it is the individual teacher who still holds the key to the successful long-term impact of change within his or her own classroom. This chapter has suggested that, if the quality of teaching in the classroom is to be enhanced, then headteachers must provide practical as well as intellectual and moral support and promote a climate in which teachers themselves can take ownership of and responsibility for innovation in practice.

Further reading

Fullan, M. G. (1993) *Change Forces: Probing the Depths of Educational Reform*, Falmer, Lewes.
Stacey, R. (1992) *Managing the Unknowable*, Jossey-Bass, San Francisco, CA.

5

The inner experience: developing self-awareness

All pigs fed and ready to fly • Learning through experience • Starting with the self: developing intrapersonal intelligence • Taking care of the self • Self-concept and self-esteem: laying the foundation stones • Messages from childhood • Taking control of stress • Interpersonal communication • Physical well-being • People, people, people . . . in conclusion

All pigs fed and ready to fly

Office humour has a wisdom all of its own. Very often it helps us to think the unthinkable and express the inexpressible. There is a sheet of A4 paper decorating the wall of many a primary school headteacher's office which simply says

Another Month Ends
All Targets Met
All Systems Working
All Customers Satisfied
All Staff Eager and Enthusiastic
All Pigs Fed and Ready to Fly

This cuts to the heart of the myth of management: the myth of the perfect manager in the perfect organization. Intuitively, of course, we know from our lived daily experience in school the sense of frustration and futility this myth is capable of engendering. Yet too many headteachers and their staff are still trapped in a belief that, if they went on the right courses, read the right books and followed the experts' prescriptions faithfully, then every day at work wouldn't be a struggle to hang on to a sense of personal competence around the difficult task of 'managing' staff and pupils. The myth of perfection deludes us into believing in a fantasy world where staff are like loyal robots – enthusiastic to discuss, plan, try out, monitor and evaluate to order. In this dangerously rosy dreamworld, teachers invite honest feedback from colleagues on their teaching, love team working and look forward to the annual appraisal interview so that they can systematically identify developmental strategies for improving their classroom performance. Pupils' learning is the ultimate goal and always at the fore of every action, decision, desire, motivation.

In this candy-coloured world, teachers never sabotage, bully, squabble or let petty dislike overcome their professional judgement. Nor do they hold grudges, take revenge, gang up, gossip, scapegoat, put each other down, avoid and deny that they participate in any such underhand, unprofessional behaviour (but other colleagues apparently do). They never threaten to resign, bring in the unions, go to industrial tribunals or simply refuse to co-operate. Neither are they fun-loving, spontaneous, intelligent, creative, capable of immense tenderness, generosity, acceptance, compassion, empathy, diplomacy, comradeship or even love towards the people around them. Kilmann (1984) supports the view that it is imperative to encourage a more honest evaluation of human behaviour in organizations, and further urges us to let go of naive assumptions about human behaviour. He warns that, unless we do, frameworks for organizational development will inevitably be as distorted as the pseudo-rationalist 'model of management' mirror we hold up presently to human nature. Kilmann claims that a more accurate set of assumptions about human nature would be as follows:

(1) Human beings are not entirely rational – they make decisions based on limited information and can only analyse a few variables at one time. (2) Human beings have limited memory and tend to distort the recall of events according to their psychological needs. (3) Human beings are often insecure – their negative feelings of self-worth and confidence result in numerous defensive reactions and a dysfunctional coping style. (4) Human beings may have a strong desire for power and control – to minimize their fears of dependency stemming from discomforting childhood experiences. (5) Human beings do not like massive change, since their security and position in life will be altered. (6) Human beings do not universally have the ability to learn – sometimes all they can do is fight to survive. (7) Human beings have a strong need to be accepted by a group, stemming from their early family experiences – they are, therefore, susceptible to doing what the group decides in exchange for group membership.

Even if we may not wish to buy in wholesale to the stark realism of Kilmann's view, it does possess the intrinsic merit of reflecting a social world that most of us would recognize. We know that the environment of a school, like others, is a place where human relationships are messy and sometimes unpredictable. Relationships ebb and flow with time and both teachers' and pupils' feelings refuse to be packed away at the end of the day neatly, like so many books and pencils in a tray. Outstanding leaders have the capacity to work with people and their feelings as they really are. The paradox of such acceptance is that it frees the other person in the relationship to give up defensive or destructive patterns of behaviour.

When people feel genuine acceptance, then and only then will they trust because they feel valued for whom and what they are.

Learn to accept people for what they are – with all their strengths and weaknesses. The degree to which you can accept others is directly proportional to the degree to which you can accept yourself. Generally, those aspects of yourself which you find most difficult to accept – laziness, cynicism, dishonesty and so on – you will find the most difficult to deal with in others. Psychologists call this process projection. Until you can understand the link between your own inability to tolerate imperfection in yourself and the inability to tolerate imperfection in others, you cannot begin to deal with your own shortcomings or theirs, in a mature, healthy, developmental way.

It should come as no surprise, then, that in our role as school management and human relations consultants, we have time and time again been confronted by headteachers and others who want the bullet point list to professional salvation. They angrily demand that we solve the problems such difficult staff relationships present. The hidden agenda is that we take away the pain that they feel when confronted by the limits of their own emotional maturity in dealing with tough decisions about other people's working lives. What else are consultants paid for? They struggle to live out the myth of perfection, unable to see that it is the myth itself which is actually the greatest source of pain. The irony is, of course, that those self-same teachers know only too well when in the classroom that no matter how skilful or expert the teacher, there is only one person who can undergo the process of learning and that is the student. In short, the day-to-day reality of school life begs us to forgo the delusion that there are any easy answers to the difficult questions about managing the self and others. Bursting the bubble that all the 'Pigs are fed and ready to fly' *or ever could be* and facing the fact that emotional maturity demands that we all become students, life-long learners about ourselves and ourselves in relationship, is the first step to developing what Goleman (1996) calls 'emotional intelligence'. Effective leaders in schools are those who are willing to engage in this process of discovery on a daily basis and accept that education consultants, research findings, management texts and so on all have a meaningful place in enhancing the learning process about the self and the self in relationships – but are not a substitute for it.

Learning through experience

Knowing *about* what constitutes the essential elements of effective interpersonal communication as part of a set of managerial competences is not the same as *using* those essential elements as part of everyday behavioural repertoires. The headteacher may know intellectually that it is counterproductive to bully staff into agreeing to curriculum innovation, but when the heat is on, and it certainly will be most days, the head will resort to the tried and tested method of 'who is boss around here anyway?' or manipulate and wheedle until the desired outcome is achieved. In order to develop the people skills necessary to lead schools as learning communities, we would urge a recognition that cognitive understanding, using knowledge and learning to frame our experience, is merely a balance to the heightened self-awareness that developing our intrapersonal and interpersonal skill brings. It is only 50% of the equation. We can draw a parallel here with learning to ride a bicycle. Knowing about the techniques of bike-riding does not help the young child learn how to ride a bike. Knowing about the techniques of management does not automatically make someone a humane, person-centred manager. All the books in the world will not prepare the child for the first wobbly, out-of-control ride, even with protective stabilizers, or the new headteacher from facing the first uncomfortable staff meeting in a new school, even with a supportive deputy. The way that the child learns to ride is a complex set of interactions; between being absolutely determined to ride a bike come what may, believing that he or she is capable of succeeding, talking about technique with other more experienced riders, watching other people ride bikes, being encouraged by others, seeing and handling bikes and finally getting on and having a go. During and after the process, the young rider needs to be given adequate feedback. This feedback should be focused on the development of skills and be delivered in a constructive, helpful way. This would prompt a conversation with the learner and encourage the articulation of feelings, talking about how it felt to learn to ride a bike.

It is not possible to short circuit this process by going from the books on bike-riding (even with a bullet point list) to being the perfect bike rider – or the books on school management to being the perfect headteacher. Performance only improves when the learner regards the first tentative journeys as learning trials. Finally, through trial and error, with care and determination, the pain and embarrassment of falling-off are replaced by the initial thrill of accomplishment that is experienced when individuals take the first steps forward in their own development process. Celebration of success at this point in the learning cycle reinforces the sense of accomplishment. Repeated experiences of being an active agent in your own personal growth promote a powerful sense of self-efficacy within the individual, that is the ability to take charge of and responsibility for the direction of a life path in meaningful ways. The development of the essential human relations skills for effective school leadership mirrors this experiential learning process.

Learning to be the sort of headteacher, deputy, or teacher we believe our pupils and parents deserve can be a difficult learning journey. We want

---

Activity 5.1: Pen portraits

Try writing two pen portraits of yourself. The first, a portrait of the kind of leader you believe yourself to be in your life right now. Write in the third person as if it were being written about you by a close colleague. For example:

Jane Brown is a deputy head in a large urban primary school . . .

Include details of personal leadership qualities, likes and dislikes, strengths and weaknesses, foibles and quirks and what Jane Brown needs to do in order to realize her full leadership potential.

Then go on to write a second pen portrait of your vision of the ideal school leader. The personal qualities, attitudes, behaviours and so on.

Finally, compare the two portraits. This discrimination between the real and ideal self will give you some helpful pointers to those aspects of yourself that you need to develop in order to fulfil your leadership potential. It is healthy to have something of a gap between the real and ideal self. However, if the gap is very wide indeed this could be an indicator of low self-esteem. If they are extremely close, it may be that you have an overly defended view of the self and may need to seek feedback from others to check your self-perceptions.

---

this book to be a friendly companion which can support and encourage your determination to be the best head, deputy head or curriculum manager you can be and to remind you that although it might from time to time be a painful journey, it need not be a solitary one.

Peck (1978) told us, 'Life is difficult' and went on to add: 'This is a great truth, one of the greatest truths. It is a great truth because once we truly see this truth, we transcend it. Once we know that life is difficult – once we truly understand and accept it – then life is no longer difficult. Because once it is accepted, the fact that life is difficult no longer matters.'

Accepting the wisdom of Peck's words can liberate us from the myth that growth is achieved easily or can be achieved without first giving up old patterns and habits in relationships. However, it is possible to isolate the conditions in which powerful learning takes place. Successful experiential learning can be characterized in the way shown in Activity 5.2.

Starting with the self: developing intrapersonal intelligence

It has been said many times that man's knowledge of himself has been left far behind by his understanding of technology, and that we can have peace and plenty and justice only when man's knowledge of himself catches up.

(Kurt Vonnegut Jr, taken from *Wampeters foma and Granfalloons*)

Activity 5.2: Experiential learning: the components of success

Reflect on the following elements which are necessary for successful learning outcomes. How far are they part of your learning repertoire and that of other members of the school community?

- *Goal or image of the desired change* – knowing what it is you want to achieve.
- *Self-efficacy* – a belief that you can control your own destiny.
- *Self-esteem* – belief in personal competence.
- *Readiness to learn* – the psychological ability to reorder personal meanings and to overcome the discomfort of the learning process.
- *Availability of appropriate role models* – individuals within the environment who display the desired skills or behaviours.
- *Availability of feedback* – immediate feedback which is situation and skill specific and encourages feeling feedback in response.
- *Self-awareness* – the learner is able to reflect on the thoughts and feelings experienced during the learning process and adjust behaviour in the light of such awareness.
- *Period of integration* – time to assimilate learning and practise skills.
- *Awareness of success* – what the desired outcome looks, feels and is understood to be in an environmental context.
- *Reinforcement of the felt sense of accomplishment* – a conscious celebratory reward system which embeds positive psychological messages of self-efficacy and encourages repeated learning trials.

Books on the development of person skills for management, and human relations training courses, are only useful if the learner is prepared to put in the necessary emotional energy essential to the process of behaviour change. Without this internalized commitment and willingness to grow, all the books and courses in the world will not improve your relationships or your capacity to lead others one iota. Old patterns in relationships need to be re-examined and this can be a difficult, sometimes painful experiential process. This is a normal part of human development. To avoid or deny that fact is unhelpful and ultimately prevents growth from taking place.

By definition, teachers are academically able individuals. But a high IQ is clearly no guarantee of the human relation skills essential when managing people. The comic portrait, familiar to those of us who have experience of university life, of the genius professor with an emotional age of around four and a half (present authors excepted) is sadly all too common. The disjuncture between intellectual development and emotional development means that too often in our academic institutions, academically able individuals rise to the top who may or may not have the corresponding level of emotional intelligence (Goleman, 1995). Howard Gardner's ground-breaking work on the theory of multiple intelligence (Gardner, 1993) extends this idea. He challenges the view that human intelligence can be measured meaningfully on a unidimensional IQ scale. He proposed that what we refer to as intelligence is actually a cluster of intelligences. He argues that there are (at least) seven intelligences which can describe our 'bio psychological potential'. Of the seven (logical mathematical intelligence, linguistic intelligence, musical intelligence, spatial intelligence, bodily kinaesthetic intelligence, intrapersonal intelligence and interpersonal intelligence) it is the last two which concern us here. He calls these the 'personal intelligences' and it is Gardner's definition of these which provides some illumination into the type of intelligence needed from teachers who have specific responsibilities for managing colleagues.

He sees intrapersonal intelligence as follows:

The core capacity at work here is *access to one's own feeling life* – one's range of affects or emotions: the capacity instantly to effect discriminations among these feelings and eventually to label them, to enmesh them in symbolic codes, to draw upon them as a means of understanding and guiding one's behaviour.

Interpersonal intelligence, on the other hand, ' . . . turns outward, to other individuals. The core capacity here is *the ability to notice and make distinctions among other individuals* and, in particular, among their moods, temperaments, motivations, and intentions. He concludes that, ultimately,

The less a person understands his feelings, the more he will fall prey to them. The less a person understands the feelings, the responses, and the behaviour of others, the more likely he will interact inappropriately with them and therefore fail to secure his proper place within the larger community.

The story of the Sufi sage, the Mulla Nasrudin, illuminates our understanding of where to begin the process of developing our intrapersonal intelligence and avoid the behavioural traps that Gardner describes:

Someone saw Nasrudin searching for something on the ground outside his house. 'What have you lost, Mulla?' he asked.

'My key,' said the Mulla. So they both went down on their hands and knees and looked for it.

After a time the other man asked: 'Where exactly did you drop it?'

'In my own house.'

'Then why are you looking out here?'

'There is more light here than inside my own house,' was the Mulla's answer.

The folk wisdom contained in this simple tale highlights the irrationality of much of our everyday behaviour. The temptation when seeking answers to difficult questions is to look outside ourselves, when all too often the solution lies within. Why do human beings so often avoid self-reflection or introspection? One answer may lie in the fact that looking 'inside our own house' calls for the determination and courage to take responsibility for developing emotional maturity. Jersild (1995, reminds us:

> A teacher's understanding of others can be only as deep as the wisdom he possesses when he looks inward upon himself. The more genuinely he seeks to face the problems of his own life, the more he will be able to realize his kinship with others . . . One broad principle is this: *To gain in knowledge of self, one must have the courage to seek it and the humility to accept what one may find.*

Self-deception is a seductive lure because it keeps us tied to comfortable fantasies about the nature of our relationships:

- 'I can't afford to be honest with X because she isn't to be trusted.'
- 'I feel unsafe with Y because he is so unpredictable'.
- 'I stay well clear of Z. He is incredibly manipulative.'

As long as we feel attached to such a vocabulary of self-deception, we can avoid the short-term discomfort that self-awareness may bring. In the long term, however, relationships fracture, colleagues avoid or distrust us, people separate themselves off from us emotionally. The pain of such isolation is far more enduring and destructive of self-esteem than avoiding the trap of self-deception. Developing self-awareness means abandoning the habit of blaming yourself and others and when things go wrong in relationships (and they will) seeing the breakdown, however temporary, as a signal that we need to readjust our perspective on the relationship, reflecting on what aspects of personal behaviour contributed to the fracture. Ironically, teachers complain that one of the most infuriating forms of pupil behaviour can be the stubborn refusal to take responsibility when relationships break down. The 9-year-old who looks the teacher square in the face and declares: 'It was nothing to do with me miss. I didn't do anything to upset her, it was all his fault', is not so very different from the teacher whose pattern is always to blame others aggressively when staffroom conflicts arise or the deputy head who after repeated failures to be appointed to a headship, blames the headteacher's reference.

Activity 5.3: Increasing self-awareness

- Keep a *personal learning journal*. Write down significant moments in your day and how you felt about them. *Reflect* on what you did well and what you could have done better. *Be truthful* with yourself. You owe it to yourself.
- Learn to welcome *feedback* and ask for it from friends and colleagues. Learn to *stay alert* to how others see you.
- Practise sensory and bodily awareness. Try out simple techniques such as eating slowly and really *tasting* the food. Spend a moment just in *seeing* what is around you. *Listen* carefully and attentively to the sounds in your environment, close by and far away. *Feel* the temperature of the place you are in and the feel of your clothes against your skin. *Smell* the odours, scents and perfumes in the atmosphere around you.
- Practise taking your awareness to your *breathing* and lengthening and deepening the breath.
- *Listen to your body* and learn to read it like an open book. It may have many unread pages.
- *Pay attention* to your thoughts, feelings and emotions but do not let them define you. You can *stay aware* of them without being controlled or overcome by them.
- *Try out* the experiential activities in this chapter or go on a human relations course.

Teachers are well aware of the importance of developing healthy interpersonal *relationships as part of their professional repertoire, but need to remind themselves that learning about what constitutes effective interpersonal relationships begins with self-awareness – a willingness to examine and re-examine our values, beliefs, attitudes and behaviours. Self-awareness can be learnt, practised and finely honed like any other skill. It can teach us, if we are prepared to listen, that we can exercise control over our emotions, fears, anxieties and not let them control us. Until we can develop such control, our relationships will be dominated by potentially unhealthy personal agendas which have their roots in fearfulness and distrust of others, rather than a healthy, mutually beneficial relationship, which occurs between emotionally mature people.*

Taking care of the self

It would appear, then, that intrapersonal and interpersonal intelligence are inextricably linked. Janus-like, it is the development of the one which looks to the development of the other. However, our experience of working with primary school teachers and headteachers shows that they very often give their intrapersonal development needs a low priority and fail to make the link between the interpersonal qualities called for in effective school leadership and self-nurturing behaviour. Stressed-out headteachers waking up at 5.00 am thinking about the school development plan, arriving in school at 7.30 am, rushing around without a lunchbreak until finally leaving at 6.30 pm with a box file full of papers for the next governors' meeting, may think that they are doing a thoroughly professional job. However, they may not be in the best emotional shape to listen carefully and attentively to the genuine needs of the struggling newly qualified teacher or the inconsolable 5-year-old whose rabbit has just died. Staff are only too well aware where they are in any set of management priorities. Many would guess somewhere between the next health and safety inspection and the leaking roof in the infant block. The concerns of pupils, staff and parents need to be handled with a sensitive touch and good judgement in delicate interpersonal situations. The failure to prioritize your own intrapersonal needs calls into question your ability to respond to others appropriately. Stress and overwork are likely to compromise your responsiveness capabilities.

For headteachers and other teachers with leadership roles it invariably comes as a shock to hear that taking care of themselves is a fundamental, non-negotiable aspect in developing the human dimension of their managerial competence. Teachers are very often attuned to acknowledging and servicing the needs of others – pupils, parents, colleagues, school inspectors and so on – but may be a lot less alert to attending to their own emotional, social, physical and spiritual needs. For the profession as a whole, it is disturbing to have witnessed the ever-increasing numbers of experienced senior staff in primary schools clamouring for early retirement. The sad truth is that more and more teachers feel that the only way to put their own needs first is by taking early retirement. On a day-to-day basis they have felt, for a whole variety of reasons, disabled from prioritizing their own personal development needs and those of their staff. How many professional development days in the last five years have been spent on building staff relationships, self-care for the primary teacher, interpersonal skills training, sharing vision and values? Our guess is very few. We would want to argue very strongly that the quality of a teacher's life will have a direct impact upon his or her capacity to fulfil the professional role. Headteachers can be outstanding at setting up support systems when it comes to pupils or their parents. They may be less good at taking care of themselves emotionally or knowing how to develop personal support systems for their staff teams. Teachers need to give themselves permission to put their own growth needs, social, emotional, physical, spiritual, at the top of the staff development agenda. School leaders can legitimate this through whole-school policy and strategically implementing formal and informal personal development plans.

Peck (1993) vividly illustrates the relationship between personal and professional achievement and self-nurturing behaviour in an anecdote from his days as a psychiatrist in the US Army:

.. the military was interested in what made successful people click, and so a dozen such people from different branches of the services were gathered together for study. They were men and women in their late thirties or early forties who had all been markedly successful. They had been promoted ahead of their contemporaries, yet they also seemed to be popular. Those who had families seemed to be enjoying a happy family life; their children were doing well at school and were well adjusted. These people seemed to have a golden touch.

These men and women took part in a series of individual and group exercises which were designed to find out what made them tick. One particular exercise required that they individually answer the question: 'What are the three top priorities in your life right now?' After careful consideration (some took more than an hour to finish), their papers were examined. It was remarkable that the number-one priority listed was identical across the group. The second and third responses produced a wide variety but the top priority was the same. All the high fliers had written that their top priority was MYSELF. When primary headteachers and their staff comment on this story their instinctive response is almost always to exclaim: 'But that's selfish!' Culturally in schools there is a deep, ingrained mind set that equates professional dedication to self-sacrifice. Yet Peck's study demonstrates the short sightedness of this way of thinking and being. Peck himself comments that their prioritizing themselves '. . . was an expression of mature self-love. Self-love implies the care, respect and responsibility for and the knowledge of the self. Without loving one's self one cannot love others. But do not confuse self-love with self-centredness. These successful men and women were loving spouses and parents and caring supervisors'.

These high fliers are an example of what Carl Rogers (1961, 1963) called the 'fully functioning' person and Maslow (1970) 'self-actualizers'. The definitions are similar. It is a person who remains open to experience, whether perceived as good or bad, pleasurable or punishing and is able to live to the full in each moment of his or her life. It is interesting to note that after major life trauma or near-death experiences, many people report a heightened sense of awareness of themselves and the world around them. They develop a healthier perspective on life (Ring, 1984). A colleague, having been through the ordeal of nearly losing a child through illness, said:

It was as though a veil had been lifted. Everything became crystal clear. I knew immediately what I had to do and where my priorities lay. School and all the jobs which the day before couldn't wait, I suddenly saw them for what they were – mostly paper exercises. Colleagues and friends were fantastic, really supportive and for the first time in a long time I cried with gratitude for the loving support

---

Activity 5.4: Getting the priorities right

Consider the following list of possible areas of priority in your life right now. Order the list to reflect your *real* priorities. This will mean thinking about the actual *time* you spend involved with them on a day-to-day, week-by-week basis, as well as considering how much you feel you *care* about them in your head:

- family
- friends
- partner
- work/school
- community
- spiritual needs
- health
- myself
- house maintenance/development
- children.

Having reordered this list, spend some time considering if you are truly happy with it. Are there any items that you would like to reorder or remove completely? How far up the priority list did you place yourself? Is it possible to move yourself up the order of priority? What changes in your life right now would you need to make to move yourself up? Reflect on any significant insights which emerge into the quality of your life right now and how you can improve it.

---

of people around me. I think the experience of my son's illness in a strange sort of way, helped all of us be more alive to the wonder of life.

For ordinary mortals, the nature of our daily routine or hum-drum existence may, to some extent, desensitize us to the wonder of the world, unless we have the capacity to remain vigilant. Interestingly, Maslow found that his 'self-actualizers' were people who regularly counted their blessings and thought of themselves as lucky to be alive. We do not need to undergo such traumatic experiences, though, to sensitize ourselves to the beauty of human experience. Read through the list in Activity 5.5 as part of an exercise in self-reflection.

Activity 5.5: How many times in the last month have you . . . ?

Check how many of these activities you took part in over the last month. Some, all or not enough? What would you add to the list which you would consider to be healthy behaviours for yourself? How might you become more focused on the development of a healthy, self-nurturing lifestyle?

- Left your briefcase at work on Friday and experienced no guilt?
- Slept like a baby and woke up refreshed the next morning looking forward to school?
- Told someone you loved them and showed them too?
- Felt loved by others?
- Enjoyed a wonderful meal in the company of good friends or family?
- Laughed until the tears rolled down your cheeks?
- Volunteered to do something freely and not resented it later?
- Felt truly lucky to be alive?
- Spent a weekend at home and not once thought about work?
- Genuinely struggled to improve a sticky relationship?
- Done something just for the sheer joy of it?
- Talked to someone about things which are really important to you – hopes or fears?
- Cried out of sorrow? Confided in someone and felt deeply understood?
- Danced, exercised, played a game, ran until you could feel your own heart beat?
- Been overcome by the beauty of the moment?
- Enjoyed the beauty of nature?
- Done something creative: painted a picture, written a poem, worked in the garden, built something with your own hands, played an instrument or sang a song?

Teachers who have responsibility for the care and development of others – and by definition this is all teachers – have a responsibility to learn how to take care of themselves. There is a clear relationship between teacher effectiveness and the individual's capacity to be self-nurturing. A commitment to self-care does not mean selfishly putting your own interests above the interests of others, nor is it self-indulgent. On the contrary, it is a necessity for those of us who wish to develop our leadership skills and wish to be emotionally, physically and spiritually fit for the purpose. Don't put off taking care of yourself until retirement. It could well be too late by then.

Self-concept and self-esteem: laying the foundation stones

The foundation to living healthy lives, emotionally, physically and spiritually, lies in the self-concept. Fully functioning adults possess a high self-esteem that demonstrates a degree of resilience even under pressure because they believe in their own coping capacity and have a hopeful, optimistic way of being that is more likely to predict success for the future than failure. Interestingly Maslow (1970) noted that such people were not what might be seen as conventionally 'nice' or 'polite'. Their behaviour was what Rogers (1962) describes as authentic or genuine. They felt free to express the uniqueness of their personality with all the quirkiness that this might reveal because they were still able to believe that others had a similar right to express themselves to the full.

Teachers with high self-esteem know how to value both themselves and others. This is quite simply because they were lucky enough to have been taught from childhood that they were deserving of love. *Unconditional* parental love. This basic sense of self-worth is internalized, deeply embedded, so is not easily susceptible to any gross distortion by life events, however calamitous. As teachers, we know only too well how few of our pupils have been on the receiving end of such life-enhancing care taking. We can also spot the effects of it in pupils' attitudes to themselves and their environment. But are we prepared to examine our own lives to look at the powerful messages we were sent about ourselves as children?

Activity 5.6: How good is your self-esteem?

How many of the following statements are true for you?
1) I have feelings and I can express them.
2) I generally maintain good relationships with my family and friends.
3) I like giving compliments and I like getting them.
4) I try to be honest with myself and other people.
5) I am clear about the values which inform my attitudes and behaviour.
6) I trust people to do a good job and people trust me to do a good job.
7) When things go wrong I can cope.
8) Making a mistake is not the end of the world.
9) I want to get feedback from other people because it helps me to learn.
10) I love and I am loved.
11) It is important to me to find out what other people want so that we can negotiate the best outcomes for everyone.
12) I am open to change and I enjoy a new challenge.
13) The future is exciting.
14) I stand up for my rights and the rights of others.
15) I am not easily intimidated.
16) Sometimes I get depressed or anxious, but it passes.
17) I don't mind not being perfect.
18) I treat people with respect.
19) I take responsibility for my own life.
20) I take the trouble to look my best.

If there were any of these statements which you found *particularly* difficult to claim for yourself, then it might prove useful talking to a trusted friend about where in your life you believe the difficulty originated and, if it seems important to you, how you can begin to find ways of improving your competence in that area.

However, when we are in the company of people with a high self-esteem, we can notice a quite miraculous effect. Being in relationship to such individuals can mean that this sense of self-worth or self-esteem is infectious. We can catch it too. You will recognize immediately from your own experience those people, partners, relatives, friends, fellow teachers or ministers whose own sense of self-esteem has fostered similar constructive feelings of self-worth in yourself. Gandhi, Nelson Mandela, Martin Luther King, Mother Teresa, Alexander Solzhenitsyn, all have shown how this unshakeable sense of self-worth can be transformational in its effect on the lives of those around them. Despite the most savage cruelties that could be inflicted, these individuals were able to maintain a sense of self-worth and personal dignity which became, in different ways, symbols of hope to people across the world. On a more personal level, it is worth while spending some time making the connection for yourself between people with high self-esteem and your own personal development. Recalling such powerfully positive influences in your own life can also be a spur into thinking about the type of role model you provide right now for those around you, colleagues, pupils, family and friends. Are you the kind of headteacher or deputy that colleagues will look to for providing inspiration for their own development? The kind of teacher that pupils will remember with gratitude in years to come? A parent or partner who provides an anchor of integrity and loving care?

We would make a guess that some readers had difficulty in remembering or choosing someone from their own lives who was supportive, nurturing, encouraging or indeed loving – and remember that generally, the

---

Activity 5.7: Positive influences from childhood

- Wherever you are right now, try to relax a little more. Perhaps take a couple of deep breaths and let any feelings of tension that you may experience in your body out with a sigh. You might want to use the image of breathing relaxation in and breathing tension out to help you. As your breathing gently lengthens, you will begin to feel the sense of relaxation deepening.
- In this more relaxed state, take your awareness back in time and try to recall those people in your life who you know have made a strong impact on you and perhaps even helped you to achieve what you have become today.
- As the memories start to unfold, try to recall what it was about their behaviour, attitudes, values, beliefs which had such a beneficial impact upon you. Recall your feelings towards them.
- In your imagination you might even want to find a way of thanking them for the contribution they made to your personal development. What words would you use to verbalize your gratitude? How would you demonstrate it non-verbally? If they are still around in your life right now, you might even take the opportunity to thank them next time you meet them.

readership of a book like this will be drawn from the 'successful' groups
of teachers. We can all work much harder at making such positive impacts
on each other's lives.

---

*Headteachers and teachers with high self-esteem are effective both in the
classroom and staffroom. In order to improve our self-esteem we need to
understand the influences upon us in our formative childhood years for
good or ill. Recalling the positive influences can remind us of the strongly
affirming quality of being in relationship to life-enhancing role models and
spur us into examining our present behaviour in the light of such insight.*

Messages from childhood

The history of our physical, emotional and social development as
individuals is crucial to understanding our attitudes, values and behaviour
as managers in the present. Whether we are aware of it or not, the way we
function daily in the school environment is a mirror of all our past life
experiences, both good and bad. The clearer we are able to see the
relationship between the past and understand how those life events have
helped to shape what we are right now, the clearer the insight we have
into our current behaviour and the behaviour of our colleagues. A primary
school colleague of ours on a human relations course designed to examine
self-esteem made a startling discovery. All her life she had a poor body
image. She believed her body to be overweight and unattractive. She was
aware of this but until that workshop unaware of the effect this poor body
image had on her teaching. She realized, with some consternation, that her
dislike of PE, dance and so on was basically because she was called upon
to wear a tracksuit and she felt even fatter when wearing it. She had
avoided these activities with her class as often as she could – not because
she didn't believe them to be worthwhile activities, but because they
reinforced her own feelings of self-doubt and negativity. Once she put the
two together, she was able to goal set a whole series of healthy ways of
dealing with this situation proactively which did not compromise pupils'
learning.

How we learn about our identity, then, is the product of a process which
goes on being defined and refined until the day we die. It is impossible to
have a totally stable self-concept, as this would imply stasis for a
phenomenon which is essentially a flow of information. Put more simply,
from the moment we are born we actively seek out information from the
world around us. The survival of the infant depends on giving clear
messages to carers and interpreting messages sent in return. An urgent cry
for food, coos of delight at physical closeness, the frustrated bellows of a
child taken from the breast are all ways in which the newborn shapes the
environment to get particular needs met. The responses to those signals
will, in very subtle ways, be giving the child indications of how accurately

he or she has conveyed the message and perhaps more important, how the parent feels emotionally towards the child's demand and thus from the child's viewpoint how the parent feels about him or her. Parents become increasingly aware that their infants can be extremely accurate barometers of any emotional pressures in the home. The infant in turn will be making evaluative interpretations of these responses which help to shape his or her self-image.

Robert Carkhuff (1983) offers us a broad interpretation of family types as being either facilitative or retarding. Facilitative parenting, he claims, offers a child a positive, accepting view of his or her own self, while the emotional insecurities experienced by the retarding parents prevent them from conveying a real sense of self-worth to their offspring. Carkhuff (1983) writes: 'The members of the facilitative family are in the process of becoming persons. The members of the retarding family are becoming nonpersons.'

As adults, these same individuals will have a tendency to replicate this broad pattern as managers. We would hazard a guess that most readers could offer examples from their own careers of working for either a retarding or facilitating headteacher and the effects that each approach had on the emotional climate of the staffroom, as well as your own sense of yourself as a valued person. The formation of the self-concept, then, is rather like the painting of a portrait – beginning with the broad brush strokes in terms of the influences from childhood and the fine detail being etched in by life experience. Many of these influences still affect us in our adult working lives, though the specific effects are not always predictable. For example, someone with a strongly dominating parent may not have the confidence as an adult to confront authority assertively. Another person whose parent displayed similar behaviours, might have learnt that domination is an appropriate pattern of behaviour and relates to colleagues through controlling them. Both are demonstrating symptoms of a poor self-concept, but the resulting behaviour is quite different. The way that you can begin to change some of these old behavioural patterns, which may be causing relationship difficulties in your life now, is to spot the behavioural signs of poor self-esteem and reflect on what might be a more mature emotional and behavioural response.

'I am: yet what I am none cares or knows' (John Clare).

Activity 5.8: The vocabulary of low self-esteem

In the following activity, we list some examples of behaviours and speech habits which are commonly displayed at work and which provide indications of low self-esteem. They probably had their emotional origins in childhood. Consider to what extent you exhibit any of these behaviours:

You habitually put yourself down
'I am hopeless at maths. I've never been any good.'
'It was nothing, really.'

You feel you lack social or interpersonal skills, or suffer from shyness or hypersensitivity to criticism
'I always come out of the meetings wishing I had said something.'
'I can't stand it when the head gets at me. He's constantly sniping.'

You habitually put others down or make jokes at their expense
'We all know how she got that job and it wasn't her IQ!'
'Manage? He couldn't manage a booze up in a brewery.'

You display false modesty or are unable to accept praise or compliments
'You like it? It was just something I bought in the sales.'
'I couldn't have done it without the rest of the team.'

You often assume disapproval of your actions or feel that you lack popularity
'None of the senior management listen to my ideas.'
'You have to be Mr Popularity round here to get promoted.'

You feel unmotivated and have a tendency to give up easily
'It's not worth the effort.'
'It's defeated me, I know when I'm beaten.'

You constantly expect the worst or present doom-laden scenarios
'It will never work. We tried it before and it didn't work then.'
'If they make anyone redundant, it's bound to be me.'

You have a tendency to deny responsibility for outcomes
'It's not my fault. It's not my job.'
'I can't be blamed for the recession.'

You search for evidence of failure or weakness in others
'Her problem is she never makes decisions.'
'He's too emotional to be in that job.'

Your non-verbal communication displays few smiles, little laughter, poor posture, sighing, lack of vitality and dull-eyedness. The messages conveyed by the tone of voice will include sarcasm, complaint, disinterest, passivity, blame and whining, as well as a general lack of confidence or interest in self-presentation.

Low self-esteem is learnt in childhood. We learn that the love from significant carers around us is conditional on obeying a set of behavioural rules which may be spoken or unspoken. We learn to adapt to such conditionality by hiding our real feelings and pretending to be someone we are not. Our adoption of these inauthentic behaviours leads to a view that our real selves are unworthy or undeserving of love. This results in low self-esteem in those aspects of our hidden selves. As adults even though it is difficult to change such long-held assumptions about ourselves, if we want to release our emotional energy to become more fully functioning in our relationships, we need to be vigilant in seeking out the signs and symptoms of low self-esteem.

Taking control of stress

It is claimed that everyday in the UK some 270,000 people take time off work for stress-related illness. Insurers report a 90% increase in claims made on the basis of psychological ill-health, citing symptoms such as severe anxiety and depression. Teachers and doctors appear amongst the hardest-hit groups presently making claims. A social worker, who was recently awarded £175,00 from his local county council employers on the basis that they failed to protect him from debilitating levels of job-related stress, may have prepared the ground for other professional groups to follow along this litigous route, if employees feel that their employers have not protected them from debilitating levels of work-related stress.

The toll that stress takes on staff relationships in schools is all too evident. There is limited research evidence to show that relationships with staff are construed as more stressful than relationships with students (Hall, Woodhouse and Wooster, 1984). Relationships in both the staffroom and classroom break down because of the pressures that teachers live with, day in, day out. Such pressures are a complex mix of internal psychological characteristics, unique to the individual and the demands placed upon him or her by events in the external environment. While we cannot always control our external world, it is possible to develop greater control over ourselves and our reactions.

Frayed tempers and taut nerves may finally snap when deadlines inexorably approach. As one deadline recedes another arises to take its place. Deadlines are called deadlines with good reason. As the pace of life speeds up, school can begin to feel like being at sea in the middle of a raging storm, when there is no sight of land to give relief from anxiety and stomach-churning nausea. Headteachers report the emotional devastation that an upcoming OFSTED inspection can wreak in a school staff and the emotional ripples that are felt long after the inspection team have packed up their laptops and left. Farber and Miller (1981) show that emotionally exhausted, burntout teachers are less sympathetic to their students and job performance is adversely affected overall. When there seems little respite from acute stress, the body has insufficient time to replenish its coping resources and very quickly we can move into a situation where the level of stress experienced becomes chronic. In the postwar years, a common phenomenon was the convalescent home. Patients recovering from chronic illness, were provided with recuperation time on the National Health at seaside rest homes. As a nation the days when we can afford such luxury appear to be long gone. However, the idea that we need recovery time from debilitating or stressful experience is a sound one. Each of us needs to discover ways in which we can provide opportunities to 'convalesce', and build them into our weekly schedule. If we fail to take responsibility for a degree of self-care then burn-out could all too easily result. Self-awareness is central to developing healthy coping strategies to reduce stress. Our bodies are barometers of our physical and emotional well-being; learning to listen to them *in an ongoing way* can be a lifesaver. The workaholic is one school-based example of failing to pay attention to the demands of the body.

Patterns of overwork, although perhaps resented at first, eventually in themselves can become addictive (Wilson, Schaef and Fassel, 1988). As the work pattern becomes established messages of fatigue from the body become fainter and fainter as the workaholic adapts him or herself to the lifestyle. Life begins to feel like being inside a windowless room. No other messages are allowed in. Inside the room are all the cares and worries we carry in our heads about school: targets, budgets, plans, meetings, repairs, appraisal and endless forms to fill in. No other messages are let in. This room labelled 'work' is cut off from the oxygen of the world outside and there appears to be no way to let in life and light and air. The world is reduced to four walls. We all have our own stories to tell of colleagues so preoccupied with work that it becomes a substitute for family or social life. This addictive behaviour has deleterious knock-on effects not only for the individual but also for his or her family and working practices within the school. Headteachers and senior staff who provide such inappropriate role models can unthinkingly produce feelings of guilt, resentment and anxiety in colleagues further down the hierarchy, who believe that they will be judged against this covert yardstick.

Activity 5.9: Self-reflection

Spend some time reflecting on your patterns of work. Do you make unrealistic demands on yourself and colleagues? Do you have a sense of perspective on your job? Do you recognize the difference between a healthy level of work involvement and workaholism? Have you discussed these issues with colleagues?

In order to exert a greater control over the extent of our experiences which we define as stressful, we need to develop a degree of flexibility or elasticity in our approach to life events and relationships. People who possess a high degree of self-esteem will already have a degree of psychological flexibility and an ability to change or alter perceptions as new information is received. Those with poorer levels of self-esteem will have a tendency to be more rigid in their views, with a marked disinclination to change or even see the necessity for it. The classic example is the introduction of IT into classrooms some years ago. Many teachers saw this as a challenge. Initially not one they welcomed, but nevertheless understood computers to be an important development in learning technology. The hardware held no terrors and they soon learnt to control the machinery, rather than let their fears of the machinery control them. Their less lucky colleagues found all sorts of rational reasons to resist the advance of technological change and found themselves left far behind, feeling incompetent and inadequate, thus perpetuating a stressful cycle of low self-esteem.

Hall, Woodhouse and Wooster (1984) reported that teachers who underwent a one-week programme of experiential human relations training, designed to increase responsiveness and interpersonal flexibility in relationships, found that they also experienced a reduction in reported levels of personal and professional stress. Similar findings were reported by Hall, Hall and Abaci (1997). The message is a clear one: you can reduce the number of events in your life you perceive as stressful by working towards being more elastic, less rigid in your ways of thinking and feeling. Proactivity is the key here. Thoughts that endlessly go round in your head need to be interrupted to prevent their stressful effects. Learning to let go of perfectionism and self-blame is a key step in beginning this process. This may seem scary at first and the determination to change needs to be reinforced by a programme of learning. This may take the form of joining a yoga class, a stress management course, reading about the signs and symptoms of stress, counselling, learning to meditate and so on.

Self-management, then, is fundamental to taking control of personal levels of debilitating stress but for managers in schools it is doubly important because they are the ones who set the tone for others throughout the hierarchy. Leadership entails providing a model for others in terms of handling your own life stressors well and also knowing how to spot the signs and symptoms of stress in others. Irritable, critical staff who don't want to co-operate with change may be sending out strong signals about the stress and fear associated with feelings of being inadequate to cope. If interpreted correctly, headteachers and others in leadership roles can do much to reassure staff, individually and collectively, that handling job-related stress is a communal responsibility and should be discussed openly and candidly. Discussions about how to handle stress in teaching should be part of the agenda for staff meetings. We have known schools where staff pool their resources to set up stress-busting courses of one sort or another, taking communal responsibility for good health. Working in teams is another obvious way to pool talents and resources across groups and this has been discussed in greater detail elsewhere (see Katzenbach and Smith, 1993).

Although we can work to gain greater mastery over ourselves to increase the degree of psychological flexibility we possess and pool our communal efforts to prompt a greater openness and awareness about the effects of stress on our institutional lives, there are still life events over which we have little or no control. In the face of such vicissitudes, perceptual flexibility is even more imperative. As the unique rhythm of our lives unfolds, we oscillate between periods of intense resistance to change, to wholesale leaps forward in personal understanding and growth. To some extent this dynamic process depends on a whole variety of factors, some of them outside our control: birth, marriage, separation, bereavement, ageing, illness. Such events are common to all human experience, although for some individuals these events will be more or less disorganizing (Mahoney, 1991). For one person, retirement from work might be seen as a traumatic loss of identity and status; for another a terrific opportunity to start afresh and move on to new challenges.

Remember from childhood the story of King Canute trying vainly to exercise his kingly power to hold back the tide? So inevitably we discover too the futility of struggling against life's natural currents. This oscillation and unpredictability, however, can and does produce higher levels of personal stress for some individuals than others. In general, the greater the degree of personal rigidity or inability to accept the experience, the greater the level of perceived stress. For example, the 60-year-old teacher who is asked to give up coaching the school's football team in favour of a younger, fitter colleague, may experience stress as a result of an emotional inability to accept the restrictions of age, despite rationally understanding the wisdom of the decision. All of us will have these areas in our life where we feel particularly vulnerable. First, developing the awareness to spot your own is the key to learning how to manage other people's areas of vulnerability. Developing empathy in this way is an important aspect of developing interpersonal skills and will be discussed in more detail in the final chapter.

Activity 5.10: Life events

Think back over the last five or six years of your life. How many of these major life events have you undergone? You may want to add one or two of your own. Spend some time reflecting upon the cumulative impact these events have had on you emotionally and physically and how you coped with them at the time. Reflect on the subsequent impact that these events had on your pattern of relationships with other people:

- serious family illness or accident
- job relocation
- bereavement in family or friends
- divorce or separation (self or close relatives)
- personal illness or accidental injury
- children being born or children leaving home
- victim of crime or legal disputes
- financial problems
- failure to achieve promotion
- redundancy or organizational restructuring
- OFSTED inspection
- school merger or school closedown
- hit 40, 50 or 60
- loss of religious belief or spiritual conversion.

Even for the best psychologically adjusted amongst us, there are times when the strain begins to tell. The dependency of staff on colleagues with leadership roles can be particularly debilitating if allowed to flourish. Staff can push leaders into parental-type behaviour at times, even against their better judgement and at times it might well feel like there is no hiding place. Inevitably the feelings get taken home. It is common for headteachers to disclose the enormous guilt they feel about taking relationship problems home with them. They describe subjecting their partners to endless hours of listening about difficulties with colleagues, while sons and daughters suffer because their mother or father has little emotional energy left over to attend to their needs. Home, traditionally the sanctuary or bulwark against the vicissitudes of everyday life, can start to feel as dangerous an emotional territory as the staffroom or classroom. Going home can feel more like work than work, when fences need to be mended instead of batteries being recharged.

Activity 5.11: Reaching out

All of us have those moments in life when we feel intensely alone and vulnerable. For those in leadership roles this may be particularly acute with the intense demands that relationships put on our ongoing ability to cope. Emotional resources get taxed to the limit and this may be the time that you feel like giving up. The pressure may feel so intense that your head literally feels ready to burst and you feel totally inadequate to meet the demands of the role. At times like these, do you have:

• Someone who will be there for you, to listen patiently and tenderly?
• Someone who you can express your innermost feelings to?
• Someone who will put their arm around you when you need it and show human kinship and understanding?

Consider:
• Am I able to offer any of the above to people in my personal or professional life?

Personal and professional support systems are an important way of both dealing with stress and promoting personal development. Where are the legitimate areas for support to be found? In the two activities outlined above, it is clear that, within limits, family and friends can be lifelines of emotional support. However, there is a danger that such support could be abused if it is the only outlet for work-based distress. Headteachers can do much to provide leadership in developing professional support systems in schools which give colleagues an opportunity to talk openly and confidentially about issues causing distress.

In the 1920s miners fought for what was called 'pit-head time'. This was the right to have paid time to wash off the dirt of the job, so they

---

Activity 5.12: Personal support systems

If you find yourself taking your relationship problems home with you too often for your partner's or family's liking, try the following strategy which enables your partner or listener to play a supportive role rather than merely be a convenient sounding board:

- First, tell your partner how much you appreciate his or her continuing support, listening, and comments on what is happening in your professional life.
- Then ask permission to take up a *limited* amount of time going through the key dilemmas which face you at present (this should be a minimum of 15 minutes, maximum of 50 minutes).
- Suggest that your partner may also wish to have some personal time for him or her to go through issues of similar personal importance when you might act in a similarly supportive capacity.
- The role of supporter primarily involves actively listening and encouraging the talker to articulate feelings as well as thoughts. It also challenges some of the basic assumptions about the situation but does not necessarily involve giving glib advice. The session should end with some tentative formulation of strategies, which look to improve the difficult relationship.
- Stick to the time limits agreed and find a way of showing your partner how much you have appreciated the time and energy he or she has spent on you – using a range of verbal and non-verbal strategies!
- Finally, suggest you both do something entirely different together, and, just as important, let the issue go and promise not to raise it again.

---

could go home to their families fresh. Such 'pit-head time' in schools might amount to small (usually around four members) peer support groups. These have the advantage of being voluntary self-help groups, free to make their own contracts regarding membership, degrees of openness, frequency of meetings, confidentiality and so on. Agendas can be negotiated by the group and time boundaries made clear. They can provide a useful sounding board for members to articulate their feelings with supportive colleagues. Venting emotion can relieve distress and feedback can give a much needed difference of perspective. Farber (1983) points to a growing body of evidence which indicates the potential of such groups as vehicles for combating teacher burn-out and stress. The impetus for such groups might come from the headteacher or staff but the decision about membership should be entirely voluntary. Many headteachers around the country have set up such professional support networks. However, it would be interesting to evaluate how personal they allow the agendas and the talk to become. Another institutionally based system is the mentoring or 'buddy system'. Such a system is particularly useful in the induction of new staff and will be discussed more fully in Chapter 7.

> *Stress is part of the human condition which can no more be avoided than breathing. Levels of perceived stress, however, to some extent can be under the control of the individual. We can immunize ourselves against some of the debilitating effects by working to increase our psychological flexibility and emotional responsiveness. Learning to articulate distress to supportive family, friends and colleagues is also a very useful strategy for alleviating some of the worst effects of individual stress. Formal and informal systems within schools can also be established to legitimate the right of all staff to express their work-based stressors.*

Interpersonal communication

Communication and management are inextricably linked. Of Mintzberg's (1973) ten managerial roles, five are explicitly tied to communication tasks. These are the roles of liaiser, monitor, disseminator, spokesperson and negotiator. These are clearly aspects of the managerial function which call for a high level of interpersonal communication skills. The others also depend on skilful communication in order to have an organizational impact. We might reasonably expect, then, to find senior managers in schools who are superior communicators, perhaps above all else. However, when groups of teachers meet informally on courses or at meetings, they invariably end up comparing 'the boss'. Comparisons are made, commiserations offered, incredulity expressed. The foibles of heads, it appears, are legendary. They are capricious and have favourites. They won't delegate or they don't take responsibility. They are paid to be the experts but they don't have any answers. They have information but won't share it. It's not unusual to hear headteachers described as power mad, manipulative, bullies or sometimes just plain crazy. The most commonly expressed view is that whatever they might say, generally *they are not to be trusted.* Teachers rarely comment on the skill of the headteacher's interpersonal communication and if they do, it is with some surprise. Over the years, when we have asked teachers what qualitites they believe headteachers should possess, the replies are fairly unanimous. They cite genuineness, the ability to listen, fairness, honesty, directness, a sense of humour and the capacity to show human warmth and caring. In short the capacities of a fully functioning human being (Rogers, 1963).

Experts may argue whether or not it is possible to measure interpersonal skills but most of us recognize highly skilled communicators when we meet them. Being on the receiving end of clean, honest communication with such people can be a very liberating process, because it enables us to trust what they say, even if we don't like it. In order to evaluate your personal level of interpersonal intelligence and skill as a communicator, try completing the interpersonal skills inventory given in Figure 5.1 (Sirin *et al.*, 1995). This will provide you with a personal checklist against which to rate yourself and, even more importantly, highlight specific skills which you feel you need to develop. You might want to take the exercise further and ask trusted friends, colleagues or staff teams to rate you along the scale. This feedback exercise has the virtue of checking out your self-perceptions against the perceptions of others. This type of upward feedback is growing in popularity amongst managerial teams in business settings, where traditionally the feedback goes down the hierarchy, not up it.

Some of you reading this chapter will have undertaken counselling courses or guidance training and recognize the similarity of these skills to what are commonly known as 'counselling skills' (Hall and Hall, 1988). To a large extent these skills have developed out of the work of Rogers (1962) and Egan (1994). In particular, Carl Rogers' enormous contribution to the study of psychology in the twentieth century was his work on the attitudinal preconditions of healthy, growthful patterns of interpersonal communication. His formulation of the 'core conditions' gives us a powerful insight into what it takes to be a first-class communicator. First, *genuineness*, the 'what you see is what you get' person. No pretences, no masks, no hidden agendas which confuse and distort communication between people. This superior communicator has the ability to understand and express feelings constructively. This means having their own feelings sufficiently under control to allow the other person a space to express him or herself fully too. Secondly, *empathy*, the ability to stand in someone else's shoes and take in the world as that person experiences it. Acceptance or non-judgemental *positive regard* values the other person's rights in the relationship and to be prized unconditionally. Harris (1973) memorably describes individuals who have the emotional intelligence to communicate from the basis of these core conditions as taking the 'I'm OK, you're OK' position. The 'I'm OK, you're OK' type values other people's rights in relationships, with no strings attached. This is an ethical as well as an emotional position and fundamentally informs the personal core value system. For senior managers in schools committed to creating a culture based upon people-centred values, then Harris' dictum needs to become a fully integrated part of their attitudes and behaviour to staff and pupils and lived out moment by moment. Another way of describing such behaviour is by calling it assertiveness. (Day *et al.*, 1993) define this as:

> . . . not merely a communication style but a way of life. Assertiveness is the lifelong dedication to pursuing the goal of open, truthful, clear communication in interpersonal relationships. The ability to be in touch with and express feelings and thoughts as they are experienced and the courage to acknowledge that other people in our relationships have the right to be themselves with all the human frailty that implies. These qualities depend upon a high level of skilled behaviours, which need to be continually reexamined in the light of experience for their

How good are your interpersonal skills? Consider how you would rate yourself in each of these categories when relating to colleagues, pupils or parents. What aspects of interpersonal functioning do you need to work on?

For each of the following activities, decide whether you consider your performance is:

E: Excellent
AA: Above Average
A: Average
BA: Below Average
W: Weak

Tick the appropriate response.

Inventory items	E	AA	A	BA	W
1) Initiating a discussion					
2) Helping the other person feel relaxed					
3) Being relaxed myself					
4) Adopting a helpful posture					
5) Maintaining appropriate distance					
6) Using touch as appropriate					
7) Maintaining good eye contact					
8) Keeping quiet when appropriate					
9) Smiling appropriately					
10) Using encouraging words: yes, um hum, go on					
11) Repeating words from the last statement					
12) Not interrupting					
13) Physical attending: nodding, use of gesture					
14) Avoiding 'why' questions					
15) Remembering what the other person has said					
16) Asking open questions					
17) Reflecting back recent statements					
18) Paraphrasing of what other person has said					
19) Avoiding talking about yourself and your own issues					
20) Being aware of your own feelings					
21) Expressing your own feelings					
22) Recognizing feelings in the other person					
23) Feeding back the feeling you recognize in the other person					
24) Pointing out differences of statement/expression of feelings					
25) Being honest					
26) Encouraging self-disclosure from the other person					
27) Accepting sensitive self-disclosure					
28) Using your self-disclosure skilfully					
29) Keeping the other person's self-disclosure confidential					

Inventory items	E	AA	A	BA	W
30) Pointing out inconsistencies in verbal and non-verbal communication					
31) Challenging the other person					
32) Challenging in a way that encourages a response					

Figure 5.1   My use of interpersonal skills inventory

effectiveness and authenticity. This requires awareness, a degree of risk-taking, discipline and a positive self-esteem – in short emotional and intellectual maturity.

Assertiveness is commonly described as a set of highly developed communication skills (Rakos, 1991). This is compared with less mature, more defended patterns of interpersonal responses such as aggression, passivity or manipulation. Key assertiveness skills are the ability to both give and receive feedback constructively. Teachers are very well aware of giving feedback as an integral part of the learning process for pupils in the classroom, but may be less aware of its significance in the promotion of healthy communication in the staffroom. Without feedback from others our ability to make sense of our lives and our relationships is seriously compromised. Pupils will go to almost any lengths to get feedback from teachers, positive or negative. It seems that any feedback is better than none at all. Many teachers have a push–pull relationship with the idea of feedback themselves. They both want it but fear it at the same time. Teacher appraisal was given a very mixed reception when it was introduced some years ago, largely because teachers felt that in some way it would be used against them, to undermine their self-esteem. However, senior managers who learn the art of giving feedback appropriately can positively enhance teacher self-esteem and improve relationships, even if the feedback is not always 100% positive. It is therefore an important communication skill to gain mastery over. Used badly or in an insensitive, ill-timed way, it can, of course, do the reverse.

How, then, to give feedback well? First, always start with the positive. Each of us needs encouragement, however high or low in the hierarchy, and a few words of thanks or encouragement from a senior teacher go a long way to help teachers feel valued in their work. This is also true for headteachers and deputies and yet interestingly teachers seem surprised when it is suggested to them that they might want to give positive feedback up the hierarchy from time to time. Our culture tends to linger on the negative and some people find it quite difficult to articulate praise or give compliments. In our haste to be critical, it is easy to take for granted behaviours we value in others. Building a reputation as someone who gives positive feedback regularly also makes it more likely that staff will listen to more difficult feedback and engage with it constructively. It is worth pointing out that the ratio of positive to negative comments should be 80% positive to 20% negative, if we really want staff to take on board the tough comments and learn from them. This is also true in the classroom. We would make a guess that in most staffrooms the ratio of positive to negative comments is reversed. The tendency is to tell people what we don't like rather than what we do like.

Skilful feedback refers to specific situations and avoids overly general, cloudy statements. The speaker should also own the comment and make it clear that it is *his or her* perception of events. For example, 'I liked the way you chaired that parents' meeting yesterday evening. You really summarized the action points clearly. We all knew what we had to do at the end. Thanks, I really appreciated your clarity'.

If you feel you need to offer tough feedback which you guess may be difficult for the other person to hear, then be sure you refer to behaviour which the listener has some control over and therefore can change. For example a statement such as 'I think you frighten the infants because you are so tall' doesn't really leave the person much room for manoeuvre.

'I might be wrong, but some of the infants seem to look uncomfortable craning their necks to listen to you. Do you think it might be helpful for them if you sat or knelt down more often when you talked to them?' In this example, the speaker personalizes the statement, using 'I', owns that it is an individual perception and could therefore be incorrect, offers an alternative desired pattern of behaviour, 'do you think it would be more helpful if . . .' and refers to specific situations. This type of feedback leaves people feeling they have a choice in the situation and so avoids the trap of defensive resistance common when people feel cornered by feedback. For example, 'Every one knows that you were rude to that parent. I just won't tolerate it in my school' invariably leads to a spoken or unspoken rejection.

Senior managers, of course, also need to encourage others to give them feedback so they too can learn how they are perceived by staff. When there is a clear power differential this can be rather daunting even intimidating for staff, so the ways in which it is to be offered need to be made safe so that there is no possibility of personal or professional recrimination. First, this can be done by modelling receiving feedback without jumping to a defensive reaction and arguing the feedback away. It may be uncomfortable to hear, but it is better to encourage a candid exchange than to have subtle, destructive patterns of communication become entrenched. Check perceptions out from a number of sources, don't just rely on one safe source, even if you respect their viewpoint or judgement. If you want information about your performance ask for it.

'I would really like to hear how I came across in the staff meeting the other day.' Decide what you want to do as a result of any feedback you receive. 'It takes two to know' goes the old saying. Feedback can extend our self-awareness which is incomplete if we only have our own self-perceptions. When we receive feedback we can assess its value, reflect on the consequences of ignoring it and finally decide how best to use it for our development.

Interpersonal skills are an essential component of managerial competence. These skills which are similar to counselling or helping skills, can be learnt, practised and honed like any other. Effective senior managers are highly skilled communicators who live out Harris' maxim, 'I'm OK, You're OK'. They are able to be assertive in their relationships and understand the importance of giving and receiving feedback appropriately.

Physical well-being

You may not be surprised to learn that there is also a link between physical health and interpersonal functioning. Rogers and Freiberg (1994) provide a useful summary of Aspey and Roebuck's research in this area and cite their conclusions that:

> Fatigue, poor nutrition and lack of physical exercise are deterrents to positive interpersonal relationships. The data from subsequent work suggest strongly that physical fitness is necessary for sustaining constructive interpersonal relationships across long periods of time. It seems that all teachers who understand constructive human relationships can be humane for short periods of time, but their levels of physical fitness determine the durability of their interpersonal facilitation.

More of their research, involving school principals, revealed some interesting findings. Given a fitness range of very physically fit to physically unfit principals, they were however rated similarly for interpersonal functioning. During the period of a week, on Monday morning all principals were achieving similar ratings for interpersonal responsiveness. However, by Friday, the physically fit principals had increased their Monday scores, while the unfit group had worsened their Monday scores. What we can learn from this work is that effective interpersonal relationships take physical stamina to sustain as well as emotional stamina. Unless teachers take responsibility for their own physical well-being then they place in jeopardy relationships with colleagues and pupils. We are all aware of the Friday afternoon syndrome, tired out, low energy, desperate for the bell, and this is when a crisis happens. Physically fit headteachers will be prepared to deal with it in a way which their unfit colleagues may not.

Activity 5.13: How committed are you to your physical well-being?

How many of the following statements are true for you? How could you improve your lifestyle? Are there any unhealthy practices that you would like to give up?

- I take a brisk twenty minute walk each day.
- I don't smoke and drink alcohol in moderation only.
- I eat plenty of fresh fruit and vegetables, preferably organically grown.
- I have a regular programme of exercise which I follow. This includes aerobic exercise, designed to increase heart rates. I do at least three sessions of aerobic exercise a week.
- I avoid crash diets or bingeing.
- My weight is about right for my age, height and gender.
- I avoid lifts and use the stairs when I can.
- I try to moderate my intake of salty, fatty or sugary foods. I avoid overly processed foods and reduce my intake of red meat.
- I drink plenty of water and moderate my intake of tea, coffee and fizzy drinks.
- I create spaces in my week for relaxation, meditation, reflection, yoga or contemplation.
- I know that it is up to me to take responsibility for my own health.
- I enjoy exercise, massage, reflexology, aroma therapy and so on because they give me a heightened sense of bodily awareness.

Learning to be a fully functioning person means learning to take care of you physical well-being as well as your psychological well-being. Caring for the physical body does not imply an unhealthy narcissism. Rather, it is an understanding of the relationship between the mind and body in terms of health and disease. It is also a mature expression of self-care and, as we have seen, can provide us with the stamina we need to maintain effective interpersonal functioning over periods of time.

People, people, people . . . in conclusion

How many of you recognize this scenario? It is 8.30 am on a cold Friday morning but the day is just beginning to hot up. Already this morning the cleaning staff have been up in arms and have threatened to walk out *en masse* unless the head sorts out that 'Hitler of a caretaker', so they can do their jobs properly. A delegation of angry parents has appeared at the office door complaining about the cars parked on the double yellow lines outside the school gates which will cause a fatal accident one of these days and why can't the head stop them. Oh and by the way, what about the neighbourhood dogs fouling the school field? When will they get some action on that? The photocopier has broken down and the secretary is in a state because she won't be able to get the papers ready for the governor's meeting after school. Standing next to the photocopier is a quietly sobbing child who has lost his new coat somewhere in the playground. The deputy races in to tell you that Mr Smith's class was due to present school assembly today but he has just called in sick. What does the head suggest? During assembly time, you had planned to have a long overdue chat with a colleague who was seriously thinking of taking early retirement and wanted to discuss her options. The icing on the cake is the arrival of the letter informing the school of the date for the OFSTED inspection. Looking at your watch you notice it's only 9.00 am. Sound familiar?

> Attentiveness rather than
> efficiency
> Gentle flow rather than speed.

> (Kazuaki Tanahashi)

The turbulence of each working day in school demands leaders who are capable of providing a still, calm centre to the whirlwind of competing, insistent demands. To be a leader who wears his or her authority lightly and with a reassuring nod, friendly laugh or moment spent in sharing a sorrow, enables others to be most fully themselves in all their glorious competence as fellow human beings. In relationships, such leaders tread with a light step and full heart. They are generous in their acceptance of others because they have the spirit to accept themselves. They stay close to the values which inspire and energize them, living them out daily and inspiring others to behave with similar high standards of personal integrity. They take each moment as it comes and always trust that whatever comes, it will be alright because they believe in their own capacity to stay responsive to the needs of the moment. They are voracious learners because they understand how much they still have to learn and every person, every situation becomes their teacher and guide. They can listen deeply and empathically because in such listening they become intimately connected to the lives of people around them and these deeply forged connections nurture and sustain them in the dark, lonely moments. At the still, calm centre of every outstanding school leader is the single most important human virtue, love.

You can be that leader. Are you right now?

Further reading

Claxton, G. (1997) *Hare Brain Tortoise Mind*, Fourth Estate, London.
Covey, S. R. (1992) *The Seven Habits of Highly Effective People: restoring the character ethic*, Simon and Schuster, New York.
Kabat-Zinn, J. (1990) *Full Catastrophe Living*, Piatkus, London.
Nelson-Jones, R. (1996) *Relating Skills*, Cassell, London.

6

Appraisal for development

Contexts of appraisal • Accountability • Continuing professional development and appraisal • Key elements • Classroom observation • The appraisal interview • Teacher autonomy • Classroom-based self-appraisal • Self-review procedures • Classroom monitoring techniques • Providing moral and intellectual support through 'critical friendship' • Managing the process • Supporting career-long development

Contexts of appraisal

In the 1970s the HMI survey of primary education (DES, 1978) asserted that it was important 'to make full use, on behalf of schools as a whole, of teachers' strengths to build on the existing knowledge of individual teachers. However the requirements of society come to be formulated, teachers have the main responsibility for responding to them'. Certainly the opportunity for individuals and institutions to engage in appraisal which enables teachers to build their knowledge and strengths must underpin all curriculum or professional development work undertaken at school or classroom level. How, otherwise, may we proceed or make decisions about future work if we cannot judge where we are now, and how worth while our past endeavours have been? So the need for appraisal as a means of achieving this would appear to be self-evident. Indeed, it may be argued that most teachers and schools are involved regularly in informal appraisal processes through events such as staff meetings, parents' meetings, pupil records, job specifications, in-service events and even conversations with colleagues. Nor should we forget the 'on-the-spot' appraisals carried out by teachers in their own classrooms which may cause them to change the direction of their teaching according to their perceptions of their own effectiveness, task balance (in relation to the demands of the National Curriculum), or the responses of their pupils.

Nevertheless, there is little doubt that the use of the term 'appraisal' continues to evoke negative responses from a significant number of teachers. The reason for this is that it is perceived as something that is usually

1) initiated and carried out by someone else in a position of authority within a school culture which may not encourage openness and trust;

2) for the purposes of making judgements in which weaknesses are highlighted;
3) not able to provide support for long-term remedial work where required or requested;
4) not embedded within a whole-school policy for continuing professional development; and
5) not for their own direct benefit.

So appraisal – even if we can understand the reason for it – is not always seen to be helpful. At the very least it means that we must disclose something more of our professional lives to others than we might like or feel necessary. After all, teachers are trained to be 'professionals'. Once they qualify they are regarded as competent and, by implication, able to plan, teach and evaluate their work. Despite the increased discussions between teachers that are necessary for ensuring differentiation, continuity and progression in the curriculum, classroom visits for the purpose of observing practice remain relatively rare occurrences.

So, although teachers are engaged daily in evaluating their pupils, by tradition it is rare for the teachers themselves to be evaluated by anyone other than themselves. It is likely, then, that teachers will operate on a model of restricted professionality. Once they have developed a personal solution to any problems of teaching they perceive – and this is usually achieved without any systematic assistance from others – it is unlikely that this solution will again be significantly questioned except during the external OFSTED inspection process. Argyris and Schon (1976) characterize the normal pattern of teacher development as 'single loop' learning, in which theory-making and theory-testing are private. In this world of 'restricted professionality', individuals protect themselves and colleagues by speaking in abstractions without reference to directly observed events. This has the effect of both controlling others and preventing others from influencing oneself by withholding access to valid information about oneself. These effects are manifested in the 'Stone Age obstructionists' (Doyle and Ponder, 1976) and other forms of resistance to change described earlier.

Formal appraisal, which involves others, clearly threatens this world of restricted professionality. Although writing in the context of programme evaluation, the American educator, Ernest House (1972), summed up neatly the ambivalent attitude most of us still hold:

> The first observation I want to make is that there is no real demand among teachers and administrators for evaluating their own programs. To evaluate kids, yes, we cannot live without that; but to evaluate ourselves and our own programs – no. At times, in that strange ideology with which we disguise our motives and cover our tracks, we educators convince ourselves that we would be overjoyed to receive data about our teaching and educational programs. After

all, what does a teacher have to gain from having his work examined? As he sees it, absolutely nothing. He is exposing himself to administrators and parents. He risks damage to his ego by finding out he is not doing his job as well as he thinks he is. Perhaps worst of all he risks discovering that his students do not really care for him, something a teacher would rather not know. The culture of the school offers no rewards for examining one's behaviour – only penalties. Since there are no punishments for not exposing one's behaviour and many dangers in so doing, the prudent teacher gives lip service to the idea and drags both feet. And this is not so strange, is it? Do we have any serious evaluations of lawyers, or doctors, or cab drivers? That there is no such demand is a corollary of a broader principle: No one wants to be evaluated by anybody at any time. Evaluate an evaluator's work and see how he reacts.

This perception continues to be exacerbated by the 'hostile' policy and media environment in which many teachers perceive themselves as living. With increasing government intervention in the curriculum, more parental involvement, diminishing resources, fewer opportunities for promotion, a plethora of DfEE documents, and restrictive conditions of service linked to salary structure, it is understandable, then, that some teachers feel sceptical of its value. Even today, more than a decade after appraisal was made a legal requirement of schools, OFSTED's report on the appraisal of teachers 1991–96 indicates the continuing difficulties with appraisal as a means of teacher and school development. Its main findings stated that the

Overall impact of appraisal on teaching and learning has not been substantial. In only 20% of schools visited by HMI had appraisal [that] led to observable improvements in teaching, and then on a minor scale for the most part.
. . . appraisal has remained too isolated from school development and INSET planning . . .
. . . only a minority [of teachers] are able to identify improvements in their teaching as a result of appraisal.
. . . Nearly half of the schools visited . . . reported delays in their implementation.
Reasons given included staff turnover, especially at senior level, and difficulties in finding time for appraisal interviews.

Surprisingly, this contradicts an independent 'benefits' study of eighteen schools in seven LEAs which identified:

• improved management
• better communication
• improved management skills among appraisers
• improved professional dialogue
• identification of staff potential

- better identification of professional development needs
- better targeting of INSET resources.

(Barber, Evans and Johnson, 1995)

The most authoritative study of appraisal surveyed 109 LEAs over a two-year period (Wragg *et al.*, 1996). Among its findings were that 49% of teachers reported that they had changed their classroom practice as a result of appraisal, and 69% that appraisal had offered personal benefits. However, the authors point out that these findings can be interpreted in different ways:

> ... A Department for Education official, when told of the findings, replied, 'That's good news. If appraisal had not taken place it would have been zero per cent who would have changed what they are doing, so 49 per cent is not bad.' It might equally be argued that appraisal should help everyone modify practice, so if 50 per cent say they did not, then this is a high failure rate. Optimists see a half full bottle, pessimists see a half empty one.
>
> (Wragg *et al.*, 1996)

Additionally,

> The difference between 49 per cent who say they altered their teaching and the 69 per cent who claim they derived personal benefits, is an intriguing one. How can people feel a process to be beneficial if it does not alter or improve what they do? ... If they set themselves goals that related to school, rather than classroom practices, then their actual teaching may not have been directly affected.
>
> ... Many [teachers] mentioned a 'boost' simply through being given attention . . . others enjoyed the therapy of an intimate conversation.
>
> (Wragg *et al.*, 1996)

Of the 27% who did not gain personal benefits from the exercise,

> ... some 27 per cent felt that they had not themselves gained a great deal from appraisal. Many of the sceptics had clearly not enjoyed good personal relationships, but some were simply cynical about the general value of the exercise, concerned about the introduction of performance related pay on the back of appraisal, or they felt they were too old to learn new tricks.
>
> (Wragg *et al.*, 1996)

The authors commented on the difficulties of personal change, the tensions between school and individual needs, the limitations of funding and available time, and issues of confidentiality:

> Appraisal should be properly resourced . . . appraisal needs proper time and money.
>   . . . One of the reasons why so few teachers changed what they did in the classroom may have been because there was not enough time, given the many demands on them, to be fully de-briefed, and appraisers were not freed to follow teachers up to see if agreed plans were actually being implemented.
>
> (Wragg *et al.*, 1996)

Accountability

As long ago as 1979 the East Sussex Accountability Project identified three kinds of accountability:

1) *Answerability* to one's clients, i.e. pupils and parents (moral accountability).
2) *Responsibility* to oneself and one's colleagues (professional responsibility).
3) *Accountability* in the strict sense to one's employers or political masters (contactual accountability).

Although the three overlap, we may say that in recent years the emphasis has moved from 'responsibility' to 'answerability' and 'accountability'. Headteachers and governors in schools have a professional, moral and continuing contractual responsibility to ensure not only that appraisal occurs but that it is also seen to occur, and that the results of appraisal are communicated in appropriate ways to appropriate audiences. As part of this, a climate of trust, support and openness must be established in which the learning and development needs of teachers as well as children must be considered. The assumption must be that the central purpose of appraisal is the professional development of teachers and, through this, the enhancement of the quality of learning opportunities for pupils in classrooms. We have discussed elsewhere in this book different school cultures which leaders can help to create and work with, the qualities and skills necessary for leadership, and the importance of consultation, collaboration and sense of ownership by staff if they are to be committed to the enterprise.

Continuing professional development and appraisal

Headteachers have a statutory obligation to supervise and participate in any arrangements within an agreed national framework for the appraisal of the performance of teachers, ensure that they have access to advice and training appropriate to their needs and provide information about the work and performance of the staff where this is relevant to their future employment. Yet legal obligations alone are unlikely to lead to quality processes or outcomes. Unless appraisal is a part of, rather than apart from, an agreed system of continuing professional development it is unlikely to achieve its purposes of contributing to the improvement of the quality of teaching and learning. Instead, it is likely to become bureaucratic, a 'paper' exercise that may be used for strict accountability and public relations purposes.

We have already asserted that appraisal is not new. Pupils, governors and parents – as well as members of the wider social and political community and teachers themselves – have been appraising teachers for years in largely informal ways. The difference now is that appraisal is expected to be formalized, systematic and an integral part of school management systems. It is important, therefore, that the opportunity to celebrate as well as assess professionalism is grasped.

What kind of appraisal system then, may contribute to a school's plans for INSET and staff development? What are the conditions necessary for establishing, implementing and monitoring the effectiveness? In order to proceed to an examination of these it may be useful to outline the key elements and stages of appraisal, the appraisal cycle, and the benefits claimed for appraisal.

Key elements

- What should be appraised?
- Who should appraise?

The headteacher has the responsibility to decide who appraises each teacher in a school. Normally, this will be the 'line manager'. Whilst this appears to be a strictly managerialist model of appraisal, it is perfectly possible within this to ensure, for example, a 'negative preference' system in which appraisees are able to exercise a choice of appraiser from within a panel. Additionally, the information or data discussed within an appraisal interview may consist of self-appraisal, peer observations of classroom action and so on.

What should be appraised?

Appraisal should clearly be based upon a teacher's (or headteacher's) job description. The central focus of all teacher appraisal should be teaching performance in the classroom, but will include contributions made to the school and wider social community, and should include the attention paid by teachers to their own development as 'lifelong learners'.

What are the key components in an appraisal system?

1) *The initial meeting*   The initial meeting between the appraiser and the appraisee is to clarify the purposes and to identify areas of work on which the appraisal might concentrate; to consider the teacher's job description; agree arrangements for classroom observation, data collection methods and timetable of events. In a very real sense, it is contract-making.

2) *Self-appraisal* (by the appraisee)   All teachers are expected to reflect systematically on their work.

3) *Classroom observation* (for teachers)   There will be at least two sessions of classroom observation taking at least one and a half hours in total. The appraisee must give a full briefing to the appraiser before the observation in relation to context, purposes, processes and intended outcomes. Feedback by the appraiser must be given within two days of the observation.

4) *Information collection*   Appraisers review other relevant information, for example the work of pupils, information about duties outside the classroom and school, and teachers' own development.

5) *The appraisal interview*   This is the cornerstone of the process, and should provide an opportunity for genuine dialogue and should be interruption free. Its purpose is to identify successes ('catch them being good'), agree areas of work to be developed and targets for action.

6) *The appraisal record*   The record of the appraisal is prepared by the appraiser in consultation with the appraisee. This is then subject to a further discussion aimed at a final, agreed document. The records are kept by the headteacher and appraisee, with access available to the chief education officer on request. *This clearly raises issues of confidentiality.* A summary of targets for professional development and training of staff collectively is kept, and the chair of the governors has access to this.

Despite the clarity of these organizational sequences, in Figure 6.1 there can be no assumption that the two central elements – classroom observation and the appraisal interview – will necessarily always be able to be conducted with skill.

Classroom observation

There are innumerable checklists of so-called 'good practice' available and this chapter contains suggestions for looking at classroom action systematically. It is important to remember that, first, apart from the 'technical' skills of observing (in an appraisal context) 'human-relating' skills are needed so that a climate of trust and understanding is able to be established in what for some teachers remains a relatively threatening

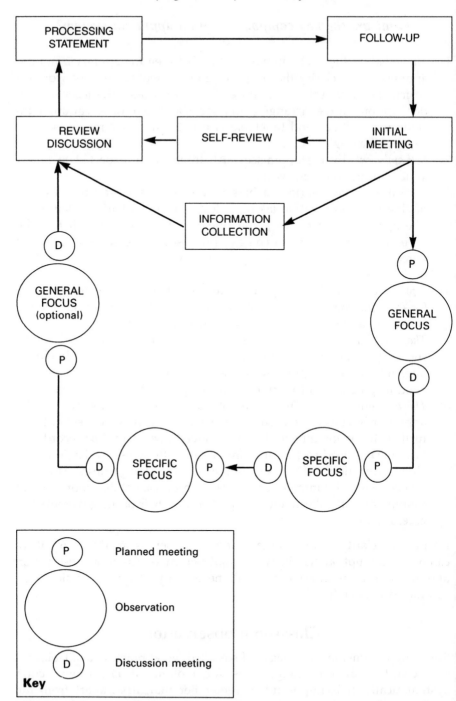

Figure 6.1 Review and development cycle, including classroom observation
Source: Somerset LEA (1987)

situation of disclosure of practice; and, secondly, where classroom observation leads to changes in planning and teaching, this in itself will not necessarily result in improved learning of pupils. Research has demonstrated that there are simply too many variables to draw a direct cause-and-effect relationship. Nevertheless, it is reasonable to infer that the clearer the teacher is about values, purposes and practices within the school development plans, the greater the opportunities for achieving a creative synergy.

In a recent national survey, the majority of LEAs 'placed great emphasis on the use of benign language when describing lesson observation, stressing the need for the feedback to be "constructive" and for the appraiser to aim to support the teacher in a "positive" way' (Wragg *et al.*, 1996).

The majority of LEAs valued this part of the appraisal process because it:

- Offers teachers feedback
- Offers teachers an extra pair of eyes
- Encourages collaboration between colleagues and exchange of ideas
- Encourages more reflection
- Encourages better lesson preparation
- Ensures appraisal interview is based on 'knowledge of a teacher's real work'
- Can lead to a common 'school' focus
- Breaks down classroom isolation
- Provides support.

(Wragg *et al.*, 1996)

The appraisal interview

Similar human relationship skills are needed here too, within the three main elements of preparation, process and follow-up. Essentially, the appraisal interview should be set against a background of trust, mutual respect and agreed purposes. It must allow the appraisee and appraiser to review the past and the present, and to set priorities or targets for the future, by the end of the interview. Consideration needs to be given to the following questions (Day, Whitaker and Wren, 1987):

1 What is the purpose of the interview?
2 When will it be held?
3 Where will it be held?
4 What form will the interview take?
5 What questions will the appraiser ask?
6 What questions will the appraisee ask?
7 What other information, documentation etc. might be required?
8 What do both participants hope to gain from the experience?
9 How will the interview end?

10 How long will the interview take?
11 How will the interview be recorded and what will happen to the interview notes?
12 How will the interview be followed up?

Additionally, and crucially, it is right for the appraisee to ask (Day, Whitaker and Wren, 1987):

What's in it for me?

- I should have a clear understanding of my job and how well I am doing it and of what is expected of me.
- I should feel secure in the knowledge that my talents are known, appreciated and exploited and that my weaknesses have been identified and constructive help has been offered to improve them.
- I should have discussed my future, including my ambitions and my career prospects, and have received guidance in achieving those aspirations.
- I should feel satisfied that all aspects of my work in and around the school have been discussed in a professional way.
- I should feel happy that everything discussed will be treated in confidence.

The problem with the two-year cycle

The appraisal of teachers and headteachers is conducted on a two-year cycle, with each successive two-year period treated as one appraisal programme. The intention is that in each second year of the programme there will be a discussion focusing on to what extent targets agreed in the preceding year have been reached. It is inevitable that a regular appraisal cycle of this kind will, at any given time, be more useful to some teachers than others. It cannot, therefore, be regarded as a substitute for a continuing professional development policy based, for example, upon a system of professional development profiling and regular review of need that characterizes schools as learning communities for teachers as well as pupils. It will be

- too infrequent for monitoring
- unnecessary for identifying low performing teachers
- so frequent that it is likely to lapse into an expensive piece of bureaucratic tokenism after the first couple of years
- unlikely to address the fundamental issues that ought to be faced in a quinquennial review
- likely to be divorced from curriculum evaluation.

(Eraut, 1989)

In addition, it diverts resources away from staff development. Not all staff will have the same needs at the same time and, by inference, a 'good' or 'moving' school will be one in which needs are constantly reviewed, practice constantly challenged and support planned accordingly. This implies particular kinds of leadership values and strategies as described in Chapter 3. It is unlikely, for example, that appraisal will be effective in a school that does not already foster openness, trust and collegiality among staff (Figure 6.2). The progress report in May 1989 of the pilot schemes then operating in six LEAs (NDC/SMT, 1989) (The Consortium of Teacher Appraisal Pilot Schemes) emphasized the importance of:

- *consultation* and school self-review in planning for appraisal;
- *climate setting* 'If the degree of mutual trust and understanding is less than perfect then awareness raising has to begin by creating it';
- *training* 'There is wide agreement that both appraisees and appraisers need preparing for appraisal . . . experience strongly suggests a need for 'on the job assistance';
- *ownership* 'We are advocating an organisational framework which gives space for individuality and freedom to develop a variety of approaches to suit the climate, style and stage of development of each school';
- *job description* 'Job descriptions are necessary for agreement; negotiation is a creative process, especially where responsibilities are shared or overlap';
- *classroom observation* 'Prompt lists of criteria for effective teacher appraisal were developed, which later became an agreed basis for planning and feedback in teaching analysis'; and
- *outcomes* 'Absolute clarity about the uses that will be made of the outcomes of the process is vital for a confident start'.

In terms of the management of primary schools, the most important of these findings is 'ownership', for if teachers do not experience the reality as well as the rhetoric of this, then they are unlikely to commit themselves to learning through an appraisal scheme. 'Ownership' implies *autonomy*.

Teacher autonomy

Accountability and autonomy, paradoxically, go hand in hand. If the assumption is made that appraisal is a form of accountability, then

Any genuine accountability procedure presupposes that the accountable subjects are capable of acting responsibly and autonomously. The imposition of external constraints and controls through external monitoring is inconsistent with a genuine accountability procedure . . . The association between 'external monitoring' and 'accountability' is . . . an attempt to legitimate social control over the teaching profession, and to influence it through power-coercive rather than rational procedures.

(Elliott, 1978)

- There should be an atmosphere of trust.
- Those involved need to be open-minded.
- The teacher's self-image is regarded as important. Appraisal should not imply a situation that is unpleasant, possesses psychological threat, and typically culminates in unrewarding consequences.
- The organizational climate needs to be positive.
- Appraisal systems need to be an integrated part of individual professional and whole-school development planning.
- Appraisal systems need to be designed and implemented through negotiation rather than imposition.
- Appraisal systems must be fair and perceived to be fair by all the parties involved.
- Appraisal systems must be economic in their use of resources (including teacher time and energy).
- Appraisal systems must ensure that tangible support for learning after appraisal is provided.
- Appraisal must begin and end with self-appraisal.

Figure 6.2 Organizational preconditions for successful implementation of appraisal

Teachers' capacity to act responsibly and autonomously will be eroded unless the planning, organization, processes and outcomes of the appraisal system itself promote this through participation in processes of negotiated needs identification and planning which signal a recognition that individual and whole-school development are complementary. It should be noted at this point that a distinction is being made between 'licence' – allowing complete freedom for teachers to do what they want, how they want, when they want, regardless of the needs expressed by pupils or society – and 'autonomy' – self-government within an ethical framework. There is no suggestion that teachers should not be accountable to society but rather that appraisal systems should be devices that enhance teachers' abilities to act responsibly and autonomously, thus empowering them to be more accountable. One way of achieving this is through the use of a 'process' rather than a 'product' model for appraisal. The product model has been described as one in which

> the main value of the appraisal process lies in the value of the product it will generate. This product is, in the first instance . . . a . . . comprehensive and up-to-date information base on teacher performance for the use of LEAs and governing bodies . . . This information base will then be used to achieve the purposes of

appraisal, namely to improve professional standards through recommendations as promotion, remediation or training.

(Winter, 1989)

Winter (1989) contrasts this with a *process* model in which

the value resides in the process of carrying it out. It is the process itself which will result in professional development. Any outcomes are unique to the individual practitioner and the specific content. Whereas the product model seeks to generate authoritative ('accurate') *assessment* of teacher performance (so that learning experiences can be prescribed, subsequently, for the teacher) the process model seeks, in itself, to stimulate effective *learning* by the teacher. It would not generate 'information' *about* teachers' work, but insight for those teachers themselves to use in improving their work.

Underpinning both these models are particular conceptions of teaching that must be made explicit in the formulation of any appraisal scheme. In the USA, Wise *et al.* (1984), as a result of an investigation of teacher appraisal practices in thirty-two cities, also associated the type of teacher appraisal with conceptions of teaching itself. They suggested the existence of four basic views of teaching (and thus teachers) that are relevant to any consideration of teacher autonomy within the appraisal process. Teaching was viewed as either *labour*, a *craft*, a *profession* or an *art*. As labour, the teachers' role is to implement schemes designed, directed and monitored by external authorities who supervise and inspect. It would not be difficult to associate with this view the OFSTED inspection system, the grading of teachers within this, and 'league' tables of test results. As a craft, it is assumed that there are specific, generalizable skills or competences defined by external authorities who monitor by periodic inspection. The introduction of national performance standards with prescribed lists of competences associated with 'the good teacher' such as those for beginning teachers, subject leaders, 'excellent' teachers, heads and would-be heads developed through the Teacher Training Agency (TTA) might be taken as one expression of this view. In contrast, in teaching as a profession it is assumed that teachers require a repertoire of qualities and skills that may be differentially applied according to the teacher's judgement. These skills and judgements will be self and peer developed and monitored; and in teaching as an art, evaluation by self or peers relies upon holistic judgements that recognize the unpredictable, personalized nature of teaching. Clearly, the process model is user-friendly, emphasizing the professional culture in which most teachers work – teaching as a profession or an art rather than a craft or labour – whereas the product model reflects the managerial culture of those who are responsible for resourcing education. Both cultures would claim responsibility for ensuring quality education for pupils.

Contract-making through negotiation and 'entitlements' could be expected to be essential features of the landscape of any appraisal system that values teacher autonomy. Entitlements are not defined in any legalistic way but rather are concerned with responsibilities and answerabilities to a variety of 'client groups'. For example, it may be that in an appraisal scheme there are six main groups who may justifiably have entitlements (i.e. the teacher, the school, the governors, the children, the parents and the LEA). The organization and process of appraisal should, therefore, be based upon a consideration of the entitlements of each of these groups. Much of the writing and most of the legislation on appraisal is focused upon the entitlements of the last five of the groups. In an attempt to redress this imbalance, here we concentrate on entitlements for teachers. Below is a list illustrating some possible teacher entitlements. It is not intended to be definitive or comprehensive, although it attempts to reflect the principles embodied in the 'process' model. Teachers are entitled to

- consultation in the design, monitoring and evaluation phases of appraisal;
- full participation in the collection of data;
- quality time for appraisal from colleagues and with colleagues;
- appropriate training and development resources in support of appraisal outcomes for professional development;
- equal rights in judgements of self, where others are involved in the appraisal;
- ownership of the appraisal process;
- time and support for training in and the implementation of self and peer-appraisal; and
- access to skilled, empathetic and knowledgeable appraisal interviewers.

In order to operationalize such entitlements, it will be necessary for managers to engage in 'contracting'. This need not be a legalistic process. 'Agreements' (a softer, more humane word than contracts) are, of course, often made informally between teachers and more formally under 'school development plans'. In cultures of collaboration encouraged by leaders who are committed to a learning community of teachers as well as children in their schools, many teachers will have experienced the value of being able to share thoughts, practices and feelings with one or more trusted colleagues. The importance of agreeing entitlements is such, however, that it may be necessary to document them for use as *aides-mémoire*. Written or at least explicit verbal contracts can do much to clarify mutual expectations as to goals and methods. In other words, in formal settings the contract may need to be explicit. Although writing in the context of interviewing, Cormier and Cormier (1979) outlined what could well serve as the basic features of such a contract:

- The contract should be negotiated, not proclaimed, by the partners involved – that is the head, staff and governors.
- The contract should be clear to all involved parties. They should know what appraisal is about.
- Some kind of oral or written commitment to the contract should be obtained.
- The contract should be reviewed as the parties progress, and revised if necessary.

One practical example of contracting is the use of action planning within the target-setting phase of appraisal. The process of helping a colleague or colleagues to think constructively about professional and curriculum concerns by supporting and challenging them through conversation is essential to the application of the results of the appraisal process to improvement. The appraisee's main task is to listen and question critically his or her colleagues whilst they

1) explore concerns;
2) focus on a specific aspect or problem;
3) consider a range of ways of looking at the problem;
4) construct a statement of intent;
5) identify and set goals;
6) generate and analyse ways of achieving those goals; and
7) plan a precise programme of action.

The task may be organized into a series of partnerships so that when the process is complete the partner is then in the position to

- implement the programme of action; and
- monitor and evaluate the programme and its outcome.

Figure 6.3 provides a framework for undertaking this.

Classroom-based self-appraisal

One of the most problematic areas for appraisal which is central to the appraisal process is classroom observation. Here, we intend to provide encouragement to leaders to ensure that observation by an outsider of the teacher's classroom is able to be placed firmly within the ongoing process of self-appraisal in the classroom by the teacher him or herself. It assumes that: '[All] teachers need help in assessing their own

Task:			
Goal(s)			
Timescale:			
Start date:		Completion date:	
Action step (including provisional times and timings)	Own strengths	Constraining factors	Strategies
1)			
2)			
3)			
4)			
5)			
6)			
7)			
8)			

Figure 6.3   Action-planning contract

professional performance and in building on their strengths and working on the limitations so identified' (HMSO, 1985). This statement implies not only that teachers have a responsibility for appraising their own teaching but that they also need 'technical' and 'critical friendship' help in doing so; for both appraisal and self-appraisal are potentially threatening since both inevitably involve self-disclosure.

The justification for ensuring that teachers appraise their own classroom thinking and practice systematically from time to time in order to increase professional effectiveness is based on three assumptions:

1. That teachers cannot be developed (by others) but only given opportunities to develop (for themselves).
2. That effective learning arises in response to the identification and confrontation of 'real' questions by the learner.
3. That decisions about teaching should stem from reflection on the effects of previous actions in relation to purposes.

The problem is often that, while teachers have the capacity to engage in self-appraisal, they are constrained in the extent to which they may do so by:

1) *practical factors*   such as time, energy, skills, resources; and conditions of work which largely define teaching as contact hours; and
2) *organizational-specific 'culture' factors*   Teachers operate within a

framework of organisational norms, expectations and values that are often at an implicit level. For example, a new teacher very quickly develops assumptions about practice from colleagues which allow him or her to cope with the complexities of teaching and being an accepted member of staff. However, since it is relatively unusual for these to be made explicit or tested, the possibilities for evaluating those assumptions that underpin the planning and practice of his or her teaching are minimal.

3) *psychological factors* It is natural to want to live in a world that is constant, that we can control and that does not threaten our self-esteem. It is not always in our best interests to probe our motivations, intentions and practices ourselves too much.

There is likely to be, therefore, a difference between what people say (their intentions or aspirations) and what they do (their practice). Most teachers have 'a capacity for autonomous professional self-development through systematic self-study, through the study of the work of other teachers and through the testing of ideas by classroom research procedures' (Stenhouse, 1975), and that while many already engage in self-study this is not as systematic as it might be. We have considered briefly some of the reasons for this. While many teachers may be described as 'connoisseurs', able with experience to distinguish, for example, between the significance of different sets of teaching and learning practices, or to recognize and appreciate different facets of their teaching and pupils' learning, they may not find it so easy to be critics who 'disclose the qualities of events or objects that connoisseurship perceives' (Eisner, 1979). The vast majority of teachers are proficient in their work, but where this implies that the challenge of new learning is minimal, proficiency itself becomes an instrument of control.

The role of the head is crucial here, for it is he or she who must provide opportunities for capacity building, for the development of the connoisseur who is also a critic. Ways in which this may be achieved are described throughout this book in relation to styles of leadership conducive to promoting professional learning cultures. Although the ethos or climate of the school will go a long way to minimizing the psychological and sociological constraints described above, it is worth remembering that the developing teacher will pass through several learning phases over a career span.

At some stage, however, the practical constraints must also be tackled – and it may be argued that this should come sooner rather than later. Heads must provide opportunities for deliberate reflection on classroom practice. The way in which they might provide these opportunities is through their own knowledge of

1) the procedures by which teachers may reflect;

2) techniques that may be used in monitoring classrooms; and
3) the means by which teachers may be provided with the moral and intellectual support necessary for self-review.

Self-review procedures

The nine questions in Figure 6.4 have been identified by teachers themselves as being essential for classroom self-appraisal. While these are not listed in order of priority they do focus attention on the three central elements of classroom life – the pupils, the teacher and the task. It is worth noting that while these questions inevitably give rise to others (for example, 'How do I find out what the pupils were doing?' or 'What did I intend to do?'), they are designed also to ensure that the teacher moves through four distinct and necessary phases:

1) *Description* – identifying and selecting events.
2) *Interpretation* – assessing the consequences of these events.
3) *Judgement* – assessing how far these events were worth while.
4) *Decision* – accepting responsibility for (1)–(3) and planning for future action.

The importance of beginning with description cannot be overemphasized since it ensures that any bias in interpretation, judgements and decisions can be checked against available observed action rather than assumptions or expectations or memories a teacher might have about the action.

The problems of potential bias will be considered later in the chapter, but before this it is worthwhile exploring evaluation procedures a little further.

Action research

In order for the teacher to answer the questions posed in Figure 6.4, it will be necessary for him or her to become engaged in action research, which has been defined as the 'study of a social situation with a view to improving the quality of action within it', and as providing 'the necessary link between self-evaluation and professional development' (Elliott, 1981). Its concern is to 'promote improvement in practice and improvement in understanding simultaneously' (McCormick and James, 1983). While this movement originated in America, it has grown in England in the last twenty-five years largely through the efforts of Lawrence Stenhouse (1975; 1979), John Elliott (1981; 1991) and in Australia through the work of Kemmis *et al.* (1981). Kemmis *et al.* (1981) describe the process of action research:

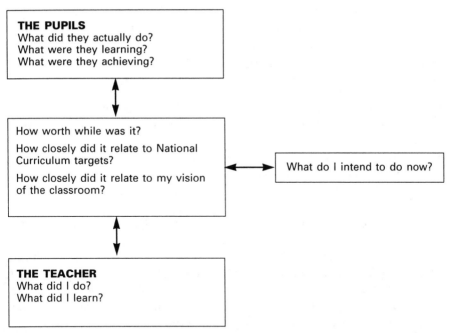

Figure 6.4 Essential self-evaluation questions
Source: Based on The Open University (1980, Block 1)

In practice, the process begins with a general idea that some kind of improvement or change is desirable. In deciding just where to begin in making improvements, one decides on a field of action . . . where the battle (not the whole war) should be fought. It is a decision on which it is possible to have an impact. The general idea prompts a 'reconnaissance' of the circumstances of the field, and fact-finding about them. Having decided on the field and made a preliminary reconnaissance, the action researcher decides on a general plan of action. Breaking the general plan down into achievable steps, the action researcher settles on the first action step. Before taking this first step the action researcher becomes more circumspect, and devises a way of monitoring the effects of the first action step. When it is possible to maintain fact-finding by monitoring the action, the first step is taken. As the step is implemented, new data starts coming in and the effects of the action can be described and evaluated. The general plan is then revised in the light of the new information about the field of action and the second action step can be planned along with the appropriate monitoring procedures. The second action step is then implemented, monitored and evaluated; and the spiral of action, monitoring, evaluation and replanning continues.

Elliott (1981) argues that the 'general idea' should be allowed to shift and that 'reconnaissance' should involve analysis in addition to fact-finding. Before moving on to discuss some of the techniques for collecting classroom observations for the purposes of professional development through action research, here is some practical advice on getting started:

- *The WHY of observation* Decide what is the purpose. Is it primarily to solve a problem or to check on the effectiveness of a particular strategy or aspect of curriculum content?
- *The WHAT of observation* This will be determined by the teachers' own interests, needs or concerns.
- *The WHO of observation* Teachers should beware of being overambitious. For example, it may be sensible, if pupils are the focus, to observe one pupil or a small group; or if observing self it may be wise to focus on one aspect of teacher talk (e.g. questioning). Figure 6.5 shows an example of a plan for investigating an aspect of teaching.
- *The WHEN of observation* Observation must be built in as a part of the teaching plan, and short concentrated periods of time for this *standing outside* actual contact with pupils may be more practical than long periods when the teacher is likely to be distracted.
- The HOW of observation Examples of techniques for collecting observations will be given later in the chapter. It is equally important, however, to find ways of organizing the activity itself so that time and energy can be focused in support of the commitment; and frameworks for recording the information gained from classroom observations must also be devised. While knowledge of evaluation procedures is important, so also is a knowledge of monitoring techniques that will enable teachers to collect, process and reflect upon classroom action.

Classroom monitoring techniques

Many monitoring techniques are easily available to most teachers, and are sufficiently flexible to cater for evidence of the unintended as well as the intended:

- *Document analysis* Teaching plans, syllabi, written work diaries, development plans, achievements may be analysed.
- *Impressionistic diaries* Of 'observations, feelings, reactions, interpretations, reflections, hunches, hypotheses and explanations' (Kemmis *et al.*, 1981).
- *Analytic memos* These are short periodic analyses which consist of 'one's systematic thinking about the evidence one has collected' (Elliott, 1981).

Step 1: Choosing the investigation.

Step 2: Asking 'What learning opportunities am I trying to provide?'

Step 3: Deciding on the questions you want to ask.

Step 4: Designing the investigation.
(a) What data do I need to collect?
(b) What should be the timing and circumstances of the investigation?
(c) What techniques should I use?

Step 5: Carrying out the investigation.

Step 6: Analysing the data.

Step 7: Reflecting on the analysis.

Figure 6.5 Investigating an aspect of teaching
Source: The Open University (1980, Block 3)

- *Lesson profiles* For example, to record teacher and pupil activity at ten-minute intervals (Walker and Adelman, 1975).

- *Checklists, questionnaires, inventories* These 'allow one to quantify people's observations, interpretations and attitudes' (Elliott, 1981) and should be used, if at all, as a means of checking against qualitative judgements.

- *The running commentary* Here the teacher who is observing an individual or group should write down as much of what he or she hears and observes as possible. This is useful for short periods of observation of at least five minutes.

- *The shadow study* This is as above, but the recorder is an observer from outside the classroom.

- *Audio/video-recordings and transcripts* Potentially, videotape is a most useful means of collecting verbal and non-verbal information. Almost certainly, however, it requires another person to be present and may, initially, cause a distraction in the classroom. However, used sympathetically and over a period of time it can provide by far the richest mine of information (Day, 1981). Audio-tape, on the other hand, is easy to use and, though transcription is time-consuming and care has to be taken in attempting to record a group of more than three or four children at work, it provides extremely valuable information.

- *Interviewing* It is very useful to interview pupils for their responses to a lesson and even more so to have a sympathetic outsider or 'critical friend' (Habermas, 1972) do this. The power and authority of a teacher figure must be taken into account when judging the authenticity of pupils' responses, and it is worth while for any outsider to be able to assure them that while general feedback of information to the teacher is necessary, individual comments will remain confidential.

- *Use of an outside observer (who may be a colleague)* A brief example of this is provided later in this chapter. Given a trusting and sympathetic relationship, this outside resource or 'third eye' can be invaluable.

- *Case studies* These essentially provide a set of reflections on the processes of investigation, the results specific to it and general issues that arise from it. In the context of the individual and the school, such documents may provide reference points for future as well as past work.

As far as possible the techniques used ought to enable one to look at what is going on from a variety of perspectives. This is particularly important to those engaged in what is for the most part a qualitative endeavour; for while there is no notion of achieving 'objective' views of classrooms in the narrow, quasi-scientific sense, it is important to provide a subjectively reasoned picture that is internally valid. One means of achieving this is to check 'results' with a colleague and/or pupils, or invite a colleague into the classroom to help decide whether teaching intentions are matched by teaching practices. If the colleague is also the appraiser, on a different occasion, then this can have additional benefits. Another now commonly used technique is that of triangulation in which observations or accounts of a situation or some aspect of it are collected from a variety of perspectives and then compared and contrasted. So pupils, observer and teacher may comment on the same piece of teacher talk, for example, and these comments may be checked for match and mismatch.

Providing moral and intellectual support through 'critical friendship'

It has been implicit throughout this chapter that teachers who are engaged in review, development and appraisal need support, not only at the beginning but also throughout the process. Self-disclosure may involve considerable anxiety for the teacher and the sympathetic support of colleague(s) must be built in from the beginning. It may also be that the teacher will require practical support (assistance in processing data, use of resources, time and so on) and intellectual support (advice on the design of an observation schedule, the interpretation of a transcript, etc.). The likelihood is that the teacher will also need further support in acquiring new skills and knowledge or modifying current skills. Notwithstanding OFSTED inspections and LEA support, it is likely that colleagues in the school will ultimately be the most important single factor in providing mutual support.

'Critical friendships' may be defined as practical partnerships entered voluntarily, based upon a relationship between equals and rooted in a common task or shared concern. They can be a means of establishing links with one or more colleagues to assist in processes of learning and change so that ideas, perceptions, values and understandings may be shared through the mutual disclosures of feelings, hopes and fears. Critical friendships can serve to decrease isolation and increase the possibilities of moving through stages of reflection to confrontation of thinking and practice. Reflection in itself will not necessarily lead to self-confrontation, and self-confrontation may need skilled support to be translated into new action. If individuals feel isolated they will only see what they are ready to see; they will only learn what is on the edge of the consciousness of what they already know (Thompson, 1984) In other words, significant personal change for improvement has limits! In terms of the appraisal of classroom practice, for example, a critical friend may establish and sustain a responsive, mutually acceptable dialogue about classroom events and their context. Through this, situations will be created in which the teacher is obliged to reflect systematically on practice.

The results of this kind of interaction, if successful, will be more effective knowledge and application of teaching standards; and the process will generate documented information for use by teachers as part of their appraisal. Below is a summary of some of the advantages and disadvantages of the use of a critical friend.

Advantages

Providing they are skilled and trusted, they can

1) lighten the energy and time loads for observation. They can also enable the teacher to carry on teaching providing the teacher with relief from the burden of collecting and analysing personal data;
2) be used to check against bias in self-reporting and to assist in more lengthy processes of self-evaluation;
3) offer, where appropriate, comparisons with classroom practice elsewhere;
4) move freely and see the children working in different situations;
5) focus in on an agreed issue or area of concern, for example small-group task work;
6) provide post-lesson critical dialogues;
7) act as a resource the teacher may use at times appropriate to the needs he or she perceives.

In addition,

8) children may be more open with outsiders (e.g. in interviews).

Disadvantages

If they are unskilled and not trusted, then (Day, Whitaker and Wren, 1987)

1) unless a regular visitor, their interpretations may be out of context (observers will have their own biases);
2) children may be less open with outsider (e.g. in interviews); and
3) unless they become a regular part of the classroom over time, then children and teacher may react to their presence in such a way as to cause untypical behaviour.

In addition,

4) the exercise is time consuming – observer and teacher must spend time together before and after the work observed to negotiate and fulfil the contract; and
5) skilled observers are difficult to find!

Whether teachers invite colleagues from in school or someone from outside (e.g. from a local higher education institution) will be a matter for their discretion. However, it may be worth noting that some research (Hopkins, 1986) suggests that

> It is preferable from the user's point of view to learn from a peer far enough from home so that: (1) asking for help can't be interpreted as a self-indictment; (2) invidious competition and comparison is reduced; (3) the ideas can be changed with impunity; (4) they can be credited to their new user.

Whatever the choice, elements in successful sharing will be

1) a willingness to share;
2) a recognition that sharing involves
   a) disclosure, and
   b) opening oneself to the possibility of feedback;
3) a recognition that disclosure and feedback imply being prepared to consider changing;
4) a recognition that changing is sometimes
   a) threatening (to self-esteem and current practice),
   b) difficult (it requires time, energy, new skills), and
   c) satisfying;
5) a recognition that the degree to which people are willing to share may, therefore, be restricted.

Collegiality, contract-making, entitlements and critical friendships are all elements within review, development and appraisal schemes that support rather than erode teacher autonomy and that encourage staff to respond to new demands. They reinforce a sense of responsibility by affirming confidence in teachers' professionalism.

Managing the process

The success of any appraisal scheme will depend on a number of 'human' factors. Although these have been discussed elsewhere in this book, it is worth relating some of them in the context of this chapter. Clearly it is important for head and staff to agree on the timings of the appraisal cycles (the organization of the school needs to be adaptive and the staff receptive).

It is important to allocate human and other resources over an agreed time period to the project as a high priority. It is also necessary for the work to be seen by the teachers as relevant to their own personally and professionally perceived needs as well as a means of demonstrating progress in relation to school development planning. For this reason, it should be an integral part of a scheme of continuing professional development. It should be feasible as well as desirable; uncomplicated but significant; and of ultimate if not immediate benefit to teaching and learning in the classroom. Without the commitment of the staff no amount of careful planning and organization, and monitoring and support, can ensure success. Such commitment is likely to arise in schools where there are climates and organizational structures that offer opportunities not only for interstaff development that focuses on identified school needs but also for individual members of staff to reflect systematically on individual needs – aspects of the teaching and learning in and outside their own classrooms – and be supported in these processes. This too has implications for those in leadership roles. Figure 6.6 summarizes the conditions for successful appraisal, and the final part of this chapter provides an example of how management can demonstrate commitment through supporting the career-long learning of teachers.

Aims	Reasons
1) Familiarization with the notion of appraisal	To gain and share information To lower anxieties To generate teacher commitment
2) Establishment of supportive appraisal environments	To facilitate changes in attitudes, values, role definitions and self-images To foster co-operation
3) Provision of physical and psychological space	To demonstrate support To provide time and somewhere to meet, discuss and work To encourage sustained interactivity
4) Application of agreed targets	To demonstrate management commitment

Figure 6.6 Conditions for successful appraisal
Source: Based on Davis (1981)

Supporting career-long development

Despite growing rhetoric, the means of supporting life-long learning among teachers are by and large related almost entirely to those which focus upon serving the system. Notions of the teacher as person as well as the teacher as professional, with all that is implied for progression, continuity and balance of support for development over a career span, are

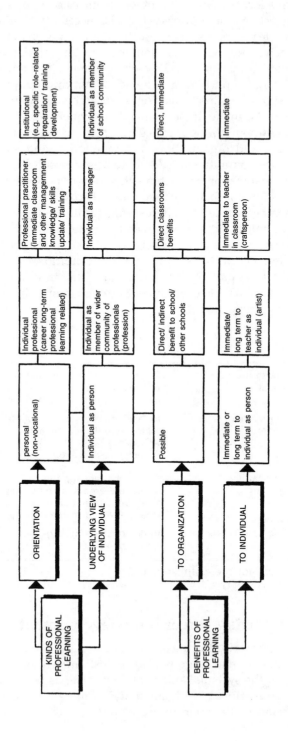

Figure 6.7 Kinds and benefits of planned continous professional development opportunities
Source: Day (1994)

limited. Competences of a functional kind are being developed; and there is a danger that policy-makers will adopt a *cul-de-sac* approach which will be counterproductive to their aims of increasing efficiency and effectiveness. The use of profiles to assess initial teacher training students seems certain to be extended into serving teachers' lives. After all, it would seem from a managerial perspective to fit neatly into the larger package of measures designed to improve schooling through monitoring procedures – teacher appraisal, school development planning, school inspection. In this way there could, the thinking goes, be a set of general competences against which all teachers might be judged, perhaps with social context as a variable relating to performance. The problem is that in such models teaching is conceptualized principally as a technical, knowledge and skill-based activity. The essential personal nature of teaching must also be taken into account in managing the career-long continuing professional development of teachers. Building and maintaining good classroom practice depends as much upon teachers' 'moral' purposes, their connoisseurship and the essential dependence of good teaching upon their abilities to connect, care and differentiate, as upon subject knowledge and teaching craft skills. We would offer *five assertions concerning teachers' and school effectiveness*:

- teachers are the school's greatest asset;
- all teachers are managers;
- personal and professional development are central to continuing effective management, and leadership is as much about the provision of effective support as it is about co-ordination and control;
- the prime function of leaders in schools is to support teachers in their management functions; and
- given the right conditions, all professionals are capable of learning from their experience of the job.

These assertions lead to a hypothesis that:

- schools are likely to be more effective if: 1) leaders actively promote processes of interaction between individual and whole-school review and development planning; and 2) teachers' personal professional development needs are recognized, supported and based upon self-managed personal development planning.

Support for teacher development must take account of teachers'

- development of professional expertise;
- cognitive development;
- developmental stages of concern/career development; and
- life cycle.

The emphasis in each of these is on progression and continuity of development.

Personal development planning over a career may be achieved through acceptance that teachers have four kinds of development needs:

- Personal (non vocational)
- Professional (career, long-term learning needs)
- Classroom practitioner (immediate knowledge, skill needs)
- Organisational role (preparation, enrichment)

(Day, 1994)

Over a career it will be important to create a 'balance' of opportunities for individual needs to be tracked and met. Figure 6.7 provides a matrix which allows management and teachers to plan and monitor such needs, indicating which are likely to have direct or indirect benefits for the individual and the school. Teachers, like their pupils, have a right to expect opportunities for development which are guided by principles of differentiation, progression and continuity, relevance and coherence and balance.

Collaborative school cultures build and develop strategies for challenge and support within the notion of teacher autonomy. They recognize the need for teachers to retain a high degree of control over the direction of their work and the confidentiality surrounding their contributions, whilst at the same time having access to appropriate critical support.

Professional development must extend beyond classroom practice, such that support for the personal and long-term professional needs of the teacher as artist, connoisseur, craftsperson and technician is legitimated. Without this, the tendency over the last decade to regard 'development' as 'training' which may be achieved in short, sharp bursts and which must be directly related to policy implementation will be exacerbated (Gilroy and Day, 1993). The consequences of adopting and developing competence-based profiling systems for use within models of appraisal designed to benefit only organizationally defined needs will be the downgrading of teachers as autonomous, responsible and accountable professionals to teachers as operatives who implement, rather than mediate, the curriculum.

Further reading

Wragg E. C., Wikeley F. J. Wragg E. M. and Hayes C. S. (1996) *Teacher Appraisal Observed*, Routledge, London.

7

Renewing the team: managing the staffing cycle

Introduction • Understanding: the impact of school culture and the staffing process • Assessing staffing needs: a whole-school process • Searching: looking for a match • Matching: the interview process • Beginning: the induction and support of new staff • Ending: when a member of staff leaves

Introduction

The days when a primary school headteacher could expect a relatively low annual staff turnover have long since disappeared. Until relatively recently, it was not uncommon for teachers to devote their entire teaching careers to one or two schools. Redundancies were rare and retirement age for the majority of teachers meant sixty-five. Stress, if experienced, was unacknowledged and educational reform meant moving desks out of rows into small groups. Young teachers emerging from training colleges and universities believed that the promise of job security and a high degree of professional autonomy was a fair exchange for relatively low salaries. This unwritten contract, however, has been torn up by two short decades of educational reform. With old certainties fractured, new incentives must be found to attract the finest teachers into our schools. We believe that the greatest incentive we can offer teachers is to join a school team which is wholly committed to the service of learning, and in this service, connect with other professionals whose values are similarly built around the life-enhancing purpose of educating our young people to be fit citizens of the world today and tomorrow. Such dedicated service must be rewarded institutionally by a relationship based on a real, rather than a cosmetic, commitment to teacher development, both personal and professional. The new contract between teachers and schools cannot guarantee permanence but it must guarantee, at the very least, to provide fulfilling development opportunities, consciously designed to promote growth and enhance competence to meet the increasing demands of a reform agenda. Selection is a two-way process. If either side reneges on the commitment to service or offers what they know can't be delivered, then the relationship is likely to break down or, even worse, struggle on with growing cynicism, resentment and despair.

One way in which this new contract is honoured is in the way that school leaders think about and prepare for the process of staffing the school. Old attitudes, which put the responsibility for presentation of self on the shoulders of the candidate alone, must be finally shed. Schools now have to learn how to *present themselves* to the profession. Headteachers must lead the inquiry and ask the question, 'is this a school worth belonging to?' 'Can we ask with integrity, teachers to commit themselves to us in an uncertain future?' We have consciously organized this chapter to enable such a profound, professional reflection to take place. Staffing is a dynamic interlinked process, which mirrors the core values and purposes of the school as an organization. We begin with *understanding*. In this section we discuss the need for senior managers to develop their competence in reading and interpreting the culture of the school. When this is possible, leaders are more able to influence the formation of culture in positive ways which enhance organizational esteem. This institutional awareness lays the foundations for assessing what is needed when staff vacancies become available and new appointments are to be made. It also makes it possible to describe the school accurately and authentically to aspiring candidates. *Assessing* deals with investigating a whole-school approach to identifying staffing needs and preparing the job and person specifications. A healthy degree of realism is encouraged by pointing to some of the potential pitfalls in idealizing or overestimating the impact that any one individual appointment can have on an existing staff team. *Searching* offers practical ways forward in the task of attracting high-quality candidates and therefore finding the best possible fit between the school's needs and the aspirations of the candidates. This includes both the management of the school's presentation to prospective candidates and the ways in which requests for references can be framed to ensure that useful information is obtained. *Matching* takes a hard look at the interview day. By this stage in the process there should be no surprises for the school interviewing teams or the candidates. Rigorous preparation and planning ensure that each candidate has an equal opportunity to present him or herself for selection and this leads to a rewarding outcome for those rejected as well as selected. All parties are able to assure themselves confidently that a fair and just process was undergone. *Beginnings* draws attention to the positive impact that a well thought-out programme of induction and continuing support, through the introduction of a mentor system, can have on initiating a new member of staff into the culture of a school. Finally, *endings* asks senior managers to consider that staff departures are as important in their own way to the dynamics of school life as staff induction. The thoughtful enactment of ending rituals can provide a vocabulary for expressing the sense of loss which often accompanies saying goodbye to a valued colleague, and in turn serves to remind the community that everyone is valued for the unique contribution he or she makes.

Understanding: the impact of school culture and the staffing process

All organizations have their own unique culture. This organizational culture is forged out of a complex interaction between the internal customs and rituals of day-to-day school life and the powerful external social, political and economic forces which impact upon its development. In a school, its history and traditions will exert a strong influence, as will the values, beliefs and ambitions of key decision-makers and influencers within the school community. Culture consists of an internalized set of values, attitudes and expectations which provide meaning and stability for members and therefore exert a powerful and enduring influence on their everyday behaviour. In other words, culture can simply be defined as 'the way we do things round here'. Established and embedded cultural norms can and do reflect the state of health of the school and, paradoxically, outsiders may be better able to read the cultural semiotics of the school than insiders. On a first brief visit to a school, pupils and their carers will pick up very strong messages from the moment they walk through the school gates. In the course of an OFSTED inspection, inspectors will be looking for evidence relating to what they call the prevailing school 'ethos'. On the other hand if you ask a teacher, school secretary or Year-6 pupil to describe the culture or ethos of the school, they are often at a complete loss. Living the culture for some means becoming habituated to its norms, taking for granted what goes on and believing implicitly that this constitutes 'normality' or 'reality'.

Senior teachers cannot afford to neglect the development of their own cultural awareness. You may recall from your natural history lessons the meerkat, an animal which is wholly attuned to read every message in its environment. Its small body literally quivers as every nerve strains to read environmental messages. The sensitivity of its physical and psychological tuning is fundamentally connected to the survival of the group. Senior teachers need a similarly high degree of awareness in relation to school culture. They need the sensitivity and intelligence to be able to both read and interpret cultural messages, learning the ways in which their own interventions influence cultural development positively or negatively. This will mean learning to listen at a profound level to what others say but also to tune in to your own intuitions and gut reactions. Leaders need to be *cultural facilitators* in order for schools to thrive. Self-consciously supporting the development of healthy cultural norms is a leadership function, critical to the success or failure of the school. Schein (1985) maintains that leadership is intertwined with cultural formation, and Duignan (in Riches and Morgan, 1989) extends our appreciation of how this process of building and sustaining schools rich in culture might be brought about:

Leaders, as culture builders, work throughout the daily management structures and routines to achieve organizational purposes or end values. Daily management transactions are not ends in themselves, but means to higher ends ... Leadership in this sense, is above all else concerned with uncovering the deeper meanings of human interaction in the organization. It deals with such questions as: what are the purposes or goals for which the organization exists? What does it mean to be a member of the organization? How is the leadership act best accomplished to help achieve common goals? How can organizational members pool their energies to achieve common goals, i.e. what structures can be established for shared leadership?

Peters and Waterman (1988) discussing the features of excellent organizations, found that organizational success was linked to strong cultures, characterized by the clear communication of objectives and superordinate goals. Put simply, in these organizations staff knew what standards were expected of them, what they had to do, why they were doing it and, as importantly, believed in the work they were doing. Such widely shared understanding leads to internal cohesiveness and increased staff motivation. On the other hand, impoverished organizational cultures will be characterized by unclear goals, poorly communicated or low expectations, mixed messages, poor interpersonal relationships and fuzzy role boundaries. This inevitably leads to a lack of an organizational focus, distrust of managers and a degree of confusion and anxiety over role performance.

Activity 7.1: Learning to read school culture – developing observational skills

- Spend some time walking around the school *as if you were an outsider*. Look at what is happening from different viewpoints: a pupil, parent, governor, inspector, social worker, police officer.
- Invite a colleague from another organization, preferably other than a school, to shadow you for an afternoon/day. Listen to their fresh impressions of the school atmosphere or ethos. What particularly impacted them about the way the staff operated with each other?
- Listen to the way in which people speak to each other in meetings, on corridors, in classrooms. Listen to the stories they tell.
- Do they speak differently to people, depending on role or status?
- Are people consistent? Do they say one thing and do another?
- Notice the way that humour is used. Is it inclusive, inviting shared fun or does it use sarcasm and put down as a way of generating laughter at other people's expense?
- What practices do staff take for granted in using shared facilities such as the staffroom? Do people compete or co-operate over the use of teaching space and resources?

Activity 7.1: Continued

- What is the atmosphere in staff meetings? Do you dread them or look forward to them?
- Use staff meetings as a way of talking about school culture. What it is and how people would like it to be. What could be done to enable cultural development?
- Can staff speak freely and honestly in their teams or in meetings? Do they talk about how they feel as well as about what they think?
- Ask pupils to tell you the best and worst things about the school.
- Ask parents or carers what reputation the school has in the area. What do people say about the school casually in conversation?
- What annual rituals do staff consider important? What don't they bother about?
- How do staff feel about the appraisal process or professional development days?
- Contemplate your own pattern of relationships within the school. Do you have strong likes and dislikes? High trust or low trust in colleagues? Do others trust you?
- Hold debriefing meetings with staff who are leaving. Talk to them about perceptions of the school from their perspective.
- Take a fresh look at the fabric of the building. Inside and out. How is it treated, decorated, maintained? Does it have clear signs, a reception area and so on?
- Is there a transparency over school systems such as promotion or how decisions are made? If there is opacity, whose interests does it serve?

Established cultural norms will also determine to a large extent staff attitudes to change and the development of new ideas for good or ill. Healthy cultures will demonstrate a congruence between values and practice. Unhealthy cultures do the reverse. A school which claims to be warm and welcoming to pupils and carers, and then employs a receptionist or secretary with poor interpersonal skills but who is terrific at setting up databases, is not living out its values.

One of the writers, when newly qualified, was attracted by an advertisement for a teaching post which declared that the school was looking for an enthusiastic, innovative teacher to join a team of similarly enthusiastic, innovative teachers. On appointment, the writer quickly came hard up against the enduring myth that the school was innovative in its approach to practice and that new ideas were always welcomed. What actually happened was that when new ideas were put forward the standard response came back: 'We tried that idea one/five/ten years ago and it didn't work then and it won't work now . . .', or 'we've been doing that for years, but we called it . . .', thus serving to preserve the illusion of an innovative culture without ever having to alter radically or evaluate existing practices. For the writer, the initiation into the real school culture, as opposed to the rosy picture presented by the job advertisement, was both swift and painful. Feelings of disappointment, anger and frustration though real, were hidden. The lesson very quickly learnt was that *in order to innovate, the last thing to do was label the process innovation* because that suggested that the staff view of themselves as radical innovators was in some way flawed. The idea *must* have been thought of previously and discarded as worthless.

In other words, the writer learnt that in order to bring about change the key skill was to *pretend* that no change was taking place. The fracture between the real and the idealized cultural norms led to a cynicism in newly appointed staff which was almost impossible to eradicate because it was self-perpetuating. They learnt very quickly that 'fitting in' meant the acceptance of a set of fundamentally dishonest ways of relating and such dishonesty inevitably erodes an individual's conception of him or herself as a person of integrity. All these years later, the writer still catches herself in the act of beginning sentences with 'but we've always done that . . .' to dynamic young colleagues, eager to implement new practice!

Organizational culture, then, will both condition staff behaviour within the school and also determine the way in which the school presents itself, interprets and in turn is interpreted by the external world.

A key leadership function is to be able to read and interpret the culture and influence its development so that there is a synergy between espoused theory – what you believe you do – and theory in use – what you actually do (Argyris, Putnam and McLain Smith, 1985). Leaders need to have the emotional maturity and sensitivity to alert staff members to the development of unhealthy cultural norms, such as the one described above. Without this synergy, the messages which are conveyed in relation to attracting new staff will result in a profound sense of disappointment and frustration. On appointment, this will very quickly lead to a feeling of having been conned or cheated in some way. This lack of congruence can be the beginning of a long slope to anger, cynicism and underperformance. Where the school culture is healthy and mature enough to present itself, 'warts and all', to prospective employees and the interview process gives a genuine chance to see the real issues the staff face on a daily basis, then the result is likely to be the recruitment of staff committed to working within a school which articulates its strengths assertively and is able to lay on the table what needs still to be done in terms of development. As Peck (1993) reminds us, 'A healthy organization – whether a marriage, a family, or a business corporation – is not one with an absence of problems, but one that is actively and effectively addressing or healing its problems.'

Assessing staffing needs: a whole-school process

The involvement of key stakeholders in the appointment process has been enshrined in legislation. The broadening role of the governing body has meant that governors, particularly the members of the pupil and personnel committee, will have the responsibility for working with the headteacher and colleagues to set the process of recruitment and selection in motion: creating the job description and person specification, framing the advertisement, deciding on the short-list and sending out invitations for interview, as well as finally debriefing successful and unsuccessful candidates. Together with the headteacher they will present the public face of the school to the candidates at the formal interview stage.

However there is an important stage which precedes this process, when a member of staff leaves and an opportunity to appoint becomes available. A recurring theme throughout this book has been the necessity to create opportunities for staff involvement in the management of the school. Given such an inclusive model of management, the needs of the individual become the needs of the organization. If the selection process is to be successful in satisfying a variety of needs, it is vital to ensure the full involvement of teaching and support staff in the recruitment and selection process. Senior managers need to ferret out ruthlessly institutional practices which cut out staff involvement and replace them with creative opportunities for responsible decision-making. Tom Peters, in *Thriving on Chaos* (1987), exhorts managers to

- involve everyone in everything;
- spend time lavishly on recruiting;
- train and retrain; and
- use self-managing teams.

Such management practices encourage us to highlight the role that each member of the school community can play in shaping their joint future and to take full responsibility for the success or failure of what is created. The Californian Task Force to Promote Self-Esteem and Personal and Social Responsibility (1990), a federally funded project from the early 1990s, recognized the importance of the workplace in building self-esteem via job satisfaction in its members. Job satisfaction includes participation in decision-making, personal recognition and individual development.

However, the question of individual development needs to be addressed before proceeding to the next stage of the selection process. It is important to consider whether, as a result of the vacancy arising, some internal staffing adjustments are desirable. Having identified current needs, consideration should be given to whether the potential to satisfy them already lies within the staff group. The departure of the school's principal musician, for example, could provide an opportunity for another member of staff with musicianship to come forward. Some teachers live in the shadow of more experienced or better qualified colleagues and allow their talents to remain unrecognized and unexpressed. When considering specialist needs, the first option should always be to give existing members of staff the opportunity to adjust their responsibilities. The departure of a key teacher can be an internal motivator, presenting other members of staff with the opportunity to move into new areas and take on new challenges.

However, once staff get together to discuss institutional priorities in relation to a new appointment, it is tempting to allow dreams to infect reality. You may recognize the frisson of excitement which is generated in a staff group when even the most liked and respected colleague decides to move on. This gives the opportunity for renewal, and the phrase 'new-blood appointment' is commonly used when staff teams get together. It is as if the new person is literally meant to transfuse life into the flagging energies of the school system. This may be possible if the organization is basically vital and healthy and only requires a fresher view. If however the system is moribund, then it would take a massive transfusion, much more than one individual could deliver without damaging him or herself in the process, to turn the system around single-handedly. During staff discussion, stay alert to the vocabulary and metaphors which are being used to describe the potential newcomer and if necessary challenge any unhelpful assumptions which are made or expectations expressed. Having unrealistic expectations about what new staff can possibly deliver will inevitably lead to disappointment.

Activity 7.2: Challenge the myths

As a senior manager, it is important to keep expectations as grounded as possible when it comes to leading discussion about replacement staffing. Here are a few common metaphors which are used and may need challenging before they become entrenched:

- *an adrenalin shot* – someone with bags of energy, a quick-fix to bump start us back into action;
- *a clone* – someone who is just like us and won't make any waves or upset any apple carts;
- *a workhorse* – someone to whom we can give all the jobs we have been trying to dump for ages;
- *a saviour/rescuer* – someone who by the power of his or her reputation is believed can single-handedly work miracles; and
- *the no-hoper* – someone whom the head wants but the staff don't.

The assessment of needs begins with an exercise to determine the perceptions of staff in relation to the current effectiveness of the school, with a specific remit to look at future staffing needs. Specifically it provides an opportunity to review the past, present and future:

- What are our aspirations and ambitions as a school?

- Where have we come from?
- Where we are at the moment?

This in turn requires an investigation of:

- What work currently occupies our thinking.
- What we need to do next in the school development cycle.

Before considering the detail of the job description and person specification, it is necessary to be reminded of the work currently in progress and of the plans due for implementation in the future. The goal will be to appoint someone who can make a positive contribution in these specific directions. The headteacher is in an ideal position to summarize the progress made in implementing plans but it is important to gather staff perceptions as well. Raising the five issues listed above in an initial staff meeting can help to provide a clear picture of current work and future tasks. The details provided by schools to potential applicants for posts rarely, if ever, give an indication of the current status of the school development programme. This is unfortunate, because it robs candidates of the opportunity to make their written applications specifically relevant to key issues and concerns.

While assessing school-wide needs can usefully involve all staff, in larger primary schools, a delegated team can take the process further by carrying out more specific tasks to do with the recruitment and selection process, particularly in drawing up the job description and person specification. Merely holding a generalized image of a 'good teacher' in the mind is likely to be the shortest route to an ill-judged appointment and an unhappy, unproductive relationship between school and appointee. The final products of a needs assessment exercise will be the job description and person specification, which will ultimately be sent out in the details to all applicants. Prospective candidates are entitled to the clearest, most professional statement about what the school requires. The job description and person specifications should supply this.

A *job description* should specify clearly the range of tasks to be undertaken and the lines of accountability that the successful candidate will be required to work within. This ensures that there can be no later misunderstandings about what the job was meant to entail. It should also specify, where necessary, details of any desired outcomes or achievements – for example, an increase in the number of school-wide drama activities or an improvement in reading scores. If there is developmental potential or the possibility of flexibility in relation to the role in the future, this should also be made clear. A rule of thumb should always be that a successful candidate should have no surprises in relation to the role he or she takes up on appointment. A clear job description also gives prospective candidates the opportunity to rule themselves out if they feel the job advertised is overly demanding or insufficiently challenging. Or simply not for them.

The *person specification*, on the other hand, should be framed to give a clear indication of the levels of competence believed by the school to be required to undertake the role successfully. This will include minimum level of professional qualification, competence and experience required for the post, and it should outline the criteria by which applicants will finally be judged at interview. The normal practice currently is to divide up these various elements into *essential* and *desirable* categories. This not only helps prospective candidates make a fully informed choice about whether they are able to meet the criteria but also provides a convenient checklist of criteria by which the short-listing team can make their selections. The interview team will also base their questions around these documents. The short-listing team will normally comprise the headteacher, a representative from the pupil and personnel subcommittee of the governing body and a staff representative or representatives. In the interests of equal opportunities, it is helpful if one member of the short-listing team has, as part of their brief, to ensure those equal opportunities criteria are adhered to and that discussion does not stray from the essential and desirable criteria outlined for applicants. LEAs now have well established procedures and training opportunities for managing the selection process, firmly setting the process within a framework of equal opportunities guidelines. These should be followed rigorously in the interests of consistency and fairness to candidates not only in the short-listing process but also throughout the whole selection exercise.

Categories	Knowledge	Competences	Interpersonal skills
Teaching			
Planning			
Creating			
Communicating			
Motivating			
Organizing			
Evaluating			
Leading			

Figure 7.1   What we are looking for in a new appointment?

The checklist in Figure 7.1 can be a useful focus for staff discussion in compiling both the job description and the person specification. However, a startling omission often made when considering who constitutes the major stakeholders in a needs assessment exercise and therefore has a right to be involved in the process, is the 'client group' themselves, the pupils. While not wishing to suggest that pupils take part at the formal interview stage, they none the less have a legitimate part to play in the process leading up to the interview. This can be considered as an important dimension to their social learning, as well as underlining their responsibility for ownership in the school as a community. Asking pupils to think carefully about what qualities they value or appreciate in a teacher, caretaker or school secretary can lead into important discussion. Discussion of itself, though valuable, may not be enough to reinforce learning. Pupils need to be actively involved in the outcomes from such discussion. One example of this might be the production of materials sent to candidates to brief them about the school. Pupils should be encouraged to take an active part in presenting the school to the candidates on or before the interview day and in the presentation of paper-based information sent out to prospective candidates. Pupils can be encouraged to talk to and question candidates, later giving staff valuable insights which they might themselves have missed. After all, pupils have most to gain or lose if a poor appointment is made. Aspy and Roebuck (1977), in their famous study 'Kids Don't Learn From Teachers They Don't Like', make the point very tellingly that it is the interpersonal, relational competences of the teacher which influence the academic and social attainment of the pupil above all else.

Another important result of highlighting pupil involvement is that of promoting what Bandura calls self-efficacy (1995) and Lefcourt (1976) locus of control. Individuals with a high internal locus of control or self-efficacy feel able to take responsibility for their own lives, have control over their own destinies and take an active part in shaping life events. The message that we send pupils when we involve them in any important aspect of the school's life is that, as adults, we value what they have to say, they can make a difference and that they can actively influence the future direction of the school community.

The non-involvement of pupils in an important school process sends very clear, if unspoken, messages about pupils' place in the school hierarchy of influence, thus reducing their feeling of control over events. The lesson they learn is that adults shape their lives and that they have little or no control over the process. Feelings of autonomy, interest and ownership diminish. It is interesting to note that Lefcourt's (1976) work into locus of control indicates that internality is related to positive self-concept, high self-esteem, greater social influence, greater self-reliance, being less anxious, having fewer psychosomatic symptoms and coping better with stress. As educators, no doubt we would wish to promote these competences in children and young people. What we need to do is avoid paying lip-service and offer real opportunities for them to make a difference. An appropriate and planned role in the staffing process can be one of these occasions.

> *Assessing needs, then, prior to advertising for a vacancy is a crucial part of the selection process. In schools where there is a policy of continuous self-appraisal it need not occupy much time or energy. What is important is that the assessing is looked at from various points of view: the needs of the pupils; the needs of individual teachers; and the needs of the staff as a whole. The intention should be to generate a realistic but comprehensive category of competences, professional and interpersonal, necessary for the post. Without this it will not be possible to match the potential skills and qualities of the applicants to the needs of the school.*

Searching: looking for a match

Whole-school policies stand or fail on the quality of each individual within the school community playing his or her part in the total process. One or two careless appointments can undo hours of well thought-through policy at the tactical level. Senior managers should try to avoid creating a hierarchy of appointments. There is a temptation to spend lavish thinking time on the appointment of a headteacher and very little on the appointment of a school secretary, although we know that each in their own way contributes to the overall effective functioning of the school. As carers, we know the pain and humiliation which can be brought about for a young child by an unthinking sour word or a scathing personal comment, not just from teachers but ancillary, support staff too. One of the writers has a child who is deaf in one ear and like most primary age children, is very sensitive to his 'difference'. During a noisy lunch time, a playground assistant tried and failed to get his attention, resorting finally to 'What's then matter with you then? Deaf are you?' He was very distressed and it was interesting to note how upset his friends were on his behalf. They too recognized insensitivity when they heard it. We've also overheard crushing comments from well-meaning secretaries to pupils such as: 'Late again with your dinner money. Can't you tell your mother to get more organized!'

School staff are only too well aware of the physical dangers that young children are subject to at the hands of adults. The emotional dangers may be less visible but are none the less as disastrous in their impact and consequences for relationships between home and school.

How then can the school ensure a suitable match between their needs and the needs and aspirations of potential applicants? This pairing process is most likely to be successful if the quality of the information provided for candidates is of the highest order. The education service has something

Activity 7.3: Preparing the further details for applicants

When preparing information for applicants the following set of questions will help you focus the team's thinking:

Type of school
- What sort of community does it serve?
- What specialist facilities does it have? Is it open plan?
- Do staff change year groups every year?
- How are curriculum decisions made?
- What is the school policy on equal opportunities?

Teaching role
- How many pupils and in what age range?
- What is the range of equipment and resources? What does the classroom look like?
- Are there policies about teaching style or curriculum guidelines?

Special responsibilities
- Is there a job description with lines of accountability made clear?
- Are there funds available for development?
- Is this a new or a replacement post?

Parents/community
- Is there a school policy on community education? What is the neighbourhood like?
- Are parents active in the school?
- Is there a PTA or parents' association?

Professional support
- Are there regular staff meetings?
- Is there a staff development policy?
- Are there regular appraisal interviews?
- Is there school-based in-service work?
- Are staff involved in policy-making?
- Is there a mentor scheme

of a poor reputation in the area of the provision of information for candidates. Potential applicants are expected to consider a major upheaval in their working circumstances on the barest of information about the job being offered, and sometimes when applicants seek an opportunity to visit a school where a vacancy exists they are received only grudgingly. The whole system of appointing staff seems to be built on the wrong assumption. Some schools and local authorities give applicants the impression that they are doing teachers a favour by offering up teaching posts for application. The opposite is true. There is widespread discontent that some teachers, having spent considerable time and care in preparing applications in response to advertisements, receive no letters of acknowledgement or even a note regretting that on this occasion they have not been successful. However, this does say something about the prevailing culture of the school and needs to be addressed.

Cost is the main reason used to explain why advertising for teaching posts is so often inadequate. All that an advertisement can be these days is an indication that a teaching post is available at a particular school and that more detailed information can be obtained on request. However, it is the first stage of the school's external presentation of itself to potential applicants and should be clear, focused and invitational in tone. The next part of the appointing exercise – the provision of the further details – is vitally important and should also be approached with the determination to provide interested teachers with as clear a picture as possible of the school, and of the teaching vacancy that has arisen within it.

The first purpose the initial details serve is to limit the number of applicants. There can be no justification for putting anyone to the time and expense of applying for a post for which they are unqualified or for which they do not satisfy the basic criteria. The aim must be to attract positively those candidates who do satisfy the identified requirements and to inhibit those whose applications will not receive serious consideration. From the details the candidate should not only be able to gain a clear appreciation of the job involved, the personal and professional qualifications required, but also, something of the values and culture of the school itself and the wider community it serves.

The list in Activity 7.3 is by no means complete, but is one that provides a useful agenda for preparing documents that supply candidates with information about, and insights into, the life and working of the school. The final pack sent to candidates might then usefully include those items in Figure 7.2.

The next stage is to prepare documentation. How the documentation is presented will convey a great deal about the value system of the school. Shoddy or hastily produced papers, which then on reading claim that the school prides itself on high standards, raise the question about lack of congruence and self-awareness. Information prepared in the first person, either singular or plural, will make a personal, more direct appeal and also serves to initiate a written conversation to which the candidate will respond in the letter of application.

Finally, the application form itself. Generally the nature, style and composition of the written application are left for candidates to decide. Most teaching posts from a main professional grade to headship are applied for in the same generalized way of completed application form plus a supporting letter. Written applications could become a much more profound and effective part of the selection procedure if steps were taken to encourage candidates to address themselves to the specific issues of the post under consideration rather than the generalized matters of concern to the profession as a whole. One step towards this end is the preparation of guidelines for the completion of the application. By specifying the issues for consideration in the application form, we ensure that the candidates' statements in support of their application actually relate to the post and

The pack to inquirers may contain some or all of the following:
- A brief vision statement from the chair of governors and headteacher.
- The job description and person specification.
- The application form, and supplementary question sheet.
- A selection from the staff handbook, which includes equal opportunities statements, the school development plan, whole-school policies, plan of the building and so on.
- Letters written about the school or a particular class from pupils – these letters might make clear *their* expectations of a new teacher.
- Pupils' statements about aspects of the school they enjoy or might want to be different.
- A school brochure with photographs of the classes at work or the areas of the building that the appointee will have responsibility for.
- A parent-teacher (or similar) association newsletter. This will also contain information about school involvement in local or national community projects, and press cuttings about recent school events; and information about formal and informal social events throughout the school year.

Figure 7.2 Sample information pack to candidates: communicating the school culture

not to wider, more general and potentially irrelevant material. The aim should be to enable the candidates to prepare an application that gives the selection team the maximum amount of relevant, focused information on which to base their final judgement. One idea would be to issue candidates with a supplementary question sheet, designed to elicit particular information not covered by the application form – the question sheet shown in Figure 7.3 is offered as an example.

It is becoming increasingly common for potential applicants to want to visit schools before committing themselves to a formal application for a post. This is a very sensible preliminary step for the teacher, providing an opportunity for the candidate to gain insights into the school and the way it works. Secondly, it provides an opportunity for the head and the staff to meet a potential colleague.

Nothing less than a half-day in a school is likely to be adequate to satisfy the candidate's needs. In arranging the visit the head and staff need to be aware of its fundamental purpose – to create conditions in which the match of person to post, and post to person, can be assessed. In the expectation that a number of candidates will accept the invitation to visit it is necessary to have agreed a procedure for managing the visit. The following checklist suggests the different elements of a visit:

- Seeing the building, inside and out.
- Visiting classrooms and talking to pupils.
- Noting specialist facilities: resources, library and so on.
- Meeting staff informally.
- Informal interview with a senior member of staff not involved directly in the selection process.

Please suggest a few strategies for improving staff involvement in curriculum development. Try to give practical examples you have been involved with.	
Please comment on your reactions to any of the National Curriculum documents relevant to this post.	
How do you suggest topic work can be improved as a central element in the primary curriculum?	
Which particular aspect of in-service training has been of help in preparing you for this post?	
What opportunities for professional development would you wish to undertake in the next few years?	
What would you regard as the single most significant contribution you have made to your present school?	

Figure 7.3   A supplementary question sheet

In organizing such a visit it is important to consider who should do the conducted tour of the school, especially if the headteacher has a full-time teaching commitment. In the interest of equal opportunities, this is best undertaken by a member of staff other than the head. It is also worthwhile for the visitor to get another teacher's view of the school and it is likely to be easier for the visitor to raise issues that might be difficult if the head were conducting the tour. In order to allow some space and time for the visitor to get a 'feel' of the school it is good to keep the tour reasonably short and then to invite the visitor to wander. This allows the candidate an opportunity just to absorb what is going on, to think out possibilities, to anticipate experiences, to sense the organizational dynamics and to reflect on impressions. Motivation will be a key consideration, and will be based on the answers to such implicit questions as, 'Am I encouraged by what I see here?', 'Can I work in this atmosphere, with these colleagues and pupils?' and 'Is this school likely to develop me and help me grow, both personally and professionally?' The discussion with the senior member of staff is in reality an interview conducted by the candidate. It is his or her opportunity to gain information on a range of issues about the running of the school and the ways in which the new member of staff is expected to contribute.

However, such an informal visit, conducted at the potential applicant's request should not take the place of a scheduled school orientation on the interview day itself. From an equal opportunity view point, it is clear that not all candidates would be able to undertake such a visit, for example if they lived a great distance from the school. Therefore it is imperative that all candidates have an opportunity to meet staff and pupils on the day of the interview. Some schools even timetable in the opportunity for candidates to work with a group of pupils, in order to gain some evidence of the candidates' classroom behaviour. If this is the case then again, candidates need to be told well in advance of the interview day what will be expected of them. The golden rule to remember is – there should be no surprises. The idea is not to catch a candidate doing the wrong thing, but to give him or her opportunities to perform at his or her best.

A *reference* or *confidential report* is a formal way of conveying information from someone who has a sound working knowledge of a candidate to an organization which is seeking to fill a vacant post. Once the short-list has been drawn up, with the short-list team using the essential and desirable criteria drawn from the job and person specification, references for the short-listed candidates will be taken up. These references will subsequently be made available to the interview team on the interview day to inform the final decision-making process. Generally, reference protocol demands that the referee give factual evidence and avoids opinion, and that references remain entirely confidential. If the referee does not take reasonable care, then it is possible that there is legal liability in negligence. Malicious references, designed to ensure that the candidate is unsuccessful, have recently been the subject of legal dispute. There may be personal liability in defamation, malicious falsehood or deceit, depending on the circumstances. Such references should always be ignored, particularly when there is no evidential basis provided to support the referee's claims.

Too often references are vague and unfocused, generally because the referees are responding to vague, unfocused questions. If specific information is not asked for then it is unlikely to be supplied, and what will be produced is a general appraisal that is characterized by excessive use of superlatives, or couched in the jargon of euphemism. What inquirers often seem to be seeking is an indication whether the candidate justifies an unreserved recommendation – a sort of five-year guarantee of good service – or not. This at best is a naive request, at worst an encouragement to be unprofessional, since it suggests that the referee is in a position to offer service guarantees, as if for a washing machine. What should be asked for is an evidentially based assessment of those skills and qualities in the candidate that specifically relate to the job under consideration.

There are a number of ways to obtain this information. First, referees should be provided with a full briefing about the post and its requirements, usually in the form of the job description and person specification, with the essential and desirable criteria; secondly, an opportunity to give information under very specific headings relating to the specifics of the post; and, finally, the opportunity to represent the candidate's interests on issues not specifically referred to in the question sheets supplied. The sample question sheets we provide here (Figures 7.4 and 7.5) are two possible routes to supplementing referees' general appraisals of candidates because they seek to gain specific information about the applicant's professional abilities, experience and behaviour. This enables the referee to offer evidence of performance rather than opinion about it. Used in combination, these two documents can provide a far more detailed and helpful appraisal of the candidate than the four or five paragraphs of general summary usually supplied.

From your experience and knowledge of the candidate, please comment on the following:
What are the applicant's particular skills in and experience of building a classroom climate conducive to effective learning?
What are the applicant's particular skills in classroom organization and management?
What do you consider having been the most positive outcomes from the applicant's work with pupils?
Which particular qualities in the applicant would you consider being especially relevant to the post under consideration?
What particular contribution has the applicant made to life in the staffroom and to staff discussion?
Which of the applicant's personal qualities have contributed most to the school?

Figure 7.4 Sample question sheet to referees (1)

Matching: the interview process

By the time the interview day arrives, scrupulous preparation will have ensured that key staff involved in the final selection process will be able to make a fair decision based on accumulated evidence, consistently rated against known criteria. In essence there should be no surprises in this process for either school staff or candidates. However given the financial, professional and educational ramifications of making a poor choice at interview, it is quite surprising that so much faith is still invested in it as a method of employee selection.

More and more private companies are using commercial assessment centres which conduct lengthy interviews and subject candidates to batteries of tests in order to assure prospective employers that the employer/employee fit is as exact as possible, and that the best possible decision in the selection of human resources is being made. It is a process which it is considered should not be left to chance, fate or clairvoyance!

From your experience and knowledge, please indicate your assessment of the applicant's qualities by ringing one of the numbers in each category.

1. Excellent   2. Very good   3. Good   4. Adequate   5. Less than adequate

Creating an effective classroom learning environment	1	2	3	4	5
Planning programmes of work	1	2	3	4	5
Building relationships with pupils	1	2	3	4	5
Matching work to the ability of pupils	1	2	3	4	5
Working with colleagues	1	2	3	4	5
Motivating pupils	1	2	3	4	5
Relationships with parents	1	2	3	4	5
Energy and commitment	1	2	3	4	5
Evaluating and monitoring work	1	2	3	4	5
Responding to and developing new ideas	1	2	3	4	5
Flexibility of approach	1	2	3	4	5
Ability to seek help and support	1	2	3	4	5
Ability to give help and support	1	2	3	4	5
Awareness of own strengths and weaknesses	1	2	3	4	5
Dealing with challenging behaviour	1	2	3	4	5

Figure 7.5 Sample question sheet to referees (2)

However, for public institutions like schools, the cost constraints of such a process would rule out assessment centres as an option, even if senior managers felt it was a principled way forward. In fact, teachers still retain a somewhat simple faith in their ability to make judgements about others' potential – in fact they spend much of their professional time doing just that! There is an enduring belief in the interview process which is likely to remain with us for the foreseeable future. Finally, interviews still remain the most cost-effective solution to the process of selection – a constraint which is unlikely to disappear. Peters (1987) claims that 'A lengthy set of interviews unmistakably demonstrates that the firm cares enough about the candidate and the working environment to get people at all levels deeply involved in recruitment'.

But irrespective of the length of the interview or the positive cultural messages it sends, how reliable and valid is it as an instrument for selection and how fair or ethical are they? Riches and Morgan (1989) remind us that we should '. . . view job selection as a procedure concerned with predicting future job performance and ensuring that the criteria the selection procedure uses have predictive validity. By predictive validity is meant that the evidence used in the selection decisions does in fact relate to performance in the real job situation'.

Estimates of the reliability of *structured interviews* are put at around 0.82, while *unstructured interviews* are estimated at 0.62. Validity estimates for structured interviews are put at around 0.62, and for unstructured interviews, 0.31. In each case, it is clear that the structured interview is the best predictor of future on-the-job performance and therefore the fairest method of selection. Both reliability and validity of interviewer selection within a structured interview (and remember that this is not an exact science) can be enhanced by four key elements: training for interview teams in interview techniques, selecting against key job requirements, systematically collecting and recording evidence; and using a standard, consistent rating scale to interpret the evidence. There are two main models of a structured interview. The *situational approach* asks candidates to consider what they would do in a variety of hypothetical situations, for example:

- 'What would you do if a pupil was threatening you with a knife?' Or,
- 'How would you respond if your headteacher tried to impose a strict dress code for staff?'

The pitfalls of this type of situational questioning are immediately apparent. The quick-thinking, imaginative candidate is advantaged by the potential in the creativity of the response; however the danger is that the response may, or may not, be the response the team wanted to hear. Coupled with this is the uncertainty as to whether the candidate would *actually* behave in that way in the real-life situation.

The maxim that *past behaviour is the best predictor of future behaviour* leads us to the second model of structured interviews, the *behavioural interview*. Such an approach aims to investigate the candidate's previous work experience with a view to eliciting what he or she did and what the subsequent outcomes were, providing evidence where possible. Questions such as:

In your letter of application, you talked about your belief in music as a means for children to express their creativity. Can you tell us how you have structured lessons to draw this element out and, if you would, also give some examples of the ways in which the children demonstrated their creativity?

In this way, it can be seen that the candidate is being asked to elaborate on an expressed belief by describing a real situation he or she has tackled, what he or she did in the situation and what the outcomes were for pupils. Clearly, though, even in this model it is possible for the candidate to talk from the perspective of the 'ideal educator' which may or may not reflect the reality of the pupils' experience.

Structured and, in particular, behaviourally based interviews, can also, and very importantly, give interview teams the confidence to proceed within an ethical framework because this type of interview ensures that the format provides an equality of opportunity for each candidate to talk about previous experience, not fantasise about what they would do in the future. What then, are the key features of structured interviews? First, that all the interview questions will be related to core competencies previously outlined in the job and person specifications. Secondly, that candidates are asked the same questions, usually in the same order. Secondary or probe questions will then clearly be dependent on the candidates' initial response. Thirdly, that candidates' replies are systematically rated by the interview team.

Unstructured interviews, on the other hand, where the interviewer relies to a large extent on his or her ability to judge candidates on the strength of inconsistent or confusing evidence, do not provide candidates with an equal opportunity framework and clearly the potential for discriminatory behaviour by the interviewer is heightened in such a situation. Questions may be asked at random, unrelated to the job specification, and impressions and hunches become key factors in the decision-making process. There is also a danger with an unstructured interview that the personality of the interviewers dominates and they can spend more time talking than the candidates. If there is a team of interviewers conducting the interview, they may also give different weighting to the same information, without a systematic agreed rating scale.

Good practice, then, is to ensure that the school's equal opportunities policy is alive and well in the selection interview. Candidates can be confident that this is a school which lives out its anti-discriminatory practices as well as produces policies on them. Unsuccessful candidates, while disappointed, will derive comfort in no small part to the satisfaction that they were rejected on a principled basis, not from the whim or fancy of a powerful individual or individuals on the interview team. This is particularly important when there is an internal candidate at interview. The emotional investment in this situation for all staff in the school can only be contained if every precaution has been taken to ensure fairness and that the procedure is transparent.

The team conducting the interview bear considerable responsibility for enabling the candidate to show what he or she is capable of and to be sufficiently at ease to provide the information the panel will need if it is to do its work well. It should always be the aim of an interviewing panel to enable candidates to perform at their best. Creating this climate conducive to bringing the best out of people is not a difficult or complicated one, although some interviewing teams in our experience find it difficult to manage. Whoever chairs the interview team should set the tone. This should be warm, friendly and courteous. An adversarial or an overly challenging manner is best avoided, as it heightens candidate anxiety and may produce competitive, macho behaviour at interview.

Introductions and handshakes set the scene and the candidate should be asked how he or she would like to be referred to. Some candidates prefer the relative informality of first names, some candidates prefer the apparent safety of formality. Cultural difference will have an impact here and interview teams should avoid making early, impressionistic judgements about a candidate's interpersonal skills at this stage. The point of common courtesies is to put the candidate at ease not to begin the selection process before he or she has even taken his or her seat.

During the course of the interview (and in the decision-making that follows it) a number of skills are utilized:

- questioning
- listening
- observing
- summarizing
- assessing
- debriefing.

Each of these will be discussed in turn.

Questioning

This includes all verbal strategies designed to promote candidate talk. There is always a danger that those interviewing will do far more of the talking than they should, thereby failing to draw from the candidate sufficient data on which to base an informed judgement.

Questions are really invitations for the candidate to talk. Sometimes the best way to facilitate this is not to ask questions at all, but to define an area upon which you would like the candidate's comments. For example, on the issue of classroom organization a possible question could be: 'What factors should be taken into account when someone is setting up a classroom for a Year-6 class?'

There are a number of limitations to this question. First, it generalizes the issue, asking the candidate to comment hypothetically on what teachers in general might regard as significant factors in classroom organization. Secondly, it invites a somewhat superficial response since situational factors will be of the essence – the size of the classroom, the previous experience of the pupils, the preferred teaching style of the school and the educational philosophy prevailing within it. Thirdly, it limits the candidate to theoretical issues rather than practical ones. Perhaps a better, behaviourally based way to frame the question would be: 'Would you like to tell us about the process you go through at the beginning of each academic year when you prepare the classroom for your new class?'

This 'open' question has a number of advantages. First, since it is not a 'closed' question designed to elicit specific, predetermined information, it does not presuppose a single correct answer. Secondly, it draws upon the most significant aspect of the candidate's capacity to do the job – his or her practical classroom experience. Thirdly, it provides an opportunity for the interviewer to match the candidate's perception of an issue with information already obtained from other sources – the visit of the head to the candidate's classroom perhaps or the specific information about classroom organization received in the confidential report. An important consideration in the interview process is the extent to which the candidate's perception of his or her work matches that of others.

In preparing themselves for selection interviews candidates are often preoccupied by the type of questions they may be asked rather than the areas they may be invited to comment upon. This emphasizes one of the myths about selection – that success depends on getting the answers to the questions *right*. Such a view misunderstands the true nature of the interview. Far more is of interest in the interview than simply the answers to questions. The basic intelligence of the candidates is rarely at issue. It is how they actually perform in the school setting which is the subject of inquiry and clarification. Candidates need to be helped to understand the fundamental purpose of the interview and interviewers can help by stating this clearly at the outset. The interview is concerned more with what they have learnt from experience and with elucidating their particular skills and competences than with mere knowledge. For this reason, it is important that invitations to talk are not merely questions requiring a simple factual answer. Obviously some factual data may need to be established during the interview and some closed questions may be necessary, but the bulk of the interview should be concerned with drawing out from the candidate the more profound aspects of professional ability and potential.

What we are trying to discover or confirm in the candidate is basically information about:

- the candidate's knowledge of, and understanding of, the processes of teaching and learning;
- the candidate's practical skills and qualities; and
- the candidate's attitudes and core professional values

There is a relationship between the phrasing of questions and the category of information elicited. Open questions will establish rapport and enable the candidate to respond more freely:

- 'What', 'when' and 'where' questions usually elicit factual information.
- 'How' questions usually elicit practical information.
- 'Why' questions usually elicit motives, attitudes and values but need to be used with care because they can be perceived as interrogatory.

Open questions can be followed up with *probes* which seek to get beneath the surface and look for evidence. They are useful in helping the candidate to focus on specifics, and increase the likelihood of providing the interview team with information on which to make an informed judgement. *Leading questions* are best avoided as they can trap the unwary candidate into giving the answer he or she believes the interviewers want to hear. Similarly with *multiple questions* candidates can feel lost, trapped or confused by a barrage of questions.

From the candidates' perspective, there is a tendency to respond to questions with what they are most comfortable with, rather than with the information that has been asked for. Interviewers need to be on their guard for this inclination to answer a different question from the one asked. When probed about attitudes and values, candidates will sometimes try to avoid that issue by offering an example from practical experience. A supplementary question is vital if the panel is to obtain a comprehensive understanding of the candidate's ability – far too often the candidate's answer is accepted and the questioning moved on to another issue or another member of the panel. It is much more profitable to stay on an issue and probe deeper into it, using the candidate's first answer as the cue for a more penetrating inquiry. When, for example, the candidate has offered a 'what' answer to a 'why' question, it is important to press the point and seek out the 'why'.

Active listening

The ability to listen effectively in the interview is of fundamental importance. Far from consisting merely of hearing what is said, listening is the active and dynamic process of attempting to gain insights into the perceptual, intellectual and emotional world of the candidate. This involves a capacity to relate the candidate's responses and to pick out the distinguishing features of the candidate's presentation. In terms of the three categories already referred to this means being able to distinguish between answers that provide factual information, those that indicate skills and qualities, and those that reveal motives, attitudes and values.

In the interview, listening operates on at least two levels. First, there is listening to make sense out of the current response – the immediate question. Secondly, there is listening to see how this answer relates to others that have come before or that will follow later. This is listening for consistency – the extent to which the candidate reveals a cohesive and compatible pattern of theory and practice. This second level of listening requires a capacity to pick out the underlying themes in the candidate's responses, in particular prejudices, ambiguities and inconsistencies.

Interviewers should demonstrate their active listening non-verbally, through an attentive body posture with a slight forward lean. This will demonstrate attentiveness on the part of the questioner and enable the candidate to talk further. If the candidate puts forward views or opinions which members of the team feel strongly about – either positively or negatively – they should withhold demonstrating either approval or disapproval. Even non-verbal indications will send strong messages to the candidate about the status of his or her response. Active listening therefore also means suspending judgements and holding off initial impressions. Keeping assumptions at bay while someone talks means that listening without prejudice becomes a possibility and the candidate will be more likely to reveal him or herself fully to you in his or her responses.

Observing and recording

The skill of observing means to draw inferences from the candidate's verbal and non-verbal behaviour during the interview. Most interviewers can detect signs of nervousness in a candidate – a somewhat stiff posture, fidgety hands, a shaky voice – but may not be so aware of other aspects of non-verbal behaviour. Since the candidate's behaviour is likely to make an impression on each member of the interviewing team, it is important to make it an explicit feature of the selection process. For example, if from the person specification it was made clear that the teacher must be approachable and welcoming in his or her manner, then it is appropriate to look for non-verbal as well as verbal indications/evidence of this competence. Interviewers should avoid making personal interpretations, for example, 'I didn't like the way she smiled all the time. Is she looking for approval, do you think?'

During the summing-up and decision-making process it is essential that these aspects of the candidate are dealt with openly, rather than left only as private but powerful impressions. The purpose of observing how people behave is to gain an understanding of why they behave as they do. The categories of non-verbal behaviour of significance in the interview will be:

* facial expression
* eye contact
* voice tone
* gestures
* body posture.

In combination these represent the candidate's 'presenting image'. There is always a danger that incorrect interpretations will be drawn and this is another reason why some discussion of this dimension is important.

Note-taking is a vital aid to effective listening in the selection interview. Since the process of interviewing itself requires considerable concentration, it is important that data is recorded so that it can be recalled during the decision-making process. A grid with a standard rating scale should be supplied to each member of the interview team, with a space to make comments against the established criteria, previously drawn from the job and person specifications.

Generally the more interviewer-friendly the rating scales the better. An elaborate scale can prove distracting and time-consuming later on, while a simple 1–5 or A–E is generally sufficient basis for discussion. A standard grid format makes for clarity and consistency between the team members. After each candidate has left the interview room, the team should take time to complete their grids with comments and scores but should refrain from discussing the candidate before all the interviews are completed.

Summarizing

From time to time during the interview it is helpful to summarize progress. This provides an opportunity to check out with the candidate ground that has been covered, and also that the candidate's view has been correctly received. In addition, it provides an opportunity for the interviewing team to assess its own progress. It is during the final decision-making discussion that the skill of summarizing is most important. The chair of the interview, when reviewing the interviews, should be able to reflect an accurate summary of the candidate's strengths and weaknesses as perceived by the team, recorded evidentially on the grid sheet. This overview will need to be supplemented later with information and assessments from visits and confidential reports.

To present such a summary requires some sort of framework. A summary could be built on the interview recording grid or the summary could be arranged under a set of categories decided upon before the interview:

- Ability to deal with the interview.
- Interview behaviour and 'presenting image'.
- Professional knowledge and understanding.
- Skills and qualities.
- Attitudes and values.
- Relationship of abilities to job requirements.
- Estimation of potential to do the job.

Wherever possible the team should be encouraged to adopt a standard procedure for summarizing and assessing each candidate. Far too often the final selection procedure rests on the exchange of personal impressions unrelated to the requirements of the job under consideration.

Assessing

This is the skill of drawing conclusions from the evidence obtained about each candidate. This part of the procedure is facilitated considerably if the summarizing described above has been of a high order. In working towards the final choice of candidate it is important to proceed by elimination – no candidate should be eliminated without discussion. If the procedures before the interview were carried out effectively, all the candidates called should have the potential to do the job. Some may not interview as well as others and the skill of assessment is about distinguishing between interview expertise and wider professional ability. It is at this stage that it is necessary to remind the team of those particular abilities and aptitudes hoped for in the successful candidate and also the important personal qualities that need to accompany them. The following checklist suggests the factors that need to be included in the assessment that precedes the final choice of candidate:

- A restatement of the current and future needs of the school.
- A restatement of the job requirements.
- A restatement of the skills and qualities hoped for.
- Summaries of the interviews of each candidate.
- Discussion of each candidate's interview.
- Presentation of information previously received.

Part of the assessment process is comparing the first-hand evidence of each candidate in the interview with reports received from other sources. It is not enough to make a choice purely on the basis of the interview itself. The interview stands as part of a comprehensive selection process and needs to be seen in the context of that wider perspective.

Most interviews for teaching seem to last between twenty and forty minutes. If the interview, as perceived in this chapter, is to succeed in becoming a more effective instrument in the process of staff selection, it is necessary to plan for interviews that are somewhat longer. This will provide an opportunity for more supplementary questioning, a chance to go into some issues in greater depth, and more scope for exploring the range of a candidate's qualities and abilities.

Feedback to candidates: debriefing

By the end of a long and possibly stressful interview day, the temptation is to inform the successful candidate and notify the others of the team's decision. However, the team have a professional responsibility to offer *all* candidates, successful and unsuccessful, the opportunity for feedback from the interview. In cases where the all candidates are still present in the school, individual panel members may be delegated the responsibility to debrief particular candidates. Where the panel's decision is communicated by letter or telephone, again it is important that candidates are given the opportunity to receive feedback. The debrief should avoid comparisons with other candidates and concentrate solely on those aspects of the candidate's performance which were related to the selection process. If the candidate wishes to ask more personal questions about how he or she might improve interview performance, then it should be made clear that such a view, if given, is from a purely personal viewpoint. The spirit in which such feedback should be offered is with the awareness that the candidate has a choice of taking up the offer or not and that he or she may well feel that shortly after the interview decision has been made known is too soon to assimilate the information properly.

Beginning: the induction and support of new staff

A planned process of induction and support should be the entitlement of new staff, irrespective of role, status or contract. If this process is skimped or the 'sink or swim' mentality allowed to predominate, then the long-term consequences for the school can be dire. Schmidt *et al.* (1992) maintain that, 'A comprehensive induction reduces start-up costs, lowers anxiety, lessens subsequent turnover, increases job satisfaction and perhaps most important, develops realistic job expectations'.

We know from both theory and practice (Tuckman, 1965; Johnson and Johnson, 1991) the importance of managing the forming stages of a group's development with an awareness of the human relations or psychological dimension to the process. Wise teachers know that it is not enough to point out what is expected of pupils at the beginning of a new school year but that they also must take responsibility for creating a social climate in the classroom which is conducive to co-operation and collaborative learning. The parallel with staff induction is clear. The process is no different when it falls to senior staff to manage induction in such a way that new staff feel welcomed and valued. A long speech from a headteacher declaring that the appointee is joining a team and what a wonderful school it is cuts no ice if, from then on in, you are on your own. Simple, thoughtful acts, like an invitation to talk over coffee, a bunch of flowers on a classroom table, being asked to join a group for lunch or 'any time you need me, I'm right down the corridor', can alleviate anxiety and promote confidence.

The induction of newly qualified staff into the school community will have a difference in emphasis from, say, that of a new deputy headteacher, but the goals remain the same: to introduce new staff to the school in terms of vision, values, culture, organization and tasks and in this caring process, demonstrate a commitment to enhancing the feelings of worth in all staff. McDougle (1982) describes the induction or orientation process as one which should promote, '. . . a feeling of self-worth, a sense of pride and confidence in both self and the organization and a desire to succeed'.

Most staff and some pupils in the school will have some part to play in the orientation process. For example, while the headteacher may wish to introduce the new member of staff to the vision, values and partnerships of the school, the caretaker might usefully be asked to show him or her all the nooks and crannies of the building. The deputy head may have conversations about systems of school organization, while the school secretary discusses the practicalities of those systems. The principle at work here is that the new member of staff should be introduced to the widest possible range of staff and the information given in digestible chunks. This also provides informal opportunities to forge interpersonal bonds with new and established members of staff, which will in turn lower levels of tension and anxiety for the newcomer. Pupils too should be allowed the opportunity to play their part in welcoming newcomers. The consideration which is generally afforded to pupils on entry into the school can then be reciprocated and lessons relating to social and personal development learnt. The sooner the individual feels drawn into the centre of the organization, instead of standing alone on the periphery, the sooner he or she will feel able to contribute most effectively in all aspects of his or her work. It is up to the school to provide opportunities for this movement to take place and up to the newly appointed member of staff to take full advantage of them.

Once the school has appointed the person they believe to be the most competent to do the job, there begins a serious professional commitment to ensure that the relationship is both profitable and developmental for each party. The process of selection will have been a costly one in terms of staff time and energy, yet ironically, relatively little thought or planning is given to the subsequent process of induction. Too often induction can literally mean being given the register, a set of keys, shown the classroom and literally thrown in at the deep end, particularly for temporary staff or supply staff, who may be seen as a disposable resource. This 'sink or swim' mentality is still far too widespread. A widely used and well respected text on school management, written as recently as 1990, talked about the induction day in terms of rooms, keys, school rules and a guided tour. We would want to argue that this mechanistic approach to the process of induction is at best ill-conceived at worst irresponsible. McDougle (1982) reminds us that 'Most experts agree that the attitudes developed during the first few days contribute greatly to the subsequent work ethic adopted'.

This process of becoming an 'insider' can be both enabled and monitored through the establishment of a mentoring system in the school. Mentoring, or the 'buddy system' as the Americans sometimes call it, is a well established system of staff support and career development in both the public and private sectors. The awareness that new staff need a formalized relationship with a knowledgeable insider to help guide them through the daunting first few weeks, months or even years in a job, has, though, taken longer to filter through into the school system. There are many working models of the mentor/mentee relationship in the workplace. Historically, a mentor was someone with a senior organizational role who was prepared to give professional advice and support, usually informally, on career development to a junior colleague. This might take the form of advice-giving, door-opening or providing a professional role model. Such relationships might also exist across organizations. We once knew a teaching colleague who wrote to a prominent public educational figure inviting him to become her mentor and the invitation was accepted! The public figure clearly felt that this was one way in which he might contribute usefully to the development of up and coming members of the profession. In this patriarchal model of mentorship, the junior colleague was often treated as a talented protégée, whom the senior colleague wished to nurture for private satisfaction. It was not uncommon, because of the predominance of men in senior organizational positions, for the mentor to be male and the junior female. The pitfalls and potential iniquities of such a relationship are self-evident.

From an equal opportunity perspective, it is essential that any mentoring system which is set up within a school is wholly transparent and that the conditions under which the scheme is operated are clear. Fears (or hopes) that the relationship might lead to promotion or career acceleration need to be seen as groundless and for this reason headteachers should not make themselves available as individual mentors. The introduction of a mentor scheme could usefully be the subject of a whole-staff discussion.

Activity 7.4: Staff discussion points prior to establishing a mentor scheme

- Who qualifies to be a mentor? Is it senior, more experienced staff or can recently appointed staff also have something valuable to offer?
- What about the personal qualities needed in a mentor? Should there be a selection process? What might that process look like?
- Is it important that mentors do not also have a supervisory relationship with their mentees?
- How long might the relationship be expected to last?
- What training might mentors be expected to undergo to equip them for the demands of the role, for example counselling or guidance skills training?
- Might mentoring be a useful development opportunity for all staff, not only for those undergoing induction?
- What degree of confidentiality might both parties expect?
- How many meetings per term? How long might such meetings last?
- How might the contribution of mentors be recognized institutionally?

Whatever the outcome of such discussions, certain principles remain constant. First, that the mentor/mentee relationship is both supportive and developmental. It is designed to introduce new members of staff into school protocols in such a way that the mentee is able to inhabit fully the role to which he or she has been appointed with enthusiasm and confidence. Secondly, it is essential that the mentor has the willingness and emotional maturity to offer genuine support, which will display the best aspects of guidance and counselling (Watts, 1986). In this spirit, agenda-setting in the conversations must be primarily dictated by the emotional needs of the mentee, not by the institutional priorities of the mentor. Finally, the institution must recognize in some way the contribution that the mentor is making to the quality of life within the school.

Ending: when a member of staff leaves

The way in which this aspect of school renewal is managed says as much about the culture and values of the school community as does the selection process. Staff departures will be due to a whole variety of reasons. Most commonly, domestic reasons, professional and career progression, a simple desire for change, lowered self-esteem resulting from feeling inadequate to meet the demands of the role, or being made to feel incompetent by others, redundancy, end of contract, pregnancy, retirement, ill-health, death and in rare cases, sacking. For headteachers, whatever the reason for staff departure, this creates an opportunity to discover more about the culture of the school. The departing member of staff may feel able to give honest feedback about his or her perceptions of the school. An hour-long debrief interview, like an appraisal interview, can afford valuable insights for both parties and brings a sense of emotional and professional closure to an employment contract.

In some schools, where the cultural taboos operating against openness are strong, the process of staff departure is kept very secret. Headteachers may actively discourage staff from sharing information relating to their career moves and inadvertently produce a covert grapevine which either embellishes or distorts simple facts. Staff applying for posts elsewhere may be reluctant to share the information in case of rejection and the resulting loss of personal and professional face, in this instance their right to confidentiality, needs to be respected. However, they also lose the opportunity to be encouraged and supported in their professional ambitions by colleagues who value them.

On each occasion a member of staff leaves, groups within the school will experience a sense of loss akin to a bereavement. Genuine grieving takes place when it is a much-loved teacher or member of the support staff. It will be possible for many of us to recall from childhood memories of the sadness and the feelings of loss we experienced when a loved teacher retired or left the school. Making the parallel with a death experience may seem overly dramatic but in fact similar feelings, varying only in their intensity, are aroused when someone we have shared our lives with, through thick and thin, moves on. The cycle of emotional reactions that we experience, though, are the same: shock, denial, anger, readjustment and finally acceptance (Kubler Ross, 1970). Withholding information about a member of staff leaving is often justified on the grounds that to tell staff or pupils too soon will only upset them in the same way that an overly protective parent can try to shield a child from the experience of death. Both behaviours deny the opportunity to come to terms with the reality of loss, which means fully experiencing and acknowledging the pain before being able to move on and, as importantly, accept the new appointment fully.

As a primary school governor, one of the writers was involved in a situation where a member of staff was accidentally killed while leading a school trip. The way in which the headteacher, deputy teaching and support staff and governors were able to respond fully and openly in a situation which was both a personal and professional tragedy was inspirational. Pupils were encouraged to express their shock and grief both verbally and non-verbally. Parents were asked to discuss what had happened openly in order to help their children make sense of an experience which, to many, seemed to make little sense. Memorials and rituals were devised collaboratively by pupils and staff, which honoured the memory of a valued colleague and bound together a community united in its grief. It was the experience of coping in shared pain and grief which brought the community together. That experience of powerful human connection was, in the end, a growthful one. Schools where school managers resist or deny the community the opportunity to share in such experiences will inadvertently stunt the emotional growth of its members.

We know from medical practice that to withhold important information from people which affects their lives actually *increases* their recovery time, as well as coming to terms with events and moving on from them. 'Moving on' for a school staff may in some cases mean that the appointee is welcomed whole-heartedly and fully supported in the induction process. Vivid examples of the destructiveness of this process if not handled sensitively are illustrated when headteachers, who having given many years of devoted service to a school, retire and a new head takes up the post. If the school community has not been given appropriate opportunities to work through the emotional, as well as the professional, implications of the loss, there will be an extremely heavy burden for the new head to deal with. Leaving rituals for staff should be planned to celebrate the contribution the individual has made – whatever his or her role in the school.

Conclusion

The untutored headteacher may see staff turnover and the recruitment and selection of new staff as a wearisome burden in an already overburdened school calendar or an impediment to the social and professional stability of the school. The more enlightened head will seize the opportunity to involve members of the school community in a process which encourages critical self-reflection and evaluation. The natural flow of staff is a cyclical process which needs to be actively and self-consciously managed with an understanding of the part that such flow plays in the recreation and sustenance of a healthy school culture.

Further reading

Katzenbach, J. R. and Smith, D. K. (1993) *The Wisdom of Teams*, Harper Collins, New York.
Marczely, B. (1996) *Personalizing Professional Growth*, Corwin Press, California.

Morgan, G. (1989) *Creative Organisation Theory*, Sage, California.
Senge, P. M. (1992) *The Fifth Discipline: The Art and Practice of the Learning Organization*, Century Business, London.

8

Connecting with communities

Promoting partnerships • Parents and families in partnership with schools • Interagency partnerships • Partnership with the LEA • Relationships with OFSTED • School and higher education partnership • Business partnerships • In conclusion: looking to the future

Promoting partnerships

Those of us who work in or regularly visit primary schools will know the ways in which they serve as community thoroughfares. Visitors stream through the school gates daily, engaged in one way or another with enhancing the quality of educational opportunity afforded to young children. Partnerships with individuals and the communities they represent, public or private, are the oxygen of primary schools. Through these relationships, headteachers and staff are able to facilitate a huge range of learning opportunities and pastoral or welfare services, which feed the school's educational goals for its pupils.

Proactive, sustained and purposeful contact with external communities is an inescapable and necessary dimension to the education of the 'whole child'. Schools which cut themselves off from this source of oxygen will seriously diminish their capacity to provide vital and essential educational services for pupils as well stimulating learning experiences. But how might headteachers and senior teachers best manage this process, so that the balance is struck between a tidal wave of uncontrolled contacts and a purposeful, negotiated set of relationships which serves the educational goals of the school? We believe that the notion of *partnership* best captures the spirit of what it is schools need to achieve. Partnership can be defined as a reciprocal relationship in which the partners place the achievement of their mutual goals above self-interest. However, there are factors which promote or inhibit the successful growth of partnerships which need to be given serious consideration. Partnerships are grounded in interpersonal relationships, and the human relations dimension to the maintenance of partnerships cannot be overstated. In this chapter, we will outline factors which may inhibit the formation and maintenance of effective working partnerships in the educational process and suggest ways of overcoming them.

First, some of the inhibiting psychological factors. 'Cocooning' was a term coined by American social trend observers to describe a phenomenon which characterized the domestic lifestyle of professionals in the 1980s and 1990s. It described an instinctive survival mechanism which was triggered in reaction to attempts to manage an unbearable rapidity of change in the workplace. Information overload, an extended working day, more public systems of accountability, all contributed to a growing perception that stress was an inevitable consequence of the work experience. People began to look to their homes to provide a sanctuary or bulwark against the invasive tide of work. People spent less time in theatres, restaurants and cinemas and more time in front of their videos with a bottle of wine and a take-away meal. Public perceptions of local and national crime as being on the increase exacerbated this tendency to social and psychological isolationism. Cocooning, however, is not just an individualized phenomenon; it also reflects an institutional trend. Organizations like schools can and do show evidence of 'cocooning behaviours', because teachers in their professional role have literally perceived themselves to be under threat from the outside world.

What constitutes a 'cocoon' in organizational terms will vary from individual to individual. For many teachers the classroom itself provides this safe haven. For headteachers it may be their office. Paradoxically, the ever-present pile of paperwork provides a ready-made excuse not to venture out of their chosen 'cocoon'. Hargreaves (1995) argues that this tendency to isolationism is a result of the fear of exposure, primarily exposure to criticism, if practice is opened up to scrutiny. This fear is then publicly rationalized as the desire for 'teacher autonomy'. Isolationism becomes an unconscious or conscious process, a short-term adaptation strategy, with which teachers guard the time and energy they need to meet the instructional demands of their work (Flinders, 1988).

The publication of national league tables, OFSTED inspections, promises to weed out 'weak teachers', the media vilifications of failing schools and so on have all contributed to a widespread perception of being in the middle of a professional and social battlefield. The concomitant of this perception both psychologically and physically has been for teachers to separate themselves off from those aspects of work which produce most emotional pain (or the prediction of pain) or do not directly appeal to their vocational identity, and legitimate this separation on educational grounds.

In the most shocking of ways, this image of being under siege has been parallelled by a growing number of physical attacks upon schools themselves. Vandalism, graffiti, break-ins are commonplace in many of our city schools. Fortress-like defence systems with closed circuit television now ring the perimeter fences in postindustrial inner-city areas where unemployment is high and wages low. The desperate, unspeakable tragedy of Dunblane seemed to validate the harsh necessity to take such precautions against the potential for violation from outside. The public gave its tacit approval to look at ways in which schools could be made safe from the communities they served as a growing feeling of societal helplessness took hold.

Defensiveness can be seen to operate on two levels, the literal level in the fortification of schools and the psychological level, through the perception of external contacts as threatening or potentially destructive. Such defensiveness can cause schools to fear contact with outsiders and predict negative outcomes from such contact. External agencies, even parents or carers, can too easily be characterized as interfering with or disturbing the normal rhythms of school life. Such interruptions become resented and relationships can quickly become soured when social workers, police, child protection workers and others are made to feel that contact with them is a distraction from the 'real' work of a school.

The challenge for headteachers and senior staff is to look for signs of 'cocooning' or 'rationalized isolationism' in their own behaviour and that of their staff. In facing up to the fear of being in contact with the world beyond the classroom lies the key to successful and enduring partnerships, which promote real learning opportunities for pupils. Isolationism is a warning sign because it points to low institutional self-esteem. It demonstrates a lack of belief in the capacity of the institution to problem-solve and tackle difficult and changing demands with the prediction of success.

However, senior teachers do need to pay attention to the ways in which the genuine anxieties of staff in relation to promoting partnerships can be heard. Unless staff have opportunities to express their feelings, both positive and negative about who should constitute appropriate partners for schools and draw up the frameworks for such partnerships, then they will be sabotaged in different ways at the informal, social or personal interaction level. Using partnerships to promote learning for teachers and pupils is a delicate balancing act and needs to be the subject of school-wide debate with teachers, parents and governors. The appropriate vehicle for discussion is in the formulation and review of the school development plan, because it requires staff to think through the aims and objectives of partnerships and consider the costs and benefits in relation to the long-term educational goals of the school. It also raises issues of staff development. Partnerships need to be co-ordinated and staff will be delegated responsibility for such co-ordination. The special needs co-ordinator, for example, in a larger primary school may be delegated the responsibility for liaising and negotiating with a whole variety of external welfare agencies on behalf of the school.

It is clear, though, that the primary responsibility for responding to, initiating and sustaining networks lies with the headteacher. The recent Teacher Training Agency publication, *National Standards for Headteachers*, (1997), spells out the 'knowledge, understanding, skills and attributes which relate to the key areas of headship'. It elucidates the core purpose of headship as 'To provide professional leadership for a school which secures its success and improvement, ensuring high quality education for all its pupils and improved standards of achievement'.

And points out that an important aspect of the role is to secure '. . . the commitment of the wider community to the school, including through developing and maintaining effective networks, for example with other local schools, the LEA (where appropriate), higher education institutions, employers and others.'

Successful headteachers are explicitly called upon to be expert relationship/partnership builders. In school, they must help to create and maintain teaching teams which are dedicated to educational achievement and outside school they must build networks of partnerships: teams with a broader focus and with a diversity of interest and expertise to complement that of the school. What are the interpersonal skills necessary for senior teachers to promote and maintain successful partnerships? The following list serves as a guide:

- Approachability, interpersonal warmth.
- Psychological flexibility, creativity and imagination.
- Enthusiasm and optimism.
- Willingness to take risks.
- Interpersonal stamina.
- Assertiveness.
- Willingness to learn.
- Provide a role model for others.
- Demonstrate high standards of personal integrity and honesty.
- Emotional maturity.

However, it is not and must not be the responsibility of the headteacher alone to forge and maintain such links. While in many primary schools it is the headteacher who has the time, energy and professional commitment to establishing partnerships, every member of the school community, pupils, teachers, ancillary staff, governors, parent helpers, will share the responsibility for sustaining and honouring the principles of partnership in word and deed. They become ambassadors for the school community and will similarly need to be able to demonstrate highly skilled interpersonal behaviour.

How can headteachers and senior staff develop principled frameworks for promoting partnerships? In fact, the essence of principled partnership is a mirror image of what makes for successful interpersonal relationships. After all, partnerships are about people. Partnership implies a relationship built on:

- *trust*, a fundamental belief in the worth of the partnership itself;
- *understanding* of the social, cultural, communication differences;
- *commitment* to the accomplishment of shared vision, values and goals;
- *belief* in the interests of the partnership over the interests of the

individual or organization;
- *respect* for the priorities, boundaries and development needs of the partner;
- *willingness* in each partner to learn from and about each other;
- *awareness* that true partnership brings about change;
- *tolerance* of difference;
- *knowledge* of each other's history;
- *empathy*, feeling the impact that perceived differences in relation to status, power and authority can have on the relationship;
- *desire* to avoid labels, judgements and negativity;
- *consciousness* that a higher purpose is being served in the creation and maintenance of the relationship;
- *forgiveness* that when things go wrong, the relationship can be repaired;
- *responsibility*, in a true partnership each partner takes responsibility for his or her part in the whole. The partnership is the sum total of what is put into it by its members; and
- *reciprocity*, a mutual dependence on each other's expertise.

At times, teachers themselves may take the lead and initiate partnerships, at other times they will be sought out to form partnerships. Teachers have an abundance of knowledge, information and expertise to share, but they never have it all, especially when it comes to the social and emotional or welfare development of the child. In seeking to enhance their learning in relation to the personal, social and academic development of children, they must first look to their closest allies, parents and carers.

Parents and families in partnership with schools

If partnership with communities and agencies is the oxygen of schools, then partnership with parents and carers is the life blood. Teachers may be the experts on education but parents or carers are the experts on their children and teachers need to hone their skills as *learners* when it comes to working in partnership with parents. Children are the super glue in the home–school relationship and senior teachers and parents or carers have a joint responsibility for ensuring that the relationship stays firmly fixed. However, teachers must take responsibility for setting the tone of and pattern for communication in the relationship at the outset. They must lead the way initially but the artistry lies in letting go of control and permitting the development of equal responsibility for its development and the growth of interdependence.

It is now highly fashionable to talk about schools being 'in partnership' with parents. As professionals, we may snort with laughter at the bad old days when school gates proudly and unapologetically displayed signs which declared 'No Parents Past This Point' and congratulate ourselves smugly on how far we have come as a profession since those days. In fact, education legislation over the last half century has morally, if not literally, compelled schools to forge bonds with parents, whether either party liked it or not. The Education Act 1944 required schools to educate pupils in accordance with their parents' wishes and the Plowden Report (DES, 1967) proved to be of seminal influence in setting out a base line for home–school communication systems. A raft of legislation through the 1970s and 1980s not only introduced notions of parents as educational 'consumers', with increased choice of school, nursery voucher schemes and so on, but also further embedded the requirement of schools to communicate formally through the governing body and informally through teacher/parent communication systems. Such systems are now bread and butter to even the most traditional of primary schools. The work of Mortimore *et al.* (1988) showed evidence that parental involvement in their children's primary education does pay dividends and cites it as one of the key determinants of school effectiveness. Wolfendale (1989) confirms this view: 'The case for involving parents in their children's development and education has been established by innumerable studies and many schools are now committed to pursuing home–school links.'

The home–school relationship, though, is too often confined to a somewhat narrow discussion of 'parent' as though members of extended family groups did not have a significant impact on the development of children. Older siblings may often, through family circumstance, be obliged to take a significant caretaking role with younger brothers and sisters, providing role models for appropriate or inappropriate nurturing behaviour. Cultural differences may also signal to some extent the importance placed on the extended family for responsibility in the child-rearing process. Grandparents, step parents, siblings, uncles and aunts, god parents or even religious leaders may be part of a complex nexus of significant carers, who also play an important role in the home–school partnership. This may be an even more urgent consideration for families with children who have special educational needs. These children will need their families and teachers to be working in close collaboration, if their success in mainstream schooling is to be assured. Hornby (1995) provides a comprehensive guide for teachers to working with parents of children with special educational needs, and he acknowledges the all-round positive impact of involving family members in the support process. This will also be true for children whose behaviour may be perceived as challenging and who, in some cases who may be at risk of school exclusion. To enhance the success of school-based interventions with pupils who demonstrate challenging behaviour, it is vital that families work together with teachers to ensure a consistency of approach to raising standards of social interaction, learning to control impulsivity and developing self-awareness (Webster-Stratton and Herbert, 1995).

However, it is the *quality* of these relationships between teachers and families, the interpersonal dynamic, which concerns us here and how the quality of interpersonal communication in the partnership can be ensured. In any relationship, good communication is the key to its long-term survival. Imagine a relationship, then, where the only news communicated was bad or superficial. Where one partner refused to take on board, or belittled, important information, ignored feedback, or never gave the other partner a chance to voice real feelings, except on his or her terms and on his or her territory. Undoubtedly, this is how some parents feel about the way in which they are forced to relate to their children's teachers. Contact from school may be limited to a summons when things aren't going too well and parents may be met with a litany of complaint from harassed class teachers. Teachers may also present themselves as experts on the child and either label or make judgements which can cause deep resentment or anger in parents. One of the writers had the disconcerting experience recently of attending a parents' meeting to be given an authoritative character sketch of her child by the teacher. The writer was told he was quiet, shy, didn't answer questions and needed to become more outgoing. This was a child the writer didn't recognize at all and checked to see if the teacher had the correct name – were we both talking about the same child? On occasions like these, where parental co-operation is being sought, teachers must avoid labelling the child or making inappropriate judgements, which imply that the teacher knows the child better than the parent or carer. This approach will generally produce either a defensive or an aggressive response. Teachers clearly possess knowledge of a child's behaviour in a context-specific situation, like a class group, but this knowledge needs to be used in tandem with, not opposition to, the parent or carer's experience. For the teacher to have prefaced the feedback with the words,

> I have been teaching your son/daughter for . . . days/weeks/months now and in my experience in lessons, I find him/her . . . How does this fit in with how he or she behaves with you at home or with friends? . . . Have you any idea why this might be the case?

would have provided the basis on which to begin a real discussion about the way the behaviour or personality of the child impacts on his or her learning and achievement. Labelling, and making premature or sweeping judgements, verbally or in written communications, and justifying them as 'feedback to parents' will be inhibiting factors in the development of an effective home–school partnership. Teachers should avoid inadvertently forcing parents into becoming apologists for their children or their children's behaviour. Frank, honest appraisal based on real acceptance and respect for the child will encourage parents and carers to disclose important knowledge which can aid the teacher's work in the educational development of the child.

Teacher attitude may, in fact, be generally a significant stumbling block in the creation of effective home–school partnerships. Turnbull and Turnbull (1986) reported that teachers found interactions with parents to be one of the major stressors in their work but, as Hornby (1995) reminds us, it is teacher *attitude* itself which may create the friction in the relationship in the first place. He cites seven commonly held perceptions of parents by teachers:

Parents as problems
Parents as adversaries
Parents as vulnerable
Parents as less able
Parents as needing treatment
Parents as causal

Parents need to be kept at a professional distance.

To this list we would add:

- Parents as interferers.
- Parents as energy sappers.
- Parents as interrogators.

However, such negative labelling goes against the grain of what research tells us about the potential and actual payoffs in schools which cultivate supportive partnerships with families. Characterizing parents in the ways that Hornby suggests will undoubtedly cause some teachers to withdraw from potentially difficult interaction with parents, for example when required to give feedback or to seek to minimize the extent of the contact they have with them. However, this is not a tenable professional option. Headteachers must eschew rationalizations which frame interactions with parents and carers as an unwelcome distraction from teaching and enable staff to reframe their understanding of the relationship. Central to pupil achievement is the ability of teachers to harness the willing co-operation of families. To some extent, this partnership may need to be choreographed by the school to put families at ease and demonstrate approachability, warmth and flexibility in patterns of communication.

If negative teacher attitudes are an important inhibiting factor in the formation of effective partnerships, the conscious adoption of positive relationship-building behaviours and strategies will help to encourage and nurture them. Empathy is one of these skills.

The emotional dimension in the relationship is seldom seriously addressed. For parents or carers and their children, schools are the inescapable bridge between the private experience of home and the public, societal, domain represented by the school. They are the first important steps to a life which functions independently of the home. It is via schools that society first presents its terms of membership to the young. Obeying school rules, developing the ability to control impulsiveness, turn-taking, working collaboratively for the collective good, becoming a group member, looking out for others, managing difference and diversity are in fact the hallmarks of citizenship, and these are part of a daily personal and social education curriculum which is outside the direct influence of parents. Schools in significant ways begin the individuation process from the home. The sense of loss at such times that both parent or carer and child experience is profound.

The experience of one of the writers when delivering her child on her first day at the local infant school may elucidate this process further. As a parent and an assertive educational professional, I confidently believed that *I* would not be cowed by the experience of handing over my child into the care of the school. I could cope. I had been a teacher, I spoke the language, I understood the jargon, I shared the values, in short, I knew the score, I knew what to expect. Sometime later, I even became a school governor. However, none of this prepared me for the feeling of utter desolation and powerlessness I experienced at the moment of letting go of my child's hand. She was kindly led off to sit on the carpet with all the other children and become one tiny member of a much larger community, which didn't contain me or my family. Some of you reading this chapter will recognize these feelings. To a greater or lesser extent, all parents and carers experience them, no matter how many times they go through the process. Parents, family members or carers will make the effort to accompany a child on his or her first day at a new school, some of them even more nervous than their children, but unhappily never to be seen again inside the school gates. The conclusion too conveniently jumped to is that these folk are disinterested, irresponsible, couldn't care less, poor parents and so on. In fact Bridges (1987), in a study tellingly entitled 'It's the ones who never turn up that you really want to see', points out that the reason for non-attendance most often cited by parents in his Cambridgeshire study was not indifference or apathy to their child's education but an emotional dread of school itself which was a hangover from their own earlier experience of school.

However, to a large extent, these strongly held emotions go by unacknowledged by the school and remain unexpressed by the parents or carers - but which surface at inappropriate moments, a situation in any relationship which bodes ill for the future. However, primary schools can use these very profound moments when parents have to let go and permit their child to begin a journey to individuality in a way which can form an enduring relationship with the school that will last probably way beyond the years the child is actually undergoing formal education. By preparing parents and children to face the emotionality inherent in the school induction process well in advance of the hand-over day, and really acknowledging how difficult a challenge they face, wise teachers will earn the gratitude of parents and carers and secure their lasting co-operation. This demonstration of empathic understanding by teachers will reinforce messages of partnership. The school can present itself as a partner who genuinely cares about parents and children's feelings and respects their need to express them and to be taken seriously. Insensitive or brusque handling in these first experiences of school will convey powerful and lasting negative impressions, which will be very difficult to undo or reverse.

Emotionally sensitive senior teachers recognize that schools need to be open to the communities they serve, well before formal enrolment begins. Joyce *et al.* (1997) provide the example of a Nottinghamshire primary school. In this school there is a self-consciously managed process of school orientation for the community which begins *before* children reach school age:

> Parents and students become acquainted with the school before the children have reached school age. In the fall of each year, the school staff holds meetings designed to build the student–parent–school partnership. In addition, neighbourhood parents of children not yet in school are invited to bring their children to school on Thursdays - to 'Thursday Club' – and they can attend every Thursday if they wish.

A particularly important aspect of the home–school partnership is the opportunity to enhance the personal, social and academic development of the child by working in concert with parents and carers on strategies to improve children's self-esteem. There is a clear relationship between high self-esteem and academic achievement as well as high self-esteem and better social adjustment (Burns, 1982). The work of Reasoner (1982) shows that the five key variables in developing and maintaining a positive self-esteem are:

- sense of purpose, meaning;
- sense of personal competence;
- sense of security;
- self-awareness, sense of identity; and
- feeling of belonging.

Home and school need to investigate the ways in which they can mutually and *coherently* undertake to support the process of enhancing pupil self-esteem in order to raise educational standards by attending to the provision of each of these variables. Teachers can take a lead here and provide families with information, advice, support, workshops and so on about how to enhance pupil self-esteem. Reasoner also presents teachers with a range of strategies for teachers to work with parents. This model of partnership identifies key mutual goals, such as fostering self-esteem in the child and jointly, purposefully, pursues that mutual goal.

However, even in the best of partnerships there will be misunderstandings, miscommunication and from time to time sheer bloody mindedness. At times like these, teachers can call on Thomas Gordon's 'no-lose' approach to problem-solving.

Activity 8.1: Gordon's no-lose problem-solving method

Steps in the no-lose strategy:
- Identify and define the problem.
- Generate alternative solutions.
- Evaluate the possible alternatives.
- Make a decision.
- Implement the decision.
- Follow up to evaluate the decision.

Person skills for the no-lose method
- Active listening.
- Clear and honest communication.
- Respect for the needs of the other person(s).
- Trust.
- Being open to new data.
- Persistence.
- Firmness in your unwillingness to let it fail.
- Refusal to accept: a) I win, you lose; or b) You win, I lose.

Source: Adapted from Gordon (1974).

It is not the task of the school to alienate a child from its family through presenting a model of education, social behaviour or citizenship which demeans any group in society. The values, implicit and explicit, that a school and its teachers espouse should be *inclusive* not exclusive and the entry and exit points for children into primary education need to be occasions which properly mark the enormous sense of personal loss that both children and their families will experience. If schools can manage these significant moments well with tenderness and sensitivity, then the tone will be set for all other patterns of communication. Parents and carers will feel both understood and heard. So communication between home and school needs to be:

- regular
- informative
- meaningful
- inclusive
- focused on the educational development of the child
- unsurprising.

It should also:

- offer a clear and simple method of home response;

- offer alternatives for contact;
- contain social as well as educational elements;
- emphasize the development of the whole child – not just academic development; and
- recognize the emotional dimension to the relationship.

Educational research demonstrates conclusively what teachers have known for a very long time, that a home–school alliance is essential in order to support the academic, social and emotional development of pupils. The challenge facing senior managers is how to promote formal and informal alliances in creative, generative ways. The maintenance and deepening of such alliances requires schools to be very sensitive to the emotional dimension of home–school communication. Judgementalism, labelling, defensiveness, confrontation or non-acceptance are teacher behaviours which militate against the development of enduring relationships.

Interagency partnerships

Interagency work has become an increasingly insistent aspect of the role of senior teachers in primary schools. The pastoral and welfare demands on teachers have grown steadily as social fragmentation and increasing unemployment have made families vulnerable to breakdown. Teachers are also only too well aware of the alarming incidences of physical, psychological and sexual abuse which are revealed to them. The incorporation of children with special educational needs into mainstream classrooms has also provided teachers with a challenge to draw together a coherent package of resources. Agencies converge to target both resources and services for the benefit of the child and family and teachers are called upon to make an input in discussions. Many teachers find these interagency meetings difficult to manage and may feel at sea, struggling to make sense of what seems like a micro-political minefield. Properly assertive leadership, modelled by a senior teacher in an interagency partnership, can do a great deal to ensure that the objectives of securing the best interests of the child are met.

When, in a recent workshop with primary teachers, the teachers were asked to storm in just two minutes the list of agencies or groups their schools worked with, the list was an impressive one, although no doubt for some readers probably not exhaustive. Here is the list they came up with as time was called:

Parents, families, governors, PTA, social workers, education welfare officers, police personnel, religious leaders in the community, educational psychologists, community safety reps., residents' associations, universities, school medical and dental services, LEA officers, DfEE, DHSS, library services, NSPCC, Child Guidance Unit, school inspectors, DARE project, Child Protection Unit, youth workers, Family First, Home Office/LEA joint-funded self-esteem project, City Challenge, Safer Cities, family of schools, leisure services, local hospital, RELATE, Dyslexia Association, probation service, youth justice

Some of these relationships are what Biott (1991) would describe as 'developmental'. They were informal, spontaneous, responsive and evolutionary in their nature. Others were what Biott describes as 'implementation partnerships': imposed, formal, mechanistic and with a specific brief or remit for action. In this section, we are concerned to look at partnerships between agencies which we would describe as 'strategic development partnerships' and in fact combine aspects of both the implementation and development partnership models. Strategic development partnerships will vary in their lifespan, but have features in common:

- Members of the group will normally represent statutory or voluntary agencies and other interested groups.
- The task of the group is to bring together otherwise disparate human, material or financial resources.
- Partners are problem-solving in their approach.
- They have a tendency towards action rather than reflection or conceptualization.
- Relationship networks created through membership enable the development of knowledge, information databases and communication systems for members and the dissemination of best practice.
- The partnership represents opportunities for policy and strategic development in the parent agencies.
- The work of the group will be delineated by time constraints.
- They will rarely have an independent or formal constitution, although there may be legislation which compels interagency co-operation (cf. Children Act 1989).
- Such partnerships are 'permanent' or enduring at senior management level but the personnel delegated to represent agencies will change in relation to the specific task focus of the group.
- Financial or resource factors will usually be a defining feature of the partnership relationship.
- Financial support for the work of the group may originate from a variety of local, governmental, European or charitable sources or a combination of these.

For headteachers and teachers used to sharing a common professional vocabulary of education, interagency work can at times present a particularly gruelling challenge to their interpersonal stamina, tolerance and empathic skills. Senior teachers who expect to enter into interagency work as if they were talking a common language will find themselves very disappointed. Social workers, education welfare officers, educational psychologists, police and so on will employ a vernacular which arises out of their own professional culture and concerns. In such partnerships, a common language has to be invented or reinvented whenever an interagency group is convened and for very busy teachers, who have little time to spare outside the classroom, this can be a frustrating process.

Partnerships founded on 'contrived collegiality' can founder because organizational self-interest can too easily dominate the agenda. Historically governmental and local authority agencies, rich in bureaucracy, have developed strong institutional identities and working practices which translate on the ground into adversarial behaviour between agencies. Sometimes the competition is over scarce resources but just as often it arises over conflicts of power and authority in relation to the child or family. Invariably, this has meant a retreat away from collaboration into adversarialism and meant an ultimate impoverishment of provision for the child or family.

Interagency partners will also have to live with and work through tensions, disagreements and sometimes seemingly intractable differences. Coupled with this will be perceptions of pecking orders or hierarchy, when none formally exists. However, informal hierarchies of 'political correctness' have recently provided opportunities for agencies to occupy the 'high moral ground' in order to gain control in a situation and achieve their own ends, rather than pursue mutually agreed goals, beneficial to the child. Agencies will have a clear perspective from where they stand of what constitutes the 'best interests of the child'. Sometimes legislation, as in the Children Act 1989, make clear how this is to be defined. More often, the best interest of the child is a more subtle, rather slippery concept which can and does get mixed up with what is in the best interest of the institution or the individual worker. The Children Act also requires agencies to work together (see *Working Together*, Department of Health, 1991) but interestingly does not indicate how such working co-operation is to be achieved (Section 27, 'Cooperation between authorities').

Making and maintaining contact with agency partners may also prove haphazard. Unless there are clear, signposted entry routes into agencies, with names attached to roles, inertia, frustration and the realities of time constraints will weaken the bonds of the relationship. You may be familiar with the frustration engendered by a phone which is never picked up or leaving endless answer-phone messages which are never responded to. Similarly, just when it seems that you have developed a relationship with one individual, he or she moves on and the effort begins all over again.

Headteachers and staff need a framework with which to make sense of and manage interagency partnership. Potentially, opportunities for miscommunication and misunderstanding are rife and relationships are all the more difficult to manage for that. The temptation in a case conference or project group, where relationships are unformed or superficial, is for the members to recreate their own organizational, habitual ways of working and try to impose them on the group or to create temporary alliances to secure a powerful base from which to operate. This may be an understandable human reaction in order to reduce anxiety when faced with a new situation (Menzies Lyth, 1988). However, it is one which will inevitably doom the group to failure, riven by conflict about work practice, rather than enabling members to tackle the fundamental objective, securing co-operation on behalf of the child or family. The first task for an interagency partnership is to consider how to preserve co-operative, intergroup behaviour, which serves the agreed best interests of the child. What these agreed 'best interests' consist of will need to be elucidated as a clear set of partnership objectives. There are three aspects to securing this co-operation which senior teachers need to be aware of and each of these will be examined in terms of factors which help or hinder interagency partnership. First, the three factors:

- organizational
- interpersonal
- development.

Organizational factors which *help* to secure co-operative behaviours are as follows:

- Keeping interagency groups small, optimally between six and eight members.
- Make any important decisions which relate to principle in open meeting.
- The chair of the group should be a key agency stakeholder, who is able to demonstrate a high level of integrity, commitment and enthusiasm and who is also capable of promoting a culture of co-operation within the group.
- Minutes should be action orientated, indicating who is responsible for taking action and reporting back to the group on progress.
- Documents relating to the interagency partnership should be carefully maintained and open to review where confidentiality permits.
- Meetings should be rotated around different agency 'territories' so that members can learn more from first hand about differences in institutional cultures.

Organizational factors which *inhibit or hinder* interagency group co-operation are as follows:

- Large, undisciplined groups, with constantly changing membership.
- Informal meetings where decisions are made in secret.
- The chair of the group lacks the full support of members and is not genuinely committed to the partnership or is inexperienced in promoting a culture of openness and honesty between group members.
- Times, dates and agendas for meetings are badly communicated and minutes not taken or circulated.
- Lines of accountability within and without the partnership are unclear.
- Key documents or records related to the work of the group are unavailable for scrutiny.

Interpersonal factors which *help* to secure interagency co-operation are as follows:

- An opportunity for members to articulate individually the values or vision which underpin their work.
- Partnership vision and values are collectively articulated, simply and concisely.
- The group remains committed to being solution orientated not problem focused.
- Members attend meetings regularly and punctually. There is a name to put with a face.
- When conflict arises members remain committed to working through the issues non-adversarially; they put the needs of the partnership before their own.
- The opportunity to discuss openly differences in perceptions about agencies' agendas.

Interpersonal factors which *inhibit or hinder* co-operation include the following:

- Disagreement or confusion over the objectives of the partnership which remain undisclosed.
- Intergroup rivalries which produce an atmosphere of competition and go by unchallenged. These may be historical rivalries which have been imported or interpersonal rivalry produced out of personality clashes.
- A rigid or unimaginative attitude towards problem-solving is allowed to take hold.
- Members give partnership meetings a low priority, are late or miss meetings regularly, thereby demonstrating low regard for other members.
- Covert personal agendas dominate the work of the group, using up emotional energy. The real client group, the child or family's best interests take a back seat.

Finally, the third aspect which needs to be considered is the opportunity for partnership development. Factors which *help foster development* include the following:

- Build in time for group development activities such as team-building.
- Partners consciously set out to find ways of understanding each other's agendas, concerns, institutional priorities.
- Reflection, review and appraisal should be part of an ongoing commitment to developing good practice.

Factors which *inhibit or hinder partnership development* include the following:

- Partners are not committed to forming a team identity and they continue to put their own institutional priorities first.
- A critical or judgemental attitude towards members or the agencies they represent. Members play out old institutional rivalries or rehearse old grievances, failing to realize the future repercussions for partnership.
- Partners deal with failure immaturely. There is a difficulty in seeing mistakes as opportunities for learning and development and the partnership gets mired into a blame culture, inhibiting growth.

Interagency partnership is essential if children and their carers are to have appropriate resources targeted and delivered efficiently to meet their individual needs. Such complex partnerships will founder if not actively and assertively managed in order to secure co-operation between agencies on behalf of their clients. Active management requires that all group members pay attention to the orgnizational, interpersonal and developmental dimensions to the partnership and take responsibility for thier organizational contribution.

Partnership with the LEA

A particularly important and enduring agency partner for primary schools has been the LEA, and this merits a more in-depth examination of the relationship. During the 1990s schools have witnessed a changing relationship with their LEAs. There has been a rapid disintegration of the traditional pattern in which schools concentrated on the educational functions and the LEA managed the necessary financial, administrative and welfare aspects. In most education authorities a flourishing advisory service was also a key aspect of their service to schools. LEAs have found themselves squeezed in two particular ways: first, through the LMS initiative which transferred a great deal of management activity from the LEA administration to the school; and, secondly, by the increasingly proactive stance of central government, generating legislation and communicating directly with schools.

In recent years we have seen schools absorbing administrative roles which were once managed by specialist staff. While their budgets may have increased to take account of these devolved responsibilities, they have not done so sufficiently for a school to be able to employ the specialists that are necessary if this non-educational work is to be done efficiently and effectively. What we find in too many schools is that the administrative work once undertaken by the LEA is diverting the attention of heads from the steadily increasing educational initiatives which flow from central government.

Schools are now faced with establishing a different pattern of relationships with their LEAs. It is important to see this developing relationship as a partnership of functions rather than a relationship of power and authority. In the past there was a tendency for schools to see themselves at the receiving end of management, with LEA officers as their employers. This was a view also held by some officers who saw schools as extensions of their own departments. What is needed in these days of high pressure and fast change is a relationship of mutual support where both school and LEA-based staff see their prime purpose as supporting the learning lives of pupils. Creating such a relationship requires the staff of the school to see themselves as colleagues of those in the central administration and to cultivate effective working relationships. A lack of clarity about roles and relationships has far too often led to misunderstandings and conflicts between schools and the central administration with heads complaining about the excessive power of 'petty clerks'. The relationship between a school and the LEA is usually much more productive and beneficial when the issues of authority and function are clearly understood.

The tendency towards new contractual arrangements, where schools are purchasers of LEA services, creates a new type of business climate, and schools can be much more explicit about exactly what it is they are seeking support for, and the success criteria which they attach to its provision.

In developing an effective relationship with LEA departments two distinct modes operate. The first is a responsive mode, where the school is providing information for the central administration. Despite the enormous weight of bureaucracy it is important to recognize that a great deal of the data required is necessary and part of the legal framework within which schools are managed. Good schools are those which recognize their responsibility to deal with a range of data and do so efficiently and accurately. The second is an initiating mode in which the school seeks something from the central administration.

This means that heads particularly should cultivate those colleagues in the central administration with whom they will be relating on a regular basis. Much of the communication between schools and central services will be by telephone, fax and email. Getting to know these colleagues is a vital prerequisite for building a sense of trust and mutual support. Although we can build effective relationships with the different voices at the end of the telephone, these are likely to be much more effective if some of the business can be conducted face to face. A number of strategies are useful to optimize this:

- Give a high priority to learning and using the names of colleagues we communicate with.
- Occasionally make a personal visit to their offices and do the business face to face.
- Invite central administration colleagues out to schools so that they can see what it is they are supporting from their office desks.
- Include central colleagues on the invitation lists to school functions, concerts, performances, etc.
- Bring colleagues in on INSET days where appropriate.

It is important that all members of staff know about the structure of central services and the roles and functions of their colleagues.

It is the advisory and inspection service of the central administration that is likely to have the most significant relationship with a school. Some LEAs have struggled to keep a substantial service intact but others have significantly slimmed them down, or reorganized them altogether on a self-financing basis. The pattern of advisory teacher work is also very varied, with some LEAs abolishing the provision completely and others creating a full team through annual or two-year secondments.

Whatever the pattern and provision, the key to effectiveness lies in having a proactive rather than a reactive relationship. As our processes of educational support move ever closer to the consultancy patterns that have existed in the business world for many years, we will begin to shift away from the idea of advisers as the driving force of school policy and practice and begin to value them as supporters and consultants. With a national framework for school inspections well established, the role of the LEA support service now becomes one exclusively focused on educational development. Advisers are not in a power and authority relationship to the schools they serve, but a responsive and supportive one, using their skills and qualities in the interests of the school and its teachers. Advisers are no longer the guardians of school standards; this is a role which is now occupied by OFSTED.

Relationships with OFSTED

Since its inception the pattern of inspections undertaken by the Office for Standards in Education has had a varied and significant impact on our schools. It has galvanized a heated debate about where the locus of control for educational development really lies and has created a climate of antagonism and antipathy to what has been perceived as a procedure to isolate and judge those schools which, for whatever reason, find themselves in difficulties. In practice schools have come through the exercise less scathed than they expected and a significant number are reported to have positively enjoyed the experience. Now that the first cycle is coming to an end it is important to learn from the experience and to introduce changes which will make the next phase more helpful to schools and more cost effective.

Any system of inspection which seems to attach more importance to failure than to success is unlikely to succeed in improving the quality of learning in schools. This perception is not one held by most of the inspectors undertaking the exercise but has been extended by the public declarations of the Chief Inspector who against all the wisdom we have acquired in recent years about good management and organizational improvement has pursued a relentlessly negative approach, questioning the integrity of teachers, emphasizing the deficiencies of schools and the failures of anything but so-called 'traditional' methodologies. This is unfortunate because it has served to create a diversion of purpose. At a time when we need more imagination than ever before to devise effective ways of educating the young in a fast changing world, we have been forced into a bitter and acrimonious debate about methodologies. Let us hope that in the next few years, through the review of the National Curriculum and the deliberations of the National Schools Standards Task Force, we shall enter into a more productive debate in which the creative exploration of possibilities becomes more important than the identification of failure and the allocation of blame.

Despite its many problems the OFSTED exercise has brought a number of benefits to primary schools. In particular it has provided a considered view of how our schools are operating to complement those held by the staff of their own working practices, and of the parents and pupils who experience its provisions. Information is always valuable, and feedback is one of the key ingredients for change and improvement. Many schools have received encouragement for their efforts, and confirmation that their thinking, planning and practice have been effective and productive.

As the next cycle approaches we need to consider how the exercise can be used to create opportunities for development, rather than a trial to be survived. In other words we need to see the whole exercise as an opportunity to learn rather than a threat. This will only work if an inspection is seen as a partnership between a school, struggling to provide the highest-quality educational experience for its pupils and a team of skilled observers who can bring insights and observations to bear on its developmental thinking. Undoubtedly there will need to be some relaxation of the strictures that inspectors are there to assess and judge and not to advise and support. Perhaps the biggest weakness of the present model is that all the funding goes into the judgement and virtually none of it into the development and support.

It is useful to see an OFSTED inspection as a key event in the strategic development of a school. It will provide a key opportunity to gather vital data about how the school is operating and how effective its strategies are in satisfying declared aims and aspirations. Rather than prepare for the inspection by a vigorous struggle to change appearances, an inspection should be regarded as the key event in that year's school development plan. The planning for the inspection should be concerned with what we want to learn rather than with what we want to conceal.

Part of the challenge in the current OFSTED experience is to separate the valuable information it provides from the sometimes sorely felt judgements about our efforts and intentions. One example of this lies in the information about how schools are managed. In the 1997 report (Annual Report of HM Chief Inspector of Schools) the Chief Inspector of Schools highlighted a number of ways that headteachers seem to fail. They

- are rarely seen in classrooms;
- do not monitor the teaching enough to know staff's strengths and weaknesses;
- fail to bring about improvements in teaching;
- are unable to delegate and spend too much time on routine paperwork;
- fail to assess whether the school is getting good value for money;
- create a lack of a sense of purpose through weak leadership;
- fail to give clear objectives and targets, thereby causing staff to waste time; and
- add to discipline problems by not laying down clear rules for pupils and by failing to support staff when they try to discipline children.

Once we can discount the somewhat damning tone of these criticisms we are offered some valuable and practically useful information. As a start we can translate this list into some principles for the effective management of schools. School management is particularly effective when headteachers:

- observe the working life of classrooms and engage with teachers in exploratory dialogue about management and methodology;
- regularly work alongside colleagues in classrooms;
- work closely with all staff to define, refine and monitor the teaching methodologies used in the school;
- work with colleagues to assess the relationship between investment and achievement;
- involve colleagues in the setting of purposes and plans and support them actively in the implementation of policies;
- seize opportunities to clarify, articulate and explain the objectives and targets currently agreed; and
- work alongside colleagues in establishing and maintaining a code of conduct for pupil life in the school.

Reframed in this positive way we can transform negative criticisms into a positive agenda for management development.

One of the great challenges in managing schools is how to take account of, and work with, the enormous quantity and variety of variables that affect the learning process. Through their observations, school inspectors can complement our own professional searches and explorations, bringing a valuable quality of detachment and objectivity to what is an essentially subjective process. In our teaching and managing work we need to be as focused and specific as possible if we are to navigate successfully through all these complex variables.

In taking note of observations about our work we need to seek for precision so that we know exactly what we need to do and what we might try. Vague terms like 'improve', 'sound' and 'satisfactory' do not help us to bring about changes in practice. We need to press OFSTED for more detail so that we can understand their terms and distinctions. We need to know exactly what we might have to do in order to change from 'satisfactory' to 'good'.

As in all practical activities, it is the insight that examples bring that are so valuable and in our discussions at feedback time we must assertively press inspectors for these so that we accumulate concrete ideas about how we can bring about a specific change. If these are not forthcoming, then in the words of the Chief Inspector above they will merely cause us to waste time. Exhortations about how we *should* be rarely bring about the improvements hoped for. What is needed is attention to the specific operational detail of our work as teachers and managers. Approaching an OFSTED inspection with curiosity and a determination to acquire detailed insights into our practice will help to make the whole exercise focus more on a school's developmental needs and will become more of a mutual endeavour to improve educational life.

School and higher education partnership

Involving others from outside the school is vital to the development of its learning life. One of the options that heads and teachers have is to build into their personal and institutional development plans the use of higher education personnel. The advantages of this are that they

- are not connected to the authority structures or inspection mechanisms of the school. This means that though passionate about education in all its aspects, they are disinterested; and
- are able to provide knowledge and skills which are complementary to those held by colleagues in school and LEAs, for example, knowledge of particular research techniques or access to a variety of research and knowledge perspectives upon, for example, methods of teaching, reading, maintaining a broad 'critical' vision of schools and schooling is an essential part of their job.

There has been in the past a felt distance between schools and institutions of higher education and a scepticism among some teachers of the relevance of knowledge produced by academics and the abilities of academics to contribute to the practical development of schools. Where this 'practicality ethic' is the staple diet of professional development, it tends to lead to isolation and a degree of parochialism, with an over-reliance on the craft of teaching, rather than on its science and artistry.

School leaders, who care about providing a balanced learning diet for themselves and their staff, have worked with higher education tutors and their departments to great effect. In addition to providing support for traditional taught post-experience courses, which provide for the intellectual and vision growth so vital, for example, for mid-career colleagues whose development may have plateaued, there are many examples of the following:

- *Limited team development consultancies,* for example related to pre-OFSTED preparation, areas of school curriculum, teaching and assessment, or team-building or appraisal.
- *External audit support,* for example where the school has identified the need for a 'critical friend' to audit an aspect of school policy, provide an evaluation of the effectiveness of a programme of study, or even the strategies for supporting teachers' professional development.
- *Knowledge about educational input,* for example about what is known nationally or internationally about whole-class teaching strategies and their effects.
- *Generating educational knowledge* in which, for example, a colleague or colleagues from higher education work alongside a teacher, teacher or headteacher in order to assist in the further development of reflective teaching practices. There are many examples of such collaborative action research work.
- *Building communities of intelligent practice* in which, for example teachers from different schools or groups work together with higher education personnel over a period of years on a project which they (perhaps with their LEA) have chosen as being essential to school development. Higher education personnel often play a number of roles, for example those of consultants, critical friends, data collectors and analysers (with teachers) and co-ordinators (the glue in the system). These can be the most rich of partnerships, since they represent *sustained interactivity* (Huberman, 1995), combining the best of many worlds: the need of teachers and schools to work on agendas relevant to them; the benefits of sharing experience and practice across school environments and cultures; the advantage of using broader research and knowledge perspectives over time. It is important to note that where they are used predominantly as a means of uncritically implementing externally imposed innovations

they can, however, limit growth and contribute to the 'technicalization' of teaching'.

Of course, there are costs to partnerships of these kinds, but in general the benefits far outweigh these. Where used wisely, with clearly negotiated agendas within agreed ethical frameworks in which all partners benefit, and where set within career-long, balanced personal and institutional planning which takes account of both rational and 'emotional intelligence' needs, they are good investments.

Business partnerships

Gleeson (1987) claims that schools have traditionally been criticized for being 'anti-industry' in their attitudes and that they 'promoted academic values in the curriculum at the expense of technical and vocational skills'. The Technical Vocational Education Initiative (TVEI) was a governmental initiative which 'front-loaded' state funds into curriculum innovation and development in secondary schools, targeted at the 14–16 age group. The agenda was to raise awareness and change practice in both teachers and pupils in relation to recognizing the relationship between the process of education and the world of work.

In many ways a similar initiative, targeted at primary schools, may have proved an equally productive vehicle through which working partnerships with business could have been built. Formal ties with the local business community, however, can be assured through membership of the governing body. The governing body is required to consider the extent to which the local business community is represented, and has the power to co-opt if necessary. While it is clear that the nations' employers and wealth creators have a legitimate interest in the education process, having an entitlement to articulate the skills and competencies which are required for the employees of the future, business or commercial involvement in schools can never be an ethically neutral process.

Teaching staff may have legitimate fears about the kind of interventions into school life that forging a partnership with local or national business interests might bring. Some teachers may seek to overdramatize such worries, presenting the case against business partnerships as if schools were being asked to sup with the devil – necessitating the use of a long spoon. While somewhat unimaginative, these fears should not be trivialized by head teachers in their general enthusiasm to bring additional resources, from whatever origin, into the school. Anxieties about business involvement or 'interference' in the education process will then be forced underground, only to emerge later as possible sabotage of partnerships. Ethical issues related to the possibilities of companies using schools to promote commercial products are real and must be fully discussed and plans for partnership negotiated by parents and governors as well as teachers. The introduction of work books or other materials bearing advertising slogans or company logos may be offensive to groups both inside and outside the immediate school community and the governing body is a useful vehicle through which to promote widespread discussion of these issues. Schools may also have a natural reluctance to form a partnership with business if they feel that through the relationship they may in some way be endorsing the company's products. Again, governors will have a vital role to play in leading this discussion. Some companies may also have political or environmental backgrounds which may make linking up with them unacceptable to some members of the school community. However, it is also naive to assume that schools will have the monopoly on ethically motivated decision-making. Increasingly, companies are describing their core business mission within an ethical framework, in precise terms which spell out their commitment to community or global stakeholders, rather than just shareholders.

It must be emphasized, though, that a company's products are not the only things which they have to offer. Many companies also support charitable trusts which fund educational action research projects. Some of the larger ones are Sainsburys, Allied Dunbar, Rowntrees, WH Smith - to name but a few. Many schools and higher education institutions have already benefited from such funded research projects and to some extent are reliant on them in an environment of tight fiscal restraint on the public purse. However, senior teachers should avoid characterizing business as a possible 'cash or resource cow', to be milked on demand.

There are real possibilities for skill sharing and support which exist beyond the level of simple resource transfer. Business does not only have products to sell but also expertise to share. The cutting edge of organizational theory in business management is envisioning companies as 'learning organizations' (Starkey, 1996). Managers' roles are characterized as coaches, facilitators, teachers, role models (Ray and Rinzler, 1993). Does this sound familiar territory? Valuable opportunities exist to promote learning in management development, recruitment and selection procedures, publicity and marketing skills, skills exchanges, job shadowing, joint consultancy and support through reciprocal manager mentor schemes. This can be a useful two-way staff development process, benefiting both partners. As business managers struggle to make sense of their new organizational role as facilitators of learning and teachers struggle to develop advanced managerial competences, there exists a genuine and profound possibility for partnership, based on a respect for the expertise and knowledge of each other.

In conclusion: looking to the future

Foskett (1992) forecasts that the following three factors will dictate the future agenda for schools and their leaders in the coming decades:

* Information technology.
* The role of parents in the joint education of their children.
* The unpredictability of socioeconomic and political pressures.

To this we would add the physical opening up of schools to their neighbourhood communities as a learning 'habitat' (Senge *et al.*, 1996). This environment will see intergenerational learning as the norm and the role of teachers will focus more on resource gathering and the facilitation of learning.

Senge *et al.* (1996) expand upon this vision of the 'learning habitat':

The habitat–community interface is permeable. The classroom extends beyond the school building, into museums, science centres, colleges and universities, health care and social service organizations, businesses and homes. Teachers move into local businesses for summers and sabbaticals, to experience more of the world they are bringing students into. Nonschool employees return to spend weeks in the learning habitat regularly, to renew their own learning, and to teach others. Gradually, the community evolves its own sense of collective intelligence, greater than the sum of its individual parts.

In the future schools can create global partnerships. The power of information technology systems to connect schools with an international, rather than a local, regional or national boundary is being increasingly realized. The challenge for headteachers and their staff is how to manage this tsunami of educational opportunity within an ethical, educational framework. While the technological revolution holds the key to a rich store of opportunity, far too many teachers are still secret Luddites and senior teachers need to find creative ways to enable staff to face their fear of technology. Computer technology, if harnessed in the service of education, can transform the learning lives of pupils and their teachers. It can open up frontiers to pupils in ways that at present we can only dream. The information superhighway and the potential development of virtual reality as a tool for learning mean that pupils from inner-city schools can visit Amazon rainforests, explore the frozen wastes of the Arctic, fly a jet plane or see the *Mona Lisa* in the Louvre.

The local, regional, national and global communities that headteachers and their staff can access with their pupils will develop partnerships rich in diversity of culture and heritage. They will enable us to promote a respect and sense of awe at the wonder of the planet we inhabit. Peck (1993) tells us that 'In and through community lies the salvation of the world . . .

Community is the way – the means and the technology – to institute a planetary culture of civility'.

The building block of such community is partnership and in partnership is laid the foundation for a richer, more profound sense of a school's purpose in relationship to the larger whole. We are all partners in our children's education, because in their education lies all our futures.

Further reading

Bastiani, J. and Wolfendale, S. (eds.) (1996) *Home-School Work in Britain: Review, Reflection and Development*, David Fulton, London.

Block, P. (1993) *Stewardship*, Berrett-Koehler Inc., San Francisco.

Waller, H. and Waller, J. (1997) *Linking Home and School: Partnership and Practice in Primary Education*, David Fulton, London.

References

Abbott, J. (1996) Chaos and Complexity: or just Education? in *Education 2000 News*, March 1996, Letchworth, Education 2000.

Annual Report of Her Majesty's Chief Inspector of Schools (1997) *Standards and Quality in Education 1995/6*, HMSO, London.

Argyris, C. (1960). *Integrating The Individual and the Organization*, Wiley, New York.

Argyris, C., Putnam, R. and McLain Smith, D. (1985) *Action Science*, Jossey-Bass, San Francisco.

Argyris, C. and Schon, D. A. (1976) *Theory in Practice: increasing professional effectiveness*, Jossey-Bass, San Francisco.

Ashton-Warner,S. (1980) *Teacher*, Virago, London.

Aspy, D.N., and Roebuck, F.N. (1977) *Kids Don't Learn From Teachers They Don't Like*, Human Resource Development Press , Amherst, MA.

Bandura, A. (1995) *Self-Efficacy in Changing Societies*, Cambridge University Press, Cambridge.

Barber, M., Evans, A.and Johnson, M. (1995) *An Evaluation of the National Scheme of School Teacher Appraisal*, DfEE, London.

Barnes, D. (1982) *Practical Curriculum study*, Routledge & Kegan Paul, London.

Barth, R. (1988) School: a community of leaders in A. Lieberman (ed.) *Building A Professional Culture in Schools*, Teachers College Press, New York.

Beare, H. and Slaughter, R. (1993*) Education for the Twenty-First Century*, Routledge, London.

Beck, L. G. and Murphy, J. (1993) *Understanding the Principalship: Metaphorical Themes, 1920s–1990s*, Teachers College Press, New York.

Bennis,W. (1989) *On Becoming a Leader*, Hutchinson, London.

Best, R., Lang, P., Lodge, C. and Watkins, C. (Eds) (1995) *Pastoral Care and Personal and Social Education*, Cassell, London.

Biott, C., (1991) *Semi-detached teachers: Building Supp.ort and Advisory Relationships in Classrooms*, Falmer Press, Lewes.

Bridges, D., (1987) 'It's the ones who never turn up that you really want to see'. The 'problem' of the non-attending parent, in Bastiani, J. (ed.) *Parents and Teachers. 1.* NFER-Nelson, Slough.

Brighouse, T. (1991) *What Makes a Good School?* Network Educational Press, Stafford.

Burns, R. (1982) *Self-Concept Development and Education*, Holt, Rinehart and Winston, London.

California Task Force To Promote Self-Esteem and Social Responsibility (1990)*Toward a State of Esteem*, Department of Education, Sacramento, CA.

Carkhuff, R.R. (1983) *The Art of Helping*, Human Resource Development Press, Amherst, Mass.

Casey, D. (1993) *Managing Learning in Organisations*, Open University Press, Buckingham.

Cormier, W.H. and Cormier, L.S. (1979) *Interviewing Strategies for Helpers: A Guide to Assessment, Treatment and Evaluation*, Brook/Cole, Monterey, CA.

Coulson, A. (1987) Recruitment and management development for primary headship, in Southworth (ed.) *Readings in Primary School Management*, Falmer Press, Lewes.

Dalin,P. & Rust, V. (1996) *Towards Schooling for the Twenty-First Century*, Cassell, London.

Davis, E. (1981) *Teachers as Curriculum Evaluators*, Allen & Unwin, London.

Day, C.W. (1981) *Classroom Based In-Service Teacher Education: The Development and Evaluation of a Client-Centred Model*, University of Sussex Education Area, Occasional Paper no.9.

Day, C. (1994) Personal Development Planning: a different kind of competency, *British Journal of In-Service Education*, vol.20, No.3, 1994, pp.. 187–301.

Day, C.W. and Baskett, H.K. (1982) Discrepancies between intentions and practice: re-examining some basic assumptions about adult and continuing professional education, *International Journal of Lifelong Education*, Vol.1, no.2.

Day, C., Hall, C., Gammage, P., Coles, M. (1993) *Leadership and curriculum in the Primary School,* Paul Chapman, London.

Day, C., Whitaker, P. And Wren, D. (1987) *Appraisal and Professional Development in Primary Schools*, Open University Press, Milton Keynes.

Day, C. (1996) Professional learning and School Development in Action : a personal development planning project, in R McBride (ed.) (1996) *Teacher Education Policy*, Falmer, London.

Department of Health (1991) Working Together (under the Children Act) London HMSO.

Egan, G. (1994) *The Skilled Helper,* Brooks/Cole, Pacific Grove, CA.

DES (1975) Report of the Committe of Enquiry appointed by the Secretary of State for Education and Science under the chairmanship of Sir Allan Bullock (A Language for Life) HMSO, London.

DES (1977a) *A New Partnership for our Schools* (the Taylor Report), HMSO, London.

DES (1978) *Primary Education in England : A Survey by HM Inspectors of Schools*, HMSO, London.

DES (1983) *Teaching Quarterly*, HMSO, London.

DES (1988) *Circular 7/88: Education Reform Act 1988: Local Management of Schools*, HMSO, London.

DES (1989b) *The Implementation of the Local Education Authority Training Grants Scheme (LEATGS): Report on the First Year of the Scheme 1987/88*, HMSO, London.

Donaldson,M (1978) *Children's Minds.* Fontana, London.

Doyle, W. and Ponder, C.A. (1976) The practicality ethic in teacher decision making, *Interchange* Vol.8, 1977.

East Sussex Accountability Project (1979) *Accountability in the Middle Years of Schooling: An Analysis of Policy Options*, University of Sussex (mimeo.) in R. McCormick (ed.) (1982) op.cit.

Egan, G. (1994) *The Skilled Helper: a problem-management approach to helping* (5th ed.) Brooks/Cole, Pacific Grove, CA.

Eisner, E.W. (1979) *The Educational Imagination*, Collier Macmillan, West Drayton

Elliott, J. (1975) The values of the neutral teacher, in D. Bridges and P. Scrimshaw (eds.) *Values and Authority in Schools*, Hodder & Stoughton, London.

Elliott, J. (1978) *Who Should Monitor Performance in Schools? (mimeo.) Cambridge Institute of Education.*

Elliott, J. (1981) Action-research: a framework for self-evaluation in schools, Schools Council programme 2, *Teacher – Pupil Interaction and the Quality of Learning Project*, Cambridge Institute of Education working paper no.1 in J. Elliott and D. Ebbutt, op.cit.

Elliott, J. (1991) *Action Research for Educational Change,* Open University Press, Buckingham.

Eraut, M.E. (1977) Strategies for promoting teacher development, *British Journal of In-Service Education*, Vol.4, nos.1–2.

Eraut, M.E. (1988) Learning about management: the role of the management course in C.Poster and C.Day (eds.) *Partnership in Education Management*, Routledge, London.

Eraut, M.E. (1989) Teacher appraisal and/or teacher development: friends or foes?, in H. Simons and J. Elliott (eds.) *Rethinking Appraisal and Assessment*, The Open University Press, Milton Keynes.

Farber, B. A., (ed.) (1983) *Stress and Burnout in the Human Service Professions.* Pergamon Press, New York:.

Farber, B. and Miller, J. (1981) Teacher Burnout. A Psychoeducational Perspective. *Teachers' College Record*, Vol. 83, no. 2, pp.. 235–243.

Flinders, D. J., (1988) Teacher isolation and the New Reform *Journal of Curriculum and Supervision* Vol. 4, no.1, pp. 17–29.

Foskett, N. (ed.) (1992) *Managing External Relations in Schools*, Routledge, London.

Fullan M G (1993) *Change Forces: Probing the Depths of Educational Reform*, Falmer Press, Lewes.

Fullan,M. and Hargreaves,A. (1992a). *What's Worth Fighting For In Your School*, Open University Press, Milton Keynes.

Fullan, M. and Hargreaves, A. (eds) (1992b) *Teacher Development and Educational Change*, Falmer Press, Lewes.

Galton, M. and Simon, B. (1980) *Progress and Performance in the Primary Classroom*, Routledge & Kegan Paul, London.

Gardner, H. (1993) *Frames of Mind*, Fontana, London.

Garratt,B. (1987). *The Learning Organization*, Fontana, London.

Gilroy, D.P. and Day, C. (1993) The erosion of INSET in England and Wales: analysis and proposals for a redefinition, *Journal of Education for Teachers*, Vol. 19, no. 2, pp..147–57.

Gleeson, D. (1987) *T.V.E.I. and Secondary Education*, Open University Press, Milton Keynes.

Goleman, D. (1995) *Emotional Intelligence*, Bloomsbury, London.

Gordon, T., (1974) *T.E.T. Teacher Effectiveness Training*, David McKay , New York.

Habermas, J. (1972) *Knowledge and Human Interest*, Heinemann, London.

Hall, E. and Hall, C. (1988) *Human Relations in Education*, Routledge, London.

Hall, E., Hall, C. and Abaci, R. (1997) The effects of human relations training on reported teacher stress, pupil control ideology and locus of control, *British Journal of Educational Psychology*, Vol. 67, pp. 483–96.

Hall, E., Woodhouse, D. A. and Wooster, A. (1984) An evaluation of in-service courses in human relations, *British Journal of In-Service Education*, 11, 1, 55–60

Hand, G. (1981) First catch your adviser: The INSET role of advisers, in C. Donoughue *et al.* (eds.) *In Service: The Teacher and The School*, Kogan Page, London.

Handy,C. (1989) *The Age of Unreason*, Business Books, London.

Hargreaves, A., (1995) *Changing Teachers, Changing Times*, Cassell, London.

Hargreaves, A. (1997) Feeling like a teacher: the emotions of teaching and educational change. Keynote Presentation, PACT, 6th National Conference in Educational Research 1997, Norway, May, 1997.

Harris, T.A. (1973) *I'm OK, you're OK*, Harper & Row, New York.

Havelock, R.G. (1971) *The Change Agent's Guide to Innovation*, Educational Technology Publications, Englewood Cliffs, NJ.

HMSO (1985) *Better Schools* (white paper), HMSO, London.

Hoffer,E., (1985) in J.O'Toole, (ed.) *Vanguard Management*, Doubleday, New York.

Home Office, Department of Health, DES, Welsh Office (1991) *Working Together – Under the Children Act, 1989*, HMSO, London.

Honey,P. & Mumford,A. (1986) *Manual of Learning Styles*, Maidenhead. Peter Honey.

Hopkins, D. (1986) *Inservice Training and Educational Development: An International Survey*, Croom Helm, Beckenham.

Hornby, G. (1995) *Working With Parents of Children With Special Needs*, Cassell, London.

House, E. (1972) The conscience of educational evaluation, *Teachers College Record*, Vol.73, no.3.

Huberman, M. (1995) Networks that alter teaching: conceptualisations, exchanges and experiments, *Teachers and Teaching: Theory and Practice*, Vol. 1, no. 2, pp.. 193–212.

Hughes, M. (1976) The professional-as-administrator: the case of the secondary school head, in R.S. Peters (ed.) *The Role of the Head*, Routledge & Kegan Paul, London.

Hughes, M. (1988) Leadership in professional staffed organisations, in R. Glatter *et al.* (eds.) *Understanding School Management*, The Open University Press, Milton Keynes.

ILEA (1985) *Improving Primary Schools, report of the Committee on Primary Education*, ILEA, London.

ILEA (1986) *The Junior Schools Project*, ILEA, London.

The Industrial Society (1983) *Action-Centred Leadership*, Education for the Industrial Society, London.

Jersild, A. T. (1955) *When Teachers Face Themselves*, Teacher's College, New York.

Johnson D.W. and Johnson, R.T., (1991) *Learning Together and Learning Alone*, Allyn & Bacon, Boston.

Joyce, B., and Calhoun, E. with Puckey, M. and Hopkins D. (1997) Inquiring and Collaborating at an Exemplary School, *Educational Leadership*, May, pp. 63–66.

Katzenbach, J. R . and Smith, D. K. (1993) *The Wisdom of Teams*, Harvard Business School Press, Boston.

Keddie, N. (1971) Classroom knowledge, in M. E. D. Young (ed.) *Knowledge and Control*, Collier Macmillan, London.

Kemmis, S. *et al.* (1981) *The Action Research Planner*, Deakin University Press, Geelong, Victoria, Open Campus Program.

Kilmann, R.H. (1984) *Beyond the quick fix: managing 5 tracks to organisational success*, Jossey-Bass, San Francisco.

Kinsman,F. (1991) *Millenium: Towards Tomorrow's Society*, W.H.Allen, London.

Kolb,D., Rubin,I., & McIntyre,J., (1971) *Organizational Psychology: An Experiential Approachs*, Prentice-Hall, Hemel Hempstead.

Kubler Ross, E. (1970) *On Death and Dying*, Tavistock Publications, London.

Lacey, C. (1977) *The Socialisation of Teachers*, Methuen, London.

Lefcourt, H. M. (1976) *Locus of Control*, Erlbaum, Hillsdale, NJ.

Lewis, M. E. (1987) *Continuation of a Curriculum Innovation: Salient and Alterable Variables* ,(paper presented to the Annual Meeting of the American Educational Research Association), Washington, DC, April.

Louis, K. S. and Miles, M. B. (1990) *Improving the Urban High School: What Works and Why*, Teachers College Press, New York.

MacDonald, B. (1973) Innovation and competence, in D. Hammingson (ed.) *Towards Judgement: The Publications of the Evaluation Unit of Humanities Curriculum Project 1970–2*, Centre for Applied Research in Education, Nottingham, occasional publication no.1, pp.88–92.

MacDonald, B. (1974) quoted in Walker, R. (1980) The conduct of educational case studies: ethics, theory and Procedures, in W.B. Dockrell and D. Hamilton (eds) *Rethinking Educational Research*, Hodder, London.

Machiavelli (1513) in A. Harris *et al.* (eds.) (1979) *Curriculum Innovation*, Croom Helm in association with The Open University Press, London

Macy, J. (1995). Working Through Environmental Despair, in T. Roszak, M. Gomes and A Kanner (eds.) *Ecopsychology,* Sierra Books, San Francisco.

Mahoney, M.J. (1991) *Human Change Processes.* Basic Books, New York.

Marshall, J. (1994). Re-visioning organizations by developing female values, in J. Boot, J. Lawrence and J. Morris (eds.) *Managing the Unknown By Creating New Futures,* McGraw Hill, London.

Maslow, A. (1970) *Motivation and Personality* (2nd ed.), Harper & Row, New York.

McCormick, R. (ed.) (1982) *Calling Education to Account,* Open University/Heinemann Educational, London.

McCormick, R. and James, M. (1983) *Curriculum Evaluation in Schools,* Croom Helm, Beckenham.

McDougle, L.G. (1982), Orientation of new employees: implications for the supervisor. *Supervision,* 44, 4, pp.. 3–5.

McGregor, D. (1960) *The Human Side of Enterprise,* McGraw-Hill, New York, NY

Menzies Lyth I.E.P. (1988) *Containing Anxiety in Institutions: Selected Essays* Vol. 1 Free Association Press, London.

Mezirow, J., 'A Critical Theory of Adult Learning and Education' in Tight,M.(ed), (1983) *Adult Learning in Education.* London. Croom Helm.

Miles, M.B., Saxl, E.R. and Lieberman, A. (1988) What skills do educational 'change agents' need? An empirical view, *Curriculum Inquiry 18,* no.2, Ontario Institute for Studies in Education.

Miller, D.C. and Fom, F.H. (1966) *Industrial Sociology,* Harper & Row, New York.

Mintzberg, H. (1973) *The Nature of Managerial Work.* Harper & Row, New York.

Mortimore, P., Sammons, P., Stoll,L., Lewis, D. and Ecob, R. Key factors in effective junior schooling, in R. Glatter, M. Preedy, C. Riches and M. Masterton (eds.) (1988) *Understanding School Management,* Open University Press, Milton Keynes.

NDC/SMT (1989) *Consortium of Teacher Appraisal Pilot Schemes,* Newsletter, May, NDC/SMT, Bristol.

Nias, D.J. (1987a) *The Culture of Collaboration* (summary of paper given at BERA Conference), Manchester, September.

Nias, D.J. (1987b) The Primary School Staff Relationships Project: origins, aims and methods, *Cambridge Journal of Education,* Vol.17, no.2.

Nias, D.J., Southworth, G.W. and Yeomans, R.(1989) *Staff Relationships in the Primary School: A Study of School Culture,* Cassell, London.

Oaklander,V. (1978) *Windows to Our Children,* Real People Press, Moab, Utah.

Open University (1980) *Curriculum in Action: An Approach to Evaluation* (P234, Blocks 1 and 3) Open University, Milton Keynes.

Papert,S. (1980) *Mindstorms – Children, Computers and Powerful Ideas,* Harvester Press, London.

Peck, M., Scott, (1987) *The Road Less Travelled,* Rider, London.

Peck, M. Scott, (1993a) *Further Along the Road Less Travelled,* Simon and Schuster, London.

Peck, M. Scott, (1993) *A World Waiting to be Born: The Search for Civility,* Arrow Books, London.

Peters, T. (1987) *Thriving on Chaos,* Alfred A. Knopf, New York.

Peters, T.J., and Waterman,R.H., (1988) *In Search of Excellence,* Harper & Row, New York.

Plowden Report (1967) *Children and Their Primary Schools,* HMSO, London.

Postle,D. (1989) *The Mind Gymnasium,* Macmillan, London.

Postman,N. and Weingartner, C. (1971) *Teaching as a Subversive Activity,* Penguin, London.

Rakos, R.F. (1991) *Assertive Behaviour: Theory, Research and Training,* Routledge, London.

Ray, M. and Rinzler, A. (eds) (1993) *The New Paradigm in Business,* Putman's Sons, New York.

Reasoner, R. (1982) *Building Self-Esteem* (Elementary Edition), Consulting Psychologists Press Inc., San Jose, CA.

Revans, R. (1980). *Action Learning,* Blond and Briggs, London.

Riches, C. and Morgan, C. (eds.) (1989) *Human Resource Management in Education,* Open University, Milton Keynes.

Ring, K. (1984) *Heading Toward Omega: In Search of the Meaning of the Near Death Experience,* Quill, New York.

Rogers, C. R. (1961) *On Becoming a Person,* Houghton Mifflin, Boston.

Rogers, C. (1963) The concept of the fully-functioning person. *Psychotherapy: Theory, Research and Practice,* Vol. 1, no. 1, pp.17–26.

Rogers,C. (1980) *A Way of Being,.* Houghton Mifflin, Boston.

Rogers, C. and Freiberg, H.J. (1994) *Freedom to Learn,* Merrill, New York.

Rogers, C.R. and Stevens, B. (1991) *Person to Person – the problem of being human,* Souvenir Press, London.

Rosenblatt ,D., (1975) *Opening Doors,* Harper & Row, New York.

Rosenholtz, S.J. (1989) *Schools, Social Organization and the Building of a Technical Culture,* Longman, New York.

Roszak ,T. (1981) *Person/Planet,* Granada, London.

Rowan,J. (1988) *Ordinary Ecstasy,* Routledge, London.

Schein, E. (1985) *Organizational Culture and Leadership,* Jossey-Bass, San Francisco.

Schiller, C. (1984) in *Christian Schiller in his own words,* C. Griffin-Blake (ed.) NAPE, London.

Schmidt, M.J., Riggar, T.F., Crimando, W., and Bordieri J.E. (1992) *Staffing for Success,* Sage, London.

Schon, D.A. (1983) *The Reflective Practitioner: How Professionals Think in Action,* Temple Smith, London.

Senge, P.M. (1990) The Leader's New Work: Building Learning Organizations *The Sloan Management Review,* Fall, pp. 7–23.

Senge, P., Kleiner, A., Roberts, C., Ross, R. B. and Smith, B.J. (1996) *The Fifth Discipline Fieldbook,* Nicholas Brealey, London.

Sergiovanni, T. J. (1990) *Value-added Leadership: How to get Extraordinary Performance in Schools,* Harcourt Brace Jovanovich, San Diego, CA.

Sergiovanni T J (1992) *Moral Leadership,* Jossey-Bass, San Francisco.

Sergiovanni T J (1995) *The Principalship: A Reflective Practice Perspective,* Allyn & Bacon, London.

Simons, H.and Elliott, J.V. (eds.) (1989) *Rethinking Appraisal and Assessment,* Open University Press, Milton Keynes.

Sirin, A., Hall, E., Hall, C. and Restorick, J. (1995) Item Analysis of the 'My Use of Interpersonal Skills Inventory', *British Journal of Guidance and Counselling* Vol. 23, No.3.

Schmuck, R. A. (1980) Interventions for Strengthening the School's Creativity, in T. Bush et al (eds) *Approaches to School Management,* Paul Chapman, London.

Skilbeck, M. (1982) School based curriculum development: a functionalist/ environmentalist Approach to curriculum change, in D. Barnes, op.cit.

Somerset LEA (1987) *Review and Development: An Introduction to Appraisal* (introductory pamphlet), Taunton.

Southworth, G. (1988) Vision and visibility, *Education,* Vol.172, no.10, September.

Southworth, G. (1990) Leadership, headship and effective primary schools, *School Organisation,* Vol.10, no.1.

Southworth G (1995) Talking Heads: Voices of Experience: An Investigation into Primary Headship in the 1990s, University of Cambridge Institute of Education, Cambridge.

Stacey R (1992) *Managing the Unknowable,* Jossey-Bass, San Francisco.

Stake, R.E. (1967) The countenance of educational evaluation, *Teachers College Record*, Vol.68.

Starkey, K. (ed.) (1996) *How Organizations Learn,* Thompson International Business Press, London.

Stenhouse, L. (1975) *An Introduction to Curriculum Research and Development,* Heinemann Educational, London.

Stenhouse, L. (1979) *What is Action-Research?* (mimeo.), CARE, University of East Anglia.

Sutcliffe J. and Whitfield, R. (1976) Decision making in the classroom : an initial report, *Research Intelligence,* Vol 2. No 1.

Tanahashi, K. (1990) *Brush Mind.* Parallax Press, Berkeley, CA.

Teacher Training Agency (1996) Consultation Paper on training for Serving Headteachers, November. TTA, London.

Teacher Training Agency (1997) *National standards for headteachers.* TTA, London.

Thompson, A. (1984) The use of video as an observation tool, in L. Thompson and A. Thompson, *What Learning Looks Like: Helping Individual Teachers to Become More Effective,* Schools Council (program 2), Longman, London.

Toffler,A. (1971) *Future Shock,* Pan, London.

Tuckman, B.W., (1965) Developmental sequence in small groups. *Psychological Bulletin,* Vol. 63, pp. 384–99.

Turnbull, A.P. and Turnbull, H.R. (1986) *Families, Professionals and Exceptionality,* Merrill, Columbus, OH.

Walker, R. and Adelman, C. (1975) *Guide to Classroom Observation,* Methuen, London.

Watts, A.G., (1986) Counselling,*Journal of the British Association for Counselling* no.57, pp.4–7.

Webb,R. & Vulliamy,G. (1996) *Roles and Responsibilities in the Primary School,* Buckingham, Open University Press.

Webster-Stratton, C. and Herbert, M. (1995) *Troubled Families – Problem Children: Working with Parents: A Collaborative Approach* , Wiley, Chichester.

Westoby, A. (Ed.) (1988) *Culture and Power in Educational Organizations*, Open University Press, Milton Keynes.

Whitaker, P. (1983) *The Primary Head,* Heinemann Educational, London.

Whitaker,P. (1993) *Managing Change in Schools,* Open University Press, Buckingham.

Whitaker,P. (1995) *Managing to Learn,* Cassell, London.

Whitaker, P (1997a) *Primary Schools and the Future,* Open University Press, Buckingham.

Whitaker, P. (1997b) *Managing School,.* Butterworth Heinemann, Oxford.

Whitmore, D. (1986) *Psychosynthesis in Education,* Turnstone Press, Wellingborough.

Wilson Schaef, A. W. and Fassel, D. (1988) *The Addictive Organization,* Harper & Row, New York.

Winter, R. (1989) Problems in teacher Appraisal – an action-research solution, in H. Simons and J. Elliott (eds.) op.cit.

Wise, A.E., Darling-Hammond, L., McLaughlin, M.W. and Bernstein, H.T. (1984) *Teacher Evaluation: A Study of Effective Practice*, Rand Corporation, June.

Wolfendale, S. (1989) *Parental Involvement: Developing Networks between Home School and Community*, Cassell, London.

Wragg E C, Wikeley F J, Wragg C M and Haynes G S (1996) *Teacher Appraisal Observed,* Routledge, London.

Zinker, J. (1977) *Creative Processes in Gestalt Therapy,* Vintage Books, New York.

Index